T0355537

IMPERFECT COMPROMISE

ALSO BY MICHAEL KARPIN

Tightrope: Six Centuries of a Jewish Dynasty (2008)

The Bomb in the Basement: How Israel Went Nuclear and What That Means for the World (2006)

Murder in the Name of God: The Plot to Kill Yitzhak Rabin (with coauthor Ina Friedman) (1998)

RELATED TITLES FROM POTOMAC BOOKS

Does Israel Have a Future? The Case for a Post-Zionist State
—Constance Hilliard

Israel vs. Iran: The Shadow War
—Yaakov Katz and Yoaz Hendel

Transforming America's Israel Lobby: The Limits of Its Power and the Potential for Change
—Dan Fleshler

IMPERFECT COMPROMISE

A New Consensus among Israelis and Palestinians

MICHAEL KARPIN

Potomac Books
Washington, D.C.

Library of Congress Cataloging-in-Publication Data
Karpin, Michael I., author.
Imperfect compromise : a new consensus among Israelis and Palestinians / Michael Karpin. — First Edition.
p. cm
Includes bibliographical references and index.
ISBN 978-1-61234-545-1 (hardcover : alk. paper)
ISBN 978-1-61234-546-8 (electronic)
1. Arab-Israeli conflict—1993—Peace. 2. Palestinian Arabs—Politics and government—1993– 3. Zionism. 4. Israel—Politics and government—1993– I. Title.
DS119.76.K269 2013
956.9405'4—dc23
2012043913

Printed in the United States of America on acid-free paper that meets the American National Standards Institute Z39-48 Standard.

Potomac Books
22841 Quicksilver Drive
Dulles, Virginia 20166

First Edition

10 9 8 7 6 5 4 3 2 1

CONTENTS

PREFACE

A PEACE AGREEMENT between Jews and Arabs is at hand. The conditions have never been more auspicious for the attainment of a regional peace agreement based on the Saudi Arabian initiative of March 2002 that was adopted by the Arab League.[1] This plan supplies both sides with excellent solutions for the achievement of compromises on critical issues. Moreover, the Arab peace initiative is what Israel's forefathers dreamed about since modern Zionism was created. By implementing the plan, fifty-seven Arab and Islamic states will recognize the Jewish state and dramatically change its international status.

The Middle East and the Arab world is now entering a lengthy period of instability. Extremists like the Iranian mullahs and the offshoots of al Qaeda are lying in wait and planning to strike at the soft underbelly of the free world. The threat of proliferation of nonconventional arms from the Middle East to the West is increasing. Oil prices will rise and impair recovery from the global economic crisis. In view of this complex situation, the United States and Europe will make efforts to foster stability in the Middle East. Such stability will depend on a large number of factors, and one of the most important of these is the state of the conflict between the Arabs and the Jews. The closer the conflict comes to a solution, the more tension in the Arab world will ease, and vice versa. One may therefore assume that the international demand for Israel to implement the Arab peace plan will become more insistent.

Of course, the question is whether Israel agrees to pay its share: withdrawing its army and settlements from most of the West Bank territories occupied in 1967 and accepting an independent Palestinian state.

For the first time, the leadership and the elites of Israel, including the right-wing elite that has set national policy for most of the years that have passed since the 1967 war, have given up the dream of a Greater Israel. The majority in the nationalist camp has grasped the reality: prolonging the occupation will create a demographic threat. If Israel continues to rule over the occupied West Bank and to retain and strengthen the settlement project, within a few years Jews will lose their majority and the power to control their own destiny. In a parallel slow but obvious manner, Israelis are realizing that the occupation leads to Israel's isolation and to its being condemned as an apartheid state. This means that most Israelis are ready to give up a considerable part of the territory they conquered in June 1967.

Simultaneously, on the Palestinian side, too, for the first time since the signing of the Oslo Accords in 1993, basic conditions have arisen that make reaching a complete peace agreement with Israel possible. Facing Israel now is a serious partner, a Palestinian Authority (PA) that is functioning reliably and responsibly on security issues, creating law and order, and combating terrorism. (The PA is the interim administrative organization governing the West Bank, while Hamas controls Gaza Strip.)

Under Mahmoud Abbas (Abu Mazen), the Authority's president, and his prime minister, Salam Fayyad, the PA is building the institutions of a Palestinian state from the foundations up, producing an economic environment of entrepreneurship and a process of self-empowerment for the West Bank's Palestinian population. The change is not a matter of image—it is a change of substance.

For the task of building harmonious relations with Israel, Abbas is an excellent partner. He doesn't challenge the legitimacy of the state of Israel, nor is he denying the connection between the Jewish people and the Land of Israel and its capital, Jerusalem. By proclaiming that, from the Palestinian point of view, the two intifadas (uprisings) had been a "terrible failure," Abbas explicitly delegitimized the use of terror. Instead of inciting violent uprisings, PA leaders have advocated passive civil resistance. In the West Bank's territories, Hamas activists have largely been neutralized.

On the Gazans' side, the leaders of Hamas, who represent the more devoted Islamists among the Palestinians, have also reduced the intensity of their objection to the two-state solution.

In the background, the moderate Arab states united in an anti-Iranian coalition, headed by Saudi Arabia, are interested in resolving the conflict with Israel. The United States, the United Nations, and the European Community, under the guidance of the Obama administration, have effectively readied the means for such a resolution.

Moreover, it is not only the Israeli-Palestinian conflict that is on the brink of resolution. A peace treaty with Syria lies on the shelf, almost ready for signing. Around 90 percent of the disputes between Syria and Israel have already been resolved, including security arrangements and normalization, and the 10 percent that remain are not impossible to resolve. On the basis of Israel pulling back from the Golan Heights, it is reasonable to assume that as the post-Assad regime settles down in Damascus and designs Syria's future relationship with the West, the peace option with Israel will be back on the agenda.

Obtaining a peace settlement between the Palestinians and Israelis as part of a regional agreement will significantly temper the severity of the global confrontation between the West and Islam, weaken the fanatics, and give the world a period of tranquility. From Israel's point of view, this should be the most important result of the Arab uprising.

As always, much lies in Egypt's hands. Post-revolution Egypt will play a more robust role as a peace broker and help move forward the stalled Israeli-Palestinian peace process, mainly by leveraging Israel's deep concerns that Tahrir Square's popular anger at the Israeli occupation will drive the ruling Muslim Brotherhood to tear up Egypt's peace accord with Israel.

Indeed, the Egyptian upheaval has set off shock waves in Israel, shaking the self-confidence of the Jews. For the first time in thirty-two years, most Israelis believe there is a danger that Egypt will freeze or even nullify the peace agreement between the two countries signed in Washington, D.C., in 1979 by Egyptian president Anwar Sadat and Israeli prime minister Menachem Begin, under the auspices of President Jimmy Carter. A return to a state of perpetual conflict with the strongest Arab country would have a material impact on the Israelis' way of life and harm their relatively high standard of living. The army would have to be strengthened, and the term of compulsory military service would have to remain at the current three years for men and two years for women. The defense budget would have to increase, and the economy would sustain damage. In the three decades since the peace treaties with Egypt and the Hashemite Kingdom of Jordan were signed, expenditure on defense has decreased, the Israeli economy has flourished, and the national mood has soared.

I do not think that the new Egypt is likely to revoke or breach the peace treaty—the largest Arab nation will be busy with itself in the coming years, and revoking the treaty would cause it tremendous economic damage. A healthy economy needs peace, and this is particularly true of Egypt. Without tourism, an open Suez Canal, oil and gas exports to neighboring states (among them Israel), and American aid—the four principal foundations of the Egyptian economy—there would be no chance whatsoever of attaining the goals that Egypt's new president set for his country in his inauguration speech.

Furthermore, the continuous internal struggles have significantly weakened the Arab countries' economies and military strength, and therefore the Arab Spring effect on Israel's defense has been positive. In the foreseeable future, the occupation with inner confrontations and power clashes would reduce Arabs' desire to hold an arms race and to wage war against the Jewish state.

Regarding Iran's threat, Israel's strategic standing has improved significantly. First, the mullahs are compelled to adapt the national economy to the international sanctions imposed on the country, and therefore the strong wind blowing into its sails from the Arab Spring would reinforce Iran's internal opposition. Second, in the wake of the Syrian uprising, the ayatollah's military options have been reduced. Syria's breakup will automatically weaken the fighting abilities of Iran's two other proxies, Hezbollah in Lebanon and Hamas in Gaza. Consequently, the Iranian Revolution's western flank would be drained of energy.

It should not be forgotten that Israel possesses enormous military might, including nuclear capabilities, and the Arab states have no chance of overcoming it in war. It would not be worth the new Egypt's while to waste its limited resources in an armed struggle with Israel.

But the sense that there's a danger of Israel returning to being a state under siege is in itself enough to arouse fear in Israelis, and therefore I anticipate that the dramatic changes in the region will lead a significant part of Israel's electorate to choose a new leadership, capable of handling this fragile situation.

Israel has a multiparty parliamentary system. Historically, each one of the consecutive parliament plenums, the Knesset, comprised 10 to 15 parties representing diverse political views. As no party has ever won a majority of the Knesset's 120 seats, the government is based on a coalition of parties. Control of the government has alternated between periods of rule by a coalition of parties headed by the left-wing Labor Party and by a coalition headed by the right-wing Likud ("unity" in Hebrew).

Currently Benjamin Netanyahu's Likud party (twenty-seven Knesset seats) governs the country together with a coalition of smaller right-wing and ultrareligious parties.[2] It is the most hawkish government Israel has ever had, and its discourse with the Arab world is bellicose. Some of the coalition's components are on the far right of the political map, and the gap between their fanatical worldview and the way of thinking prevalent in the mainstreams of important democracies today is too wide to be bridged. The manner in which the Netanyahu government froze negotiations with the PA showed that it is not capable of coping with complex tasks. It's clear that if the Netanyahu government had not cut off the talks with the PA, Israel would be facing the new Middle East under much better conditions. But Netanyahu hesitated and refused to freeze construction in the settlements, and negotiations ground to a halt. The opportunity has passed by, and Israel will now have to sign on to a peace deal with the Arab world that will not be as good as the one it could have achieved before Mubarak's ouster.

The Netanyahu government bungled its reaction to the Egyptian uprising as well, not only betting on the wrong horse by expressing support for President Hosni Mubarak but also by publicly leveling criticism at the backing that the Obama administration voiced for the uprising.

Paradoxically, the values that President Obama was trying to instill in Egypt are precisely the same values that form the foundation of the informal alliance between America and Israel; the Jewish state is the only bastion of freedom and democracy in the Middle East, which is the reason why most Americans feel a sense of identification with Israel. However, out of anxiety that the Egyptian revolt would worsen their situation, the Israelis did not notice that they were pulling the rug out from under their feet with their own hands. If Israel's leaders were not able to identify with a nation's demand for freedom, how could they argue that their values were identical to those of the United States? With all of the obvious reservations one may have regarding the future of the Egyptian revolution and the risks (so far unseen) that the new situation may create, Israel should have at least symbolically joined in the displays of support for the protestors in Tahrir Square shown by America and European countries. Obama did not think that it was the job of the United States to initiate a revolution in Egypt. It was up to Egypt's citizenry to do so, and they took the task upon themselves with great courage. But from the moment the revolution broke out and it became clear that the elite headed by Mubarak was not capable of managing the crisis, a new reality had been set. Whether the United States wanted it or not, the Egyptian revolution had created a new situation, and there was therefore no point in trying to stabilize the Mubarak regime.

The change in Egypt caught the Israeli leadership totally by surprise, and in its panic the Netanyahu government could not grasp how an American president could abandon his loyal ally. They immediately came to a conclusion: if America could leave its Egyptian ally in the lurch, who is to guarantee for us that he will remain faithful to Israel?

This lack of understanding demonstrates the extent to which the Israelis are unaware of the ideological roots of the American Revolution and the fundamental values that guide U.S. foreign policy. Moreover, a large number of Israeli governmental, intelligence, security, and media factors failed to decipher the DNA code of America's relationship with Egypt. It was precisely the strong links between the U.S. defense establishment and Egypt that enabled Obama to dovetail his idealistic worldview with the correct amount of realpolitik and to guide the Egyptians in carrying out their transition in an orderly and gradual manner. Thus, as the free world looked on in high emotion as millions of both proud and humble Egyptians of all walks of life and ages demonstrated for their basic rights with exemplary order and discipline that would have been appropriate for more developed societies, public opinion in Israel rapidly aligned behind anxiety that the Egyptian revolt signaled an existential danger for them. Netanyahu's negative and fearful initial response was to warn of a takeover by radical Islamists, as had happened in Iran when the hated shah was overthrown in 1979: "Our concern is that when there are rapid changes, without all aspects of a modern democracy in place, what will happen—and it has happened already in Iran—will be the rise of an oppressive regime of radical Islam. Such a regime will crush human rights and will not allow democracy or freedom and will constitute a threat to peace."

Netanyahu's typically Pavlovian reaction evinced a patronizing political incorrectness. A more accurate historical equivalent was the French Revolution. The rebels in Tahrir Square demanded liberty, justice, and dignity, and on the list of their interests, the Israeli-Arab conflict was relegated to a marginal position, if it was there at all. Only a manipulator could draw a parallel between the Iranian Revolutionary Guards and the young people who rose up in Egypt. The Khomeini revolution did free the Iranian nation from the dictatorship of the shah and his secret service, the SAVAK, but from the beginning it was meant to institute an extremely patriarchal and constraining interpretation of sharia law. The young initiators of the Egyptian revolution had the opposite intention—to replace oppression with freedom.

Of course, in the short term stability will be shaken in Egypt, but after an interim period and once civil governance is built up, there will be a consensus based on dialogue between interest groups. And if, as is to be expected, the consensus is expressed in a policy whose goal is to improve society and the economy, there is no reason why the peace agreement should suffer. Peace with Israel is not and will not be a burden for a democratic Egypt, but rather a strategic asset of prime importance.

Actually, even before the uprising in Egypt, Israel and the Arabs had entered the last stretch of the course leading to a comprehensive settlement, and this is one of the main subjects dealt with in this book: the riveting process undergone by Israeli society since the conquest of the West Bank in June 1967. The perspective of over forty years makes it possible to explain how the occupation led to disaster and suffering, especially of the Palestinians but also amongst the liberal part of Israel's citizenry, and how the disaster has spurred most of the Israelis, albeit in a slow and nerve-wracking process, to rid themselves of the mystical illusion that a "Greater Israel" could be created, and to return to a course that is realistic and sane.

Without understanding the bellicose and chauvinistic zeitgeist that took root in Israeli Jewish society after the glorious victory of 1967, there is no possibility of grasping how complicated it was to return to sanity. It was a kind of a mass metamorphosis, inspired by an unnatural and illogical drive, for which a significant part of the responsibility lies with the Orthodox and ultra-Orthodox communities in Israel that over the years tended toward messianic faith and today are threatening to drain Zionism of its secular and liberal elements. Without understanding the transformation that the Jewish religious communities went through, it is difficult to understand the extent to which the occupation has corrupted the country.

And without understanding how the occupation has alienated Israel's Arab minority—a fifth of the population—from its country, it is impossible to grasp how so large and talented a community has failed to be integrated into the society, the economy, and the culture of the state, and has been left shut up within its own ghetto.

Lancing the boil that the occupation has created will signal the start of a repair that is likely to bring the Zionist revolution back to its original vision, which was based on secular and tolerant values. The successful uprising in Egypt is likely to project itself onto the repair that Israel owes itself and encourage it to renew itself.

I have to admit that many experts and analysts in Israel relate to my predictions with disdain. They say that the true picture is precisely the opposite of the one I am sketching, that the current uncertainty casts doubt on my optimistic forecast and that Middle Eastern reality now is like a powder keg with a burning fuse. The correct conclusion, these Israeli pundits say, is that the powerful stabilizing factors in the region have disappeared or declined, and the extremists are in the ascendancy—the Muslim Brotherhood in Egypt, the antimonarchical opposition in Jordan, Hezbollah in Lebanon, Hamas in the Gaza Strip, and of course the Revolutionary Guard in Iran. Only a fool cannot see that the new Middle East has become more extreme in its attitude toward the West in general and Israel in particular, and the logical conclusion is that the new Middle East is not interested in absorbing Israel but rather wants to vomit it out.

I'll respond by exhibiting my credentials. I am presenting here a firsthand testimony of a journalist who was born in the region in 1945 and has lived and breathed the conflict ever since. I was a soldier in the earlier wars and covered the later ones for radio and television, as well as all the major episodes of negotiations. In my books and documentary films, I covered various angles of the conflict.

My expertise in the politics of the region and American involvement in it found expression in my book *The Bomb in the Basement: How Israel Went Nuclear and What That Means for the World.*

My familiarity with Israeli society and the history of the State of Israel found expression in my book *Murder in the Name of God: The Plot to Kill Yitzhak Rabin* (with coauthor Ina Friedman), in which we bared the sophisticated campaign of incitement conducted by right-wing and ultra-Orthodox circles in Israel and the United States against the Oslo Accords before the assassination of the prime minister.

My knowledge of Jewish history found expression in my book *Tightrope: Six Centuries of a Jewish Dynasty*, which relates the history of the Jews in Galicia (now part of the Ukraine), the largest Jewish Diaspora prior to the Second World War. I am closely acquainted with American society, having been a student at UCLA in the 1960s. My interest in American Jewry and its complex relationship with the State of Israel led to my 1996 television series entitled *Distant Relatives*. I became familiar with European politics when I was Israel Television's bureau chief in Germany in the 1970s and in Moscow in the 1990s.

This book is not a piece of theoretical research by an ivory tower academic, and neither is it an analysis by a fellow of a Washington think tank working with reports from the field. It is a work that is based mainly on my own work and encounters with primary sources. It is not freighted with ideological baggage.

Relying on my experience, I am convinced that the revolutions in North Africa and the Middle East are not a reason for dismay but rather signal a historic opportunity to uproot the evils that have brought catastrophe after catastrophe upon the Arabs, weaken the Revolutionary Guard in Iran and their protégés in Lebanon and the Gaza Strip, and complete a political settlement between the Jews and the Arabs. A Middle East with fewer dictators is a better Middle East—more rational, calmer, and therefore more at peace. The more democratic the region becomes, the more integrated with globalization, the broader the agreement will be to make peace with Israel.

In 1933, my paternal grandparents emigrated from Berlin to Tel Aviv, motivated by Zionist idealism. They did not feel that they were leaving home. For them Germany was exile, and they saw their move to Palestine, the Land of Israel, as a homecoming. In the 1920s and 1930s, antisemitism had spread throughout Europe, and tens of thousands of

Jews were driven to Palestine, then ruled by Great Britain, under a mandate from the League of Nations.

Many of the Zionist pioneers of the early twentieth century were influenced by a romantic-Marxist ideology, holding that the "ignorant" Arab peasants, who were being exploited by the effendis ("landowners" in Turkish), would willingly ally themselves with the European new settlers as a unified working class that would defy the capitalists.[3] However, my grandparents' world view was not socialistic. In Germany they owned hotels and carried with them to Palestine a significant amount of capital. They had faith in free market values and were influenced by European colonialist ideology. The educated and progressive Jews, with their advanced economic abilities and high morals and values, my grandparents were certain, would be accepted by the natives as saviors. Both socialists and capitalists alike were optimistic, with good reason. During most of the 1920s, the relationship between Jews and Arabs in Palestine had been peaceful. The British administration governed Palestine well, and the economy expanded.

Like my German grandparents, most of the Zionists chose to close their eyes and totally ignore the fact that hundreds of thousands of Arabs with deep roots inhabited Palestine. They simply ignored the Arabs' national aspirations, and this is why since the creation of the modern Zionist movement approximately 120 years ago a myth has grown in which the first Zionists settled in a country almost empty of inhabitants.[4] The implications of these views would be fateful in the future relationship between Jews and Arabs.

Indeed, within a short time the illusions that the Jewish newcomers had were shattered. In the autumn of 1936, the leadership of the Palestinians responded against the Zionist migration by organizing a massive assault, and my grandfather, who had fought for Germany in the First World War, had to take up arms. The violence abated while the Peel Commission (the British Royal Commission of Inquiry set up to find a solution to the Arab-Jewish conflict in Palestine) deliberated and eventually recommended partition of Palestine. While the Zionist leadership announced its readiness to divide the territory, the Arab Higher Committee rejected the proposal. Consequently, the Arabs intensified their revolt, and it waned only two years later, in 1939, when the world's attention was diverted by Nazi Germany's preparations to conquer Europe.

Seventy years later, the same principle of partition is still guiding the two sides through their peace negotiations, and one may only imagine how much agony and blood could be saved by accepting the reasonable compromise that the Peel Commission recommended in the mid-1930s.

Between 1940 and 1946, my father served in the Royal Air Force's Middle East Command in Cairo. My mother accompanied him, and I was born in a British Army hospital in Heliopolis.

When the Second World War was over and the magnitude of the Holocaust was revealed, world public opinion lined up behind the underdog and pushed enlightened leaders to solve the Jewish problem once and for all. Once again the partition solution was recommended to both sides, this time by the United Nations General Assembly, and once again the Zionist side endorsed it while the Arabs refused. David Ben-Gurion, the leader of the Jewish pioneers, declared the State of Israel, and the Arabs declared war.

In 1948, in what the Israelis call the War of Independence and the Arabs call the Naqba, or "catastrophe," my father was an officer in the air force. I did my required army service in the Israeli Defense Forces' paratroopers in the early 1960s. My wife served in the headquarters of the armored forces. When my eldest son was born in 1974, just after the Yom Kippur War of October 1973, I said to my wife that he was lucky because there would be no more war when he grew up. I was wrong, of course. As required of every Israeli, he and his younger brother both joined the army when they were eighteen. My daughter served in the Education Corps. Now, my grandchildren are being born, and it looks as if they too may have to fight. However, if the central thesis of this book is in fact correct, their children, my great-grandchildren, may belong to the first generation in a Middle East at peace.

ISRAEL

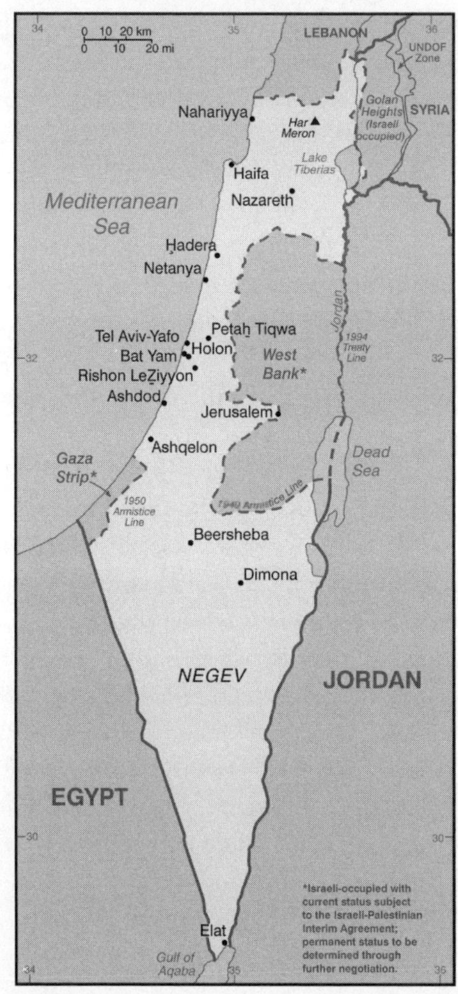

34
35
36
0 10 20 km
0 10 20 mi
LEBANON
UNDOF Zone
SYRIA
Golan Heights (Israeli occupied)
Nahariyya
Har Meron
Lake Tiberias
Haifa
Nazareth
Mediterranean Sea
Ḩadera
Netanya
Jordan
Tel Aviv-Yafo
Petaḩ Tiqwa
Holon
Bat Yam
Rishon LeẔiyyon
West Bank*
1994 Treaty Line
32
Ashdod
Jerusalem
Ashqelon
Dead Sea
Gaza Strip*
1950 Armistice Line
1949 Armistice Line
Beersheba
Dimona
NEGEV
JORDAN
EGYPT
30
*Israeli-occupied with current status subject to the Israeli-Palestinian Interim Agreement; permanent status to be determined through further negotiation.
Elat
Gulf of Aqaba

AUTHOR'S NOTE

THE READER WILL find that sources for some quotations in the text are not cited in the notes section. These quotes are attributed in the text to primary sources and are taken from my own previous journalistic reporting and books, as well as from my own documentaries.

PART I

A Post-Zionist Analysis

1

Historical Correction

ONE SCAB AFTER the other, we peel off the myths and legends that have accumulated over the one hundred years of conflict—the contradictory narratives that the warring sides insist on repeating over and over, although parts of them run counter to the facts; the distortions of history and the lies that the sides have spread about one another; the exaggerations, deceptions, and pretexts; the hopes that are based mainly upon wishful thinking; the aspirations that clearly will never be realized—and it becomes clear to whoever manages to peel off the factitious coverings and to bare the source and foundation of the conflict. What we are dealing with here is a fairly frequent historical phenomenon, the likes of which have occurred across the globe dozens of times (hundreds, if the ancient tribal past is taken into account). It is a dispute over a patch of land that can be solved only by partitioning it. It sounds so simple, so pragmatic, that a reasonable person will think, "Let the sides choose an honest arbitrator and rid themselves of this trouble that has caused so much suffering to so many, mainly to themselves."

In this case, however, reason is not the predominant element in the arguments that the sides present. The opposite is true. Reality has been diluted by traditions and remembrances, some of which are imaginary and others inflated beyond their true dimensions. Out of these fictions, myths have evolved from which the leaders of the two sides today cannot free themselves in order to distinguish between realizable solutions and dreams that can never come true. Thus, although it is clear that the Palestinian refugees will not return to their homes inside Israel and most of the Jewish settlements on the West Bank will be evacuated and the territory handed over to Palestinian sovereignty, both sides have done, and are continuing to do, everything in their power to prevent the only realistic solution from reaching fruition. The Palestinians have forced the refugees to keep living at the lowest level, in temporary camps, so that no other solution but their return to their homes is conceivable, and the Jews have planted over 120 settlements in the land of the West Bank in order to thwart any possibility of withdrawal.[1]

This is why the conflict is generally dominated by irrational conscious and subconscious motives—nationalist fanaticism, ethnic hatred of the other side, and utopian, mystical, and messianic faith. The Hebrew Elohim and the Muslim Allah watch the battle from above, their vicars on earth—the rabbis and the mullahs—hand their orders out to their followers, and common sense falls by the wayside. On the one hand, there is the biblical promise to Abraham that the Land of Israel will belong to his seed for eternity, and on the other is the Koran's precept of jihad against infidels who have occupied Islamic territory.

The Zionists, both religious and secular, present the Hebrew Bible as the title deed to the land, proof that it is theirs. History bears witness to this fact, according to the Israeli Declaration of Independence.[2] This title deed, however, is obviously amorphous. It has a literary-historical value. Its validity as a legal argument is dubious.

Moreover, it is also uncertain whether the Zionists' claim that their family roots are embedded in ancient Palestine can be scientifically proved. It is clear to the experts that the early forebears of most Jews lived in the Middle East—there's no doubt that they are of Semitic origin, and the structure of their DNA is similar. But for many generations, these Jews were dispersed throughout the world. Many of them intermarried and assimilated into the surrounding populations. It is highly doubtful that a clear link can be established between the Jews who inhabited the land of Judea and the hills of Samaria in the days of the Bible and those Jews who migrated in the twentieth century from the lands of the dispersion to what they call the Land of Israel and the Arabs call Palestine.

Thus it is not only the Jewish title deed that lacks validity: the geographical connection between the people and the land they call their "historical homeland" is also controversial.

Unlike the Jews, many Palestinians can produce authentic title deeds, handwritten official documents signed by pashas, the governors of the districts of the Ottoman Empire. The Turks ruled the Holy Land for four hundred years, from 1517 to 1917, and in 1848 they established a statutory land registry, known as the Tabu, tasked with listing the owners of all real estate and issuing each of them with a title deed, or *kushan.* These documents are valid legal proof of ownership. Can they be overruled on the strength of the Jewish kushan, the Bible? Imagine a member of the Lenape tribe standing up in a Manhattan courtroom and demanding ownership of Grand Central Station because that's where his forefathers' tepee stood. The judge and everyone else would die laughing.

Though it cannot be denied that the Palestinian Arabs were there when the Jews began arriving, they never possessed sovereignty over any part of the land; furthermore, on the one or two occasions during the last century when they were offered sovereignty over parts of Palestine, they chose not to accept it. Great Britain took the land over from Turkey in 1917–1918, and when it withdrew from it in 1948, Palestine was partitioned—the Jews declared independence in the part allocated to them by the UN, and the Hashemite dynasty took over the part along the Jordan River, known as the West Bank, in effect annexing it to their Kingdom of Transjordan, now known as Jordan. Egypt then took possession of the Gaza Strip.[3] The Transjordanian monarch at that time was King Abdullah I, and he gave the West Bank Palestinians Jordanian citizenship though some of their leaders were opposed to this, as they feared it would quell the nationalist impulse to expel the Jews and set up an independent state of Palestine.[4]

In June 1967, when Israel conquered the West Bank and the Gaza Strip, Palestinian sovereignty was not an issue on the agenda. Soon after the war ended, the government of Israel proposed handing the territory back to the Kingdom of Jordan in exchange for a peace treaty. In response, the leaders of eight Arab states convened in Khartoum, the capital of Sudan, and came up with their three famous nos: no recognition, no peace, and no negotiations with Israel.[5]

So the Palestinians cannot show any past sovereignty over Palestine,[6] but there is no questioning their claim to possession of it. The Israeli claim is weaker, as until the Jews began arriving and purchasing land and settling on it,[7] they had no rights of possession, apart from their ancient connection, which is of doubtful validity in terms of modern law.

From where does the State of Israel derive the legitimacy for its sovereignty over its territory? Just as in many similar historical cases, from reality, from the status quo: we are here, we are in control, and we are strong. Most of the classical colonialists came from afar and took over their territory in a variety of ways—purchase, lease, forcible seizure, expulsion of the natives. The Jewish pioneers coming to Palestine did the same, and this truth cannot be prettified, even if we take into account the tragic circumstances that led to the Jewish migration to Palestine and the establishment of the Israeli state: a hated and persecuted community, whose members were scattered over the globe and millions of whom were murdered in extreme cruelty by the Nazis and their helpers, marked out for itself a territory in which it hoped to realize its national aspirations. In the mid-twentieth century, after a struggle for national self-determination that had lasted fifty years, the leaders of the community seized a historic opportunity. At a time when countries all over the world were reorganizing after World War II, they persuaded the Great Powers to grant the Jewish people part of the territory of Palestine, which at the time was without a sovereign but ruled by the British under a mandate from the United Nations. Were it not for the shock prevailing in much of the world over the slaughter of the Jews during the Holocaust, it is unlikely that this course of events in the Middle East would have happened.

And indeed, the argument is often voiced by Palestinians that the powers forced the Palestinians to give up parts of their land to mollify the Jews because during the 1930s and 1940s the world had done nothing to help them while they were being persecuted and murdered by the Nazis. We paid the price of the Holocaust, say some Palestinian thinkers.

It is my belief that history will describe the establishment of the State of Israel as being in that nature of a historical correction.[8] Moreover, history will adjudge this correction as having been essential. "The Jewish problem" bothered the Christian world, and against the background of the need to reorganize the Middle East, the establishment of a national home for the Jews in a part of Palestine seems to have been a reasonable solution.[9]

The powers were sympathetic toward the founding of the Jewish state. Public opinion in the West admired the courage displayed by the "new Jews" who were still recovering from the horrors of the Holocaust when they were called upon to repel the Arab onslaught. In 1948, the media in Europe and the United States described the battles as a fight between the Jewish David and the Arab Goliath: a few defenders standing up to invaders on three fronts; Holocaust survivor refugees disembarking from immigrant ships and being sent immediately to the front; and Jewish volunteers from the United States and Europe (World War II veterans) assisting the fledgling army in a cruel war of survival.

But for the sake of accuracy, it must be made clear that in the eyes of the world, this solution was conditional. If the Jews had not won the 1948–1949 War of Independence, they would not have obtained their state—that much is clear today, and it was clear then too. Three years after the end of the world war, no one expected any government in the world to volunteer to send its troops in to rescue the Jewish army if the Arabs had them in a corner. The powers would have wrung their hands in sorrow, and their spokespersons would have expressed regret that the attempt to found a Jewish state had failed. Arabists and diplomats in the West would have shrugged their shoulders and observed nonchalantly, "Well, we told you the Jews didn't have a chance."

But the Jews fought well, and the world watched how David slew Goliath, and applauded enthusiastically. After all, the smoking embers rescued from the Holocaust had managed to establish a national homeland and defend it. The reports from the front lines played down the disastrous outcome on the Arab side, the Naqba, that resulted in some three quarters of a million refugees—some of whom were forced to flee while others were driven out by force—and hundreds of abandoned Arab communities. The world media depicted the Jew as a victim who had returned from Hell and survived and triumphed.[10] The success of the 1960 movie *Exodus* showed how dramatic the Jewish aspect of the story was, and it was much more photogenic.

Should the Palestinians have paid with their birthright and their property for the injustice that the Christian world had inflicted upon the Jews for generations and the apathy with which the world had responded to the destruction of the Jews during the Holocaust? Of course not, but in the wake of big wars, empires have dissolved, states have been wiped out, others have arisen in their place, and vast populations have had to migrate from one land to another, and this is what happened here too.[11] Just as had occurred in Europe, everything that had been true of the politics and geography of the Middle East before the war was turned upside down. The British Empire lost its assets, and France had to give up its influence in Lebanon and Syria, and following the development of the oilfields in the Persian Gulf, for the first time the United States had a major strategic interest in the region.[12] The Jews gained a national home, and almost three quarters of a million Arab inhabitants of the country had to give up their birthright and scatter into the neighboring Arab lands. During precisely the same period, some nine hundred thousand Jews left the Arab countries and settled in Israel. Similar population exchanges on the basis of ethnicity had taken place between Greece and Turkey in 1922 (when the dispute that had caused a war between those countries in 1919 was resolved)[13] and between India and Pakistan in 1947 when Great Britain departed from the subcontinent and those two states divided up the territory that the British evacuated.[14]

The Jews, of course, were unable to admit even to themselves that they had dispossessed the Palestinians of their birthright; this was a blatantly immoral deed, and the people who claim that their forefathers invented the universal moral code as embodied in the Ten Commandments would have had to explain how they perpetrated upon the Arab inhabitants of the country similar injustices to those that had been inflicted upon them throughout history. The Zionist movement therefore had to devise a new historical narrative, aimed at proving that there had been a continuous Jewish presence in the country from ancient times right up until the present day and to define the return to Zion as a perfectly natural event: the Jewish people coming back to its birthplace, where its identity had been formed and from which it had been expelled. This new narrative simply erased the two thousand years that had gone by since then. Only a few Jewish leaders were ready to admit that the Jewish state was established at the expense of the Palestinians. One of them was Moshe Dayan, the late Israeli military leader and politician who on April 1956 made a famous speech at the funeral of an Israeli kibbutz member, Roy Rutenberg, who was killed by Palestinian infiltrators on the border with Gaza. In his poetic eulogy, Dayan pondered about the reason for the Palestinians' "terrible hatred of us." His explanation was candid and exceptional for that period: "For eight years now [since the Palestinian refugees were forced to leave their homes in

1948] they have sat in the refugee camps of Gaza and have watched how, before their very eyes, we have turned their lands and villages, where they and their forefathers previously dwelled, into our home." Then he said that Israel must be "ready and armed, tough and harsh."

But like all historical narratives, the Zionist one could not last forever. As long as the Jews never felt certain that Israel was securely embedded in its place, they needed to brandish the new narrative, mostly in order to toughen themselves and to bolster their self-confidence in the face of the neighbors who wanted to eject them. But as time has elapsed and the existential danger diminished, this need has subsided. Early in the second decade of the third millennium of the Christian era, the roots that Israel has grown in the soil of the Middle East are strong enough for its people to admit that the creation of the independent Jewish state was achieved at the expense of the Palestinian people, within the framework of the massive population exchanges that took place across the globe after World War II. Accepting this reality indicates strength, and therefore, the earlier Israelis admit their responsibility to the 1948 Palestinian exodus, the better their chances will be to reach a territorial compromise with the Palestinians.

2

Without Compassion

THE ACHIEVEMENT OF self-determination by the Jews did indeed cost the Arabs of Palestine dearly. From their point of view, a despicable act of robbery has been taking place in their country since the start of the twentieth century to this day. The Jews came from far away, at first in small groups and then in a large stream. At the initial stage, during the first half of the century, the Jews secured control of most of the western, coastal strip of Palestine, as well as parts of the Galilee and the Negev. It was done mainly through classical colonization methods: investing capital in industrial enterprises in the cities and purchasing pieces of rural land. In 1924, the Zionist movement established a land purchasing instrument—the Palestine Jewish Colonization Association (known by its Hebrew acronym PICA)—with the purpose of facilitating the settlement of incoming Jews. At that time, most of the agricultural territory in Palestine was owned by about 150 Arab land owners, the effendis. Their agricultural enterprises were conducted under a semifeudal system in which the fellahin (Arabic for "peasants"), the majority of the rural Muslim population in Palestine, were directly connected to the land owners in a state of serfdom.

The challenge posed by Zionism played an important role in shaping the Palestinian identity. On the one side, the relatively huge investments of Jewish capital and know-how helped change the Palestinian's social and economic structure by rationally utilizing great parts of rural land and turning many Arab fellahin (and Jewish immigrants) into wage laborers.[1]

On the other hand, the rapid Jewish immigration and settlement encouraged anti-Zionist resentment and crystallized nationalist sentiment among the Palestinians. In order to maintain their identity, Palestinian nationalists struggled against the Zionist newcomers and the British mandate's authorities, initiating occasional outbreaks of violence during a period that lasted almost twenty years. On November 29, 1947, in an effort to end the continuous circle of violence, the UN General Assembly recommended the termination of the British Mandate and the partition of the territory into two states, a solution that the Jewish side accepted and the Arab side rejected.

Israel declared its independence and sovereignty on the portion partitioned by the UN for the Jewish state. On that day—May 14, 1948—the armies of Egypt, Jordan, Syria, Lebanon, and Iraq invaded the new Jewish state, thus starting the 1948 Arab-Israeli War. Six months later Israel controlled most of the portion of Mandatory Palestine west of the Jordan River. The remainder of the Mandate territory consisted of the West Bank, controlled by Jordan, and the Gaza Strip, controlled by Egypt.

This was the first stage of the Jewish takeover of the greater part of Palestine's territory. The second stage started on June 5, 1967, as the Jews took advantage of the errors of the Arab leaders and conquered the West Bank and Gaza as well. Since then, in an unbroken process, Jewish settlers have been seizing control of more and more of the West Bank land. Now, of the original land of Palestine, the indigenous population controls less than a third, and the Jews have taken over the rest.

Is this description an exaggeration? Not at all. Would it be possible to roll things back to their original state? Again, the reply is negative. But it would be possible to limit the damage and compensate the victims.

It would in fact be difficult to exaggerate in describing the injustice caused to the Palestinians by the decades of ongoing colonizing activity in the West Bank. Israel has implemented its occupation policies in four spheres. First, the state has taken control of lands, some of it privately owned, and erected civilian settlements there, some of which rose on land that the state itself had declared should not be taken over. Second, the state has practiced collective punishment on a vast scale against Palestinian civilians. Third, the state has applied laws that discriminate between Israeli settlers and Palestinians and has given the Israelis privileges that are reminiscent of apartheid policies. Fourth, the state has stood idly by and watched while fanatical individual Jews and groups of Jews acted violently against Arabs.

Taking control of land was the most influential tool used by the occupation. Using various pretexts, the state seized private Palestinian land, dispossessed its owners, and gave it to Jewish settlers, who have built towns and villages there. According to official data of the Israeli Civil Administration, which is the government agency in charge of the settlement in the occupied territories, nearly 32 percent of the total land area on which the settlements were built is privately owned by Palestinians. In dozens of locations, the settlers have taken over lands, and the state has then given them the rights of ownership, mostly in an official and ostensibly legal manner and sometimes with just a wink of the eye.

Moreover, an official report commissioned by Prime Minister Ariel Sharon and written by Talia Sasson, a former senior prosecutor at the State Prosecution office, describes how government officials confiscated Palestinians' land in the territories, including privately owned land, and turned a blind eye to "blatantly illegal" activities done by settlers. On March 2005, the Sasson Report was endorsed by Sharon's cabinet, although in practice, the same wrong procedures are still carried out by the authorities these days.

In August 2011, Israel's High Court of Justice ordered the state to dismantle within eight months an outpost called Migron, which was built by settlers on private land owned by Palestinians on a hill northeast of Jerusalem. Three months later, in a surprise switch, Prime Minister Netanyahu ordered the formation of a committee of jurists with the aim of finding ways to legalize settlements that were built on private Palestinian land so that the execution of the High Court order would be evaded. Commenting on this legalization committee, Sasson wrote in an op-ed piece on October 18, 2011:

> Perhaps the time has arrived for Netanyahu to explain why his government is seeking a way to launder the theft of property committed in violation of the state's own rules. It was bad enough that the state didn't do anything to prevent these criminal, illegal acts. It was bad enough that the state helped finance these acts time and again. Yet, now we have reached the point where, in the government's view, theft could even become legal, and nobody is amazed. And nobody will even protest.

In this case, Sasson's fears have not yet materialized. Indeed, the government-appointed legalization committee said that there is no occupation and the settlements are legal, but eventually the High Court of Justice set an ultimate evacuation date and the authorities complied. On September 2, 2012, the outpost's fifty families were peacefully evacuated and the stolen territory given back to its Palestinian owners. Nevertheless, the removal of Migron was an exception. More than a hundred settlements and outposts are still placed on private Palestinian land.

Frequently, settlers have destroyed the crops of Arab farmers, setting light to their fields and cutting down the trees in their fruit orchards and olive groves, often the only source of livelihood for whole families. On the margins of the occupied territories, in remote areas, settlers have violently attacked Arabs, beating up passers-by and shepherds.

The lawlessness of the Wild West has prevailed in the territories. The army and the police force usually side with the settlers. Complaints of crimes committed by Jews against Arabs have gone uninvestigated or are only cursorily probed. Convicted and sentenced Jewish murderers of Palestinians have been pardoned. The military government has segregated travel on certain roads, some of which were built especially for the exclusive use of Israelis. As Arab resistance to the occupation grew, the army took more and more extreme measures in response. Over the years, in order to suppress Palestinian terrorism, the army divided the West Bank into sectors, and the free passage of Palestinian residents from one sector to the other became almost impossible. On the outskirts of the cities and on main roads, the military set up dozens of checkpoints that brought economic activity to a standstill. Israelis passed through the roadblocks quickly, but Arabs were held up for checking. The delays were generally prolonged, and they created an enormous resentment among the Palestinians. The army blocked the vehicular traffic into and out of scores of Arab communities by throwing up hundreds of dirt barricades across their approach roads.

In recent years, in some areas, violent attacks by settlers against Arab villagers have been a common occurrence. Generally the Israeli media have made do with bare-bones reporting of such events, but after the Netanyahu government froze settlement in the territories in November 2009, the volume of coverage has swelled. In mid-December 2009, settlers set fire to a mosque in the Arab village of Yassuf near the city of Nablus and spray painted in Hebrew on the floor, "We'll burn you all" and "Get ready for the price tag," meaning, we'll be sure to punish innocent Palestinians if the Israeli government dares to stop us from setting up settlements or expanding them. The Israeli newspapers led their front pages with the story, and the electronic media opened their news broadcasts with it. In September 2011, another Palestinian mosque in the West Bank was damaged in a "price tag" attack.

A common event in which settlers put the "price tag" principle into practice happened in late January 2010. Inspectors of the Defense Ministry's Civil Administration had demolished a small structure built in the settlement Givat Menachem in the northern Judean Hills, not far from the city of Ramallah, that was in violation of a temporary construction freeze imposed by Netanyahu's government. Revenging the demolition, a band of settlers perpetrated a small pogrom in the Arab village of Bitilu, near the settlement.

The inspectors came to the settlement in a convoy that included heavy demolition machinery and police and army details. On the main road they were met by several dozen young settlers, most of them wearing masks. In Israel, the youngsters of this ilk have become known as the hilltop youths. Several hundred of them have settled in the northern West Bank, in settlements they have established on the slopes of the Samaria mountains near the city of Nablus. Other bands of hilltop youth have deployed in the Judean hills, near Hebron, in the southern West Bank. They are easy to identify. They are vocal and present the picture of arrogance. They wear large skullcaps and carry rifles slung over their shoulders, and as they walk, the long white tassels of their tzitzit, or fringed ritual garments, flutter from their waists. In the winter they all wear similar khaki parkas.

On that clear, cold morning in January, the hilltop youth posted observers on the high ground on both sides of the road and planned to hold the convoy up before the settlement's entrance gate, but the Civil Administration's inspectors tricked them and approached from a different direction. Within fifteen minutes the machines had demolished the illicit structure, and the resentful youths turned their anger on the residents of the neighboring Bitilu. Several score of them attacked one of the houses on the outskirts of the village, throwing rocks and breaking windows. A young Arab came out of the house and was wounded in the head by a stone. A strapping settler, wearing the uniform parka, ran up to the house and threw a burning torch through a window. In the yard, three or four masked youths ripped the branches off of olive trees. Panic prevailed in the village. Within minutes, the schoolyard emptied of children. Two shopkeepers quickly locked their stores and made off. Jews from Eastern Europe have given similar descriptions of pogroms carried out in their neighborhoods by antisemites.

The terrorist action took no longer than five minutes, and when the Jewish youngsters withdrew, the family quickly doused the blaze in their home. The army unit that had been guarding the demolition in the settlement chased after the fleeing hilltop youths, but they quickly vanished into the hills. Not one of them was caught. At exactly the same time another group of yarmulke wearers rebuilt the structure that the inspectors had demolished.

The following day a spokesperson for the Israel Defense Forces (IDF) commented on the Bitilu incident: "This activity is improper legally, morally, and normatively," the spokesperson said. "Central Command is determined to take full, legal action against the rioters." It was mere rhetoric. To this very day, none of the rioters in the village of Bitilu has been punished, simply because not one of them was captured.

Early in 2010, activists of a nongovernmental organization (NGO) called Breaking the Silence published testimonies taken from dozens of women who had served as soldiers in the territories.[2] Their names were not divulged, and the establishment therefore discounted their evidence, but the organization is considered credible. The women told of a large number of incidents in which soldiers and police officers used violence systematically against Palestinians, humiliated them, stole money and valuables from them, and how in some cases their superiors glossed over investigations into complaints.

The women had served in a variety of different positions, including roadblocks at the seam line between Israel and the territories and other points where Palestinians undergo checks, on patrols along roads and in population centers, in ambushes along the seam line for Palestinians infiltrating into Israel, in operations to arrest Palestinians residing illegally in Israel, in police actions against demonstrators, and in settling altercations between settlers and Palestinians.

One woman who had been in the Border Police told of the routine operations against the Palestinians who were working illegally or seeking work inside Israel: "In a single half hour you can round up thirty people without even trying." Some of them were young and some elderly, and there were also women and children. After they were caught, it was hard to decide what to do with them. They couldn't be released immediately as if nothing had happened, but there were no orders saying they should be jailed, and so they were usually lined up and "forced to sing Hebrew songs about the Border Police, to jump up and down as if they were rookies in a boot camp, and if anyone laughed, they were punched. What are you laughing at? Punch. . . . It could go on for hours," the witness said, and she explained, "It depends on how bored they are. The shifts are eight hours long; you have to fill the time somehow."

Another woman, who served at the Erez border crossing between Israel and the Gaza Strip, said that violence against Palestinians was embedded in the day-to-day routine. "There was a procedure whereby before a Palestinian was released into the Gaza Strip he was taken into a tent to be beaten up. Sometimes Border Police troops and soldiers beat children," the woman said, "and sometimes they intentionally damaged Palestinians' belongings."

The worst evidence was given by women who had served in the Hebron district. They spoke of policemen and soldiers who shot at Palestinians, including children, in violation of standing open fire regulations and then coordinated their stories before being questioned. A former Border Police worker told of soldiers' routine procedure of removing the rubber coating of riot dispersal rounds so that they would cause graver injuries. She added that despite clear orders to fire in the air or at demonstrators' legs, the soldiers would routinely fire at their stomachs.

Another woman told of an incident in which a Palestinian female journalist photographed a soldier holding a plastic toy pistol to the head of a Palestinian child. When the commander of the company heard about it, he sent a detail to locate the journalist and to confiscate her film. The soldiers came back with their loot, the witness said, adding that they had perhaps given the journalist money or threatened her. The film was destroyed, and the company commander had said that it would have been very bad if the photographs had reached the Israel Defense Force's spokesperson.

The spokesperson responded to the accusations:

> These are anonymous testimonies, without any specific dates or places, making it impossible to check their veracity in any way at all. The IDF

> is a monitored state institution that studies and draws conclusions and cooperates with any serious body with the joint aim of exhaustive checking whenever that is required. The forces of Central Command [which is responsible for the IDF's activities in the West Bank] are waging a day to day war against terrorist organizations. The troops undergo professional training including special attention to contact with the Palestinian population, mental preparation under professionals in the field, continual routine guidance by their superior officers, and are subject to constant monitoring. An additional aspect of the IDF's activities is the investigative-legal aspect. There are a number of bodies inside the IDF whose task it is to investigate cases where there is a suspicion of conduct in contravention of orders—turning to these bodies is the right and also the duty of each soldier and commander who feels that any activity is being carried out in violation of orders. Female soldiers and commanders receive the same training that male soldiers receive.

The IDF response gives an accurate picture of the situation, but apparently the witnesses were speaking the truth. How to bridge the contradiction? It would be impossible to prove that there is an official policy of encouraging soldiers and police officers to treat Palestinians harshly, but it is doubtful that the command has succeeded in getting the troops to internalize the orders. Frequently, journalists have heard from soldiers and officers testimony of aberrant behavior, similar to the incidents described by the witnesses in the Breaking the Silence report.

The descriptions given by the female soldiers are reminiscent of the abuses perpetrated by American prison guards against Iraqi prisoners in the Abu Ghraib prison in Baghdad in 2004. The American command certainly did not initiate or encourage the maltreatment, but it took no measures to ensure that bored and sadistic prison guards would not take the opportunity to do what they did. There are enough grounds to believe that cases similar to Abu Ghraib have frequently occurred in the territories occupied by Israel, but it is more than doubtful that the military command has responded with determination. The American military has handled such irregular conduct more effectively, perhaps because in the United States there is greater sensitivity to human dignity and freedom than there is in Israel. It could have been expected that the IDF's educational and law enforcement agencies, and in particular the exposure that Israeli youth undergoes to the atrocities of the Holocaust, would have moderated the harsh behavior of troops and police toward human beings. Reality has shown that in some cases, the sensitivity of certain senior IDF officers and of the military legal system to violations against the bodies, property, and dignity of innocent Palestinians has not met the criteria that should prevail in democratic societies.

In the occupied Arab part of Jerusalem, the Israeli authorities have taken a more aggressive stand. In everything to do with the Eternal City, Israel's appetite has been great. Governments have dreamed of a great and magnificent Jerusalem—after all, it is the capital of the state, and for two thousand years Jews have yearned to live there. Therefore, soon after it was conquered from the Jordanians in 1967, Israel annexed the city's Arab neighborhoods and twenty-eight surrounding townships and villages. In subsequent years, further areas were added to the city, making a total of 27 square miles (70 square kilometers) of the West Bank that were annexed to Jerusalem (area ruled by the Kingdom of Jordan between 1949 and 1967 and incorporated into the municipality of Jerusalem after 1967). The annexation added around 66,000 Palestinians, 24 percent of the city's population, then to Jerusalem. Since the annexation the Palestinian population in the city quadrupled, and today 35 percent of the inhabitants are Palestinians. The world does not recognize Israel's sovereignty over East Jerusalem, and according to international law the annexation of these lands was illegal.

In practice, throughout the four decades-plus of the occupation, the Israeli government, the Jerusalem municipality, and certain Israeli and foreign associations have been incessantly working at Judaizing Arab Jerusalem. In the first years after the conquest, the government and the city confiscated land from Arabs for the construction of new Jewish neighborhoods. These neighborhoods surround the city and are inhabited by some two hundred thousand Jews. At the same time nationalistic and religious associations, some registered in the United States, have invested considerable resources to buy properties and settle hundreds of Jewish families in the heart of Arab neighborhoods. The various national and municipal governments have generally supported these activities, some of which were carried out using deceptive means. Moreover, in order to reduce the number of Arabs in the city, the Israeli Interior Ministry has deprived thousands of Arab residents of the city of the right to live there. Most of the Jerusalem Arabs planning to build homes in their own neighborhoods have been refused building permits, compelling many of them to build without obtaining a permit.

Despite the annexation and despite the aspiration to exalt and glorify "united Jerusalem"—as the nation's leaders call the city in their attempts to stress their devotion to the national heritage—the government and the municipality have invested only paltry sums in the development of the Arab areas, and a deep gap has therefore been created between the two sides of the city. Judicially, the annexation of the Arab parts of Jerusalem to Israel imposes on the ruling authority obligations for a proper level of educational, social, and health systems, but the Arab part was not integrated into the city. Since June 1967, the extended annexation's process has been an utter political act, not a practical measure. In some of the Arab neighborhoods of the capital of Israel, sewage flows in the streets, garbage is not regularly disposed of, and the streets and sidewalks are derelict. In the Arab neighborhoods there are not enough schools or clinics, and the environmental development is minimal. About half of the Arab children of school age don't go to state or city schools, but to private institutions where there is no official supervision. And some ten thousand Arab children are not known at all to the educational authorities, who are therefore not aware if they go to any school at all.

The lust for annexation has cost Israel dearly. The Arab residents of annexed East Jerusalem, which is one of the poorest locations in Israel, have been given the status of permanent residents[3]; most of them are not Israeli citizens and therefore do not have the right to vote in elections for the Knesset, and although they may vote in municipal election, most refrain from doing so.[4]

As they are permanent residents, most of the state's laws apply to the Arabs of East Jerusalem, including those referring to social welfare. They are entitled to educational and health services and social security benefits, including unemployment payments. As a result, a quarter of a million people, about a third of the population of the capital city, who lack any affinity for the state; who will never be Israeli citizens; and in all likelihood, in the wake of a peace agreement, who will become citizens of the state of Palestine, are enjoying Israeli welfare payments, even though their contribution to the state coffers is relatively small. What sense is there in granting financial benefits to people who are not destined to become citizens and are instead to become the citizens of another state? And what logic lies behind the decision to increase the Arab population of Israel by a quarter of a million? Only foolhardiness can account for the taking on of such a great economic and security burden, a burden that brings no rewards other than a feeling of nationalist pride. In Jerusalem, extremist Israeli and American Jewish circles have taken control of the political agenda and shoved it into a dead end, in more senses than one.[5]

In late January 2010, the author David Grossman took part in a demonstration in Sheikh Jarrah in East Jerusalem against the eviction of Arabs from their homes. Grossman is a top-flight writer, and his books sell well in Israel. Addressing the demonstration, he said, "Sometimes it is impossible to sit by in silence. The settlers and the Right, with the massive support of the government, the legal system and economic forces, abuse the Palestinians in a thousand and one ways. They are entangling the situation to the extent that any peace agreement has become impossible and generally destroying our future." Grossman described the manner in which the settlers are taking over East Jerusalem as "impertinent even by their own standards, perhaps because Jerusalem is so emblematic and sensitive, and anything that happens here has enormous implications."

Grossman's lecturing met with apathy. Israeli public opinion has protested against the policy of prolonging the occupation only rarely, and it would be correct to say that it has consented by its silence to injustice. Most of the Israeli within the Green Line, as the 1967 border is known, have subscribed to the belligerent attitude towards Palestinians in the occupied territories that has evolved into a natural reality in the territories, and they have thereby enabled the settlers to dispossess Arabs of their homes and lands. During the early years of settlement, from 1975 to 1990, the Israelis and their leaders regarded the settlers as pioneers and pathfinders. You go ahead and take control of the West Bank in our name and push the Arabs out—that was what the leadership was signaling to the settlers with a wink—and when the diplomatic conditions ripen, we'll annex these territories to the state. This was the general consensus. Many of the people who were very careful about protecting the rule of law within the country, including jurists, distinguished in their minds between the territories, where might was right, and Israel proper, where the law ruled.

Jewish history will not look with pride at the chapter that deals with the occupation. How could a people that for generations upon generations had cried out that it was being discriminated against, persecuted, abused, and plundered perpetrate exactly the same things that it considered so hateful against another people, just at the time that the world community had indulged it and granted it a place where it could finally establish a homeland? The settlers were the spearhead of the conquest by force of the territory, but the responsibility surely lies on the shoulders of the entire Israeli society. History has once again been up to its tricks, giving the Jews a famous victory in 1967, a victory that has sown only tribulation.

3

The Messiah Is Back

THE WAR IN June 1967 was a fateful turning point in the history of Zionism. In a lightning campaign, Israel defeated the combined forces that had deployed to attack it from the territory of three neighboring states: Egypt, Jordan, and Syria, with the assistance of military units dispatched by Iraq, Saudi Arabia, Sudan, Tunisia, Morocco, and Algeria. The outcome of the war was decided in its first hours, after the Israeli Air Force had devastated the air forces of Egypt and Syria. Israel's exclusive control of the skies enabled its land forces to advance rapidly into the territory of its enemies. After only six days, the enormous forces that had threatened to destroy the State of Israel had been defeated, and the whole world thrilled to the achievements of the Jewish army.

The period preceding the 1967 Six-Day War had been dragged out for three anxiety-ridden weeks. Fear of the possibility of another Holocaust played a critical role in causing panic and confusion. Israel's prime minister and his cabinet of ministers were radiating hesitancy and self-doubt, and the home front was overcome by a sense of despair and despondency. The economy had slowed down, and there were shortages of basic foodstuffs. Huge numbers of casualties were expected. Tens of thousands of additional beds were prepared in hospitals, and rows of graves were dug in a Tel Aviv park. The alert declared in all the Arab countries in the region, the movement of the armies of Iraq and Saudi Arabia in the direction of Israel, and the reports of the use of poison gas by the Egyptian army in Yemen all combined to erode the morale of the Israeli population.

It was unsurprising, therefore, that many religious Jews (those belonging to the modern orthodox camp) saw the victory as divine redemption. Only one generation before had seen millions of defenseless Jews herded into ghettoes, sent in cattle trucks to death camps, and brutally murdered. Now, miraculously, a little over twenty years later, soldiers of the newly created Jewish state had defeated superior numbers and conquered territories three times larger than the state of Israel. An intoxication took hold of the country and the Jewish people everywhere, and in its wake an ancient idea broke out of its shell once more, an idea that had seemed to have been overshadowed by secular Zionism: through this mighty victory, God was signaling to his Chosen People that messianic redemption was at hand.

Messianic faith had been the basis of the worldview of the Orthodox rabbinate in the eighteenth and nineteenth centuries, when it had done battle with the Haskalah (enlightenment) movement and also in the twentieth, when it fought tenaciously against secular Zionism. The fundamental messianic idea is that the redemption of the Jews from exile is totally in God's hands, and only he is capable of returning the Jews to the land that he had promised them, something that he would do only if and when they proved worthy of salvation by demonstrating their faith, their piety, and their righteousness. Only then, in the Last Days, after the war of Gog and Magog, would God redeem them by returning them to their land, bringing the messiah (a descendant of the house of King David) to rule them, building the Holy Temple in Jerusalem, reviving the dead as prophesized in Ezekiel 37, and bringing joy and prosperity to the world. Until then, the rabbis taught their flocks, the Jews must wait in the Diaspora, deepen their faith in God, study his Law, and await the savior.

The Zionist thought is the absolute antithesis of messianic faith. It is not God who will redeem the Jews from their exile, but the Jews themselves. Redemption (i.e., political independence), joy, and prosperity must be achieved not through a passive faith in a mystical, amorphous being but through hard work, migration to the Land of Israel, building it up, industry, agriculture, and if necessary, an armed struggle to conquer it. This was the essence and the foundation of the Zionist idea: total rejection of the messianic ideology.

During the latter part of the nineteenth century and first half of the twentieth, the Zionists—including a small number of Modern Orthodox nationalists—were in the minority, and the strictly orthodox anti-Zionists were the majority, but in the middle of the twentieth century the balance changed in favor of the Zionists. When the Zionists managed to achieve the establishment of the Jewish state, it was clear that the ultra-Orthodox rabbis had lost and that the "waiting for the messiah" ideology had no chance of attracting masses of Jews, or so it seemed. And indeed, when I was a child and teenager in Jerusalem in the 1950s and the early 1960s, the messianists were generally on the fringes of the margins of Israeli society and hardly evident at all. Israeli elites related to them as a kind of anachronistic joke, the way Americans look at the Amish. It was clear that a liberal and secular society was growing up in Israel, one that had totally thrown off the messianic burden and had kept the ultra-Orthodox rabbinate far from the hubs of power and was assiduously occupied in realizing the dream of the founder of the Zionist movement, Theodor Herzl, who envisioned a pluralist Jewish state, secular and technologically advanced with equality for Jews and non-Jews. That was the common belief until the war in June 1967. Then, as the sense of euphoria over the brilliant victory swept the Jewish world, secular Israelis began to comprehend that their common belief was wrong: the messianic rabbis who were kicked out the front door managed to sneak in through the window.

The basic messianic doctrine regarding the occupied territories was formulated by the spiritual founder of the main settlers' movement, Gush Emunim (Bloc of the Faithful), the late Rabbi Zvi Yehuda Kook, in 1968: "I tell you explicitly that the Torah forbids us to surrender even one inch of our liberated land. There are no conquests here, and we are not occupying foreign lands. We are returning to our home, to the inheritance of our ancestors. There is no Arab land here, only the inheritance of our God, and the more the world gets used to this idea, the better it will be for them and for all of us."

Rabbi Kook's messianic tendencies had not remained locked up inside the ultra-Orthodox camp. On the contrary, his preaching had also been lurking within the subconscious thoughts of influential circles in society, both Modern Orthodox and secular. Messianists came out of their closets and inflamed broad audiences. While, broadly speaking, the ultra-Orthodox remained theologically opposed to Zionism, many religious Zionists, who until then had repressed their messianic ideas in the depths of their consciousness, and secular Zionists joined the messianic camp, including intellectuals and leaders who had been brought up as socialists, even Marxists, and who until that time were seen and saw themselves as complete rationalists. The whole Jewish population was like someone suffering from bipolar disorder. The sharp transition from a sense of fear and despair before the war—when the president of Egypt, Gamal Abdel Nasser, arrayed his armored divisions in Sinai and threatened to destroy the Jewish state—and the catharsis that the Israelis experienced when the dimensions of their victory became clear found expression in unusual behavior: triumphalism, arrogance, and power worshipping.

Against this backdrop of elation, there were only a few people who correctly foresaw the future and dared to sound the warning that taking over the West Bank was not an act of redemption but one of occupation, and a continuous occupation of another nation's land must necessarily end in corruption.[1]

And indeed, the occupation did corrupt. It has caused terrible damage to Israeli society and taken a heavy price in both material and ethical terms. A state that in its early years attributed to itself lofty principles and values, and whose first prime minister, David Ben-Gurion, admonished its citizens to be "a light unto the nations," became one of the most abhorred and deplored countries on the face of the earth.

For more than forty years, Israel evaded a decision on the future of the West Bank, apart from a brief period between the election of Yitzhak Rabin as prime minister in July 1992 and his assassination in November 1995, a period that saw mutual recognition between Israel and the Palestinian Liberation Organization (PLO) and resolved agreement on a two-state solution, known as the Oslo Accords. Israel held onto the occupied territories and encouraged young people to settle there, but nevertheless out of fear of the international response, it held back from annexing the territories officially. Most of Israel's governments pulled the wool over the eyes of the world. To the external world, Israel never negated the possibility of returning the conquered lands to Arab sovereignty, but internally its leaders winked at its citizenry and systematically allowed the settlers to set up more and more communities in those lands. One after the other, the prime ministers voiced their desire to make peace with the Arab world, while at the same time they were creating a reality in the territories that would make restoration of their previous borders impossible. The Right and the Left worked hand in hand. The nationalistic Right held the view that the lands of Judea and Samaria would never be separated from the "land of our forefathers," while the left and the center were ready in principle to give up land, but only on condition that the Palestinians could ensure Israel a "secure peace," the practical meaning of which was the continued occupation of most of the West Bank in order to assure Israel of what it termed "strategic depth," or the expansion of its territory eastward deep into the Palestinian lands, so that the new common border would be drawn as far as possible from Israel's large population centers.

The two worldviews, the fundamentalist and the secular, united therefore at a decisive point: both expressed a refusal to withdraw from the lands that had been conquered. This reality was exploited by the settler camp's leaders, and they determinedly deepened their penetration into the occupied territory and polarized relations with the indigenous Arab population. Over the years, the territories were populated by dogged messianic believers who forcibly and violently drove the Palestinians out of areas where they had farmed and grazed herds for long years, and created a mass of Jewish settlements, all out of an aspiration to create a reality that could not be overturned in the future.

The engine behind the settlement movement, Gush Emunim, was set up in 1974 as an extraparliamentary wing of the National Religious Party, with the aim of colonizing the territories with Jews. For four decades, Gush Emunim has invested vast sums—most of it the taxpayers' money that the leadership, in its foolhardiness, has allocated to it—to establish about 120 settlements inhabited by some 330,000 souls plus approximately 100 small outposts inhabited by another 4,000 settlers, or 4.2 percent of the 7.94 million inhabitance of Israel (as of August 2012). Along with the settlement enterprise, Gush Emunim worked hard to create a positive image of the settler in the eyes of the rest of the population of Israel and the Jews of the Diaspora. They were depicted as the new Zionists, who are emulating the pioneers of the early twentieth century, as the representatives of the entire Jewish people. As long as the Palestinians obeyed the occupation authorities and worked hard at their jobs in Israel (mostly in the construction industry; to this day some of them are still employed at building settlements in the territories) it was easy enough to seduce public opinion in Israel into believing that the settlement enterprise was good for the country, or at least did not endanger it. The leaders of the national camp gave the settlement movement momentum, and at the same time the PLO did not manage to create a critical mass of pressure on Israel in the territories, the Arab states, or the world arena. In fact, during the first twenty years of the occupation (1967–1987) the PLO succeeded only infrequently in challenging the Jewish state, when it sent terrorist squads to attack Israeli targets in Europe, mainly passengers of El Al Airlines at international airports. Israel held the occupied territories in a firm grip. Its secret services used its special techniques effectively and averted a rebellion.

A coalition of three forces gave the settlers political, economic, and moral backing. First were the moderate Orthodox believers who during the early years of the state had followed a path of modernity and toleration, and had now changed direction and within ten to fifteen years, in a gradual process, had become more pious and had adopted the messianic ideology. They differed from the ultra-Orthodox in their Zionism and in their readiness to build the state and serve in the army.

The second group included most of the ultra-Orthodox, known in Israel as Haredim, or the "God fearing." They had been the allies of the social-democratic Left as long as the latter ruled the country and held the budgetary purse strings but now became more extremely religious and more nationalistic, and they shifted their support to the Right, although they were theologically still committed to the belief that the Zionist state was illegitimate.

The third group consisted of the secular nationalists who had at first been pushed by the Left onto the margins of political life but in the new reality created after the military victory their ideology had acquired powerful momentum.

This was how what became known as the "national camp" was formed, which in the last two decades of the twentieth century gathered strength until it accounted for some 50 percent of the population. Groups of religious Jews in the Diaspora, mainly in the United States and to some extent also in France, and powerful Evangelical Christian communities in America gave this national camp political and economic support.

In practice, after the victory and the conquest, the nationalist and religious camps united behind a single ideological platform: the new territories were part of the State of Israel. When it suited them, they brandished religious elements and used them to shape their identity, but it also worked the other way, with religion exploiting secular nationalist elements. Religion and nationalism therefore served as catalysts for each other, and together they bolstered the natural tendency within each camp toward isolationism and arrogance.

The national camp adopted a catchy but isolationist slogan, "The whole world's against us," and preached to the Israelis that they should withdraw into their fortress and muster to face the hostile world. This simplistic thesis held that influential liberal groups in Europe and the United States had joined up with the Muslims with the aim of eliminating Israel's gains in the 1967 war. This was an anti-Jewish conspiracy, claimed the adherents of seclusion, and if Israel wanted to protect its assets and survive, it must tenaciously hold its ground. These proponents of isolationism gave voice to a worldview prevalent among circles that tend to highlight the painful chapters in Jewish history—exile, persecution, pogroms, and suffering—and naturally advocate the national religious outlook that stood for the notion that the Jews are a "chosen people."

The secular nationalists contributed to this isolationist trend the historical claim that the captured territories had been part of the realm of King David, while the religious ones brought the messianic element, stating that the new borders were the fulfillment of God's promise to his people. This metaphysical-nationalist concoction that combined the "chosen people" myth with the "the whole world's against us" slogan dovetailed nicely with the victim syndrome. On this complex issue, Israeli political thought turned reality upside-down on an Orwellian scale. The assailant represented himself as the victim and the victim as the assailant.

The victim syndrome fixed itself deep inside Israeli consciousness, mostly as the moral to be drawn from the Holocaust, and became a central element in its world outlook. The logic behind such thinking is that the world owes the Jews a never-ending debt because while the Nazis were murdering six million of them, the rest of the human race did nothing to stop them, and therefore, when the surviving few are fulfilling their historical and religious heritage in the land of their forefathers, and especially when they are defending themselves against their enemies, the world must support them unconditionally. On occasion, fanatics have used this reasoning to justify racist acts against the Palestinians, as in, "This is the way the goyim [gentiles] treated us when we were the victims, so we can use the same methods."

The efforts to assimilate the victim syndrome into the Zionist ethos cannot be reconciled with the two basic ideas that guided Zionism before the 1967 war. The first was the cultivation in the Jewish state of a new kind of Jew, secular and educated, modern and productive. The second was to establish an exemplary society: sovereign, secular, democratic, free of the ailments of the European Diaspora, with its narrow-mindedness, petty provincialism, and its focus on religious studies and rituals. In effect, the coalition that the believers formed with the right wing, with the goal of Judaizing the territories in mind, has emasculated the fundamentals of Zionism. It has restored to Jewish life elements that Zionism had tried with all of its power to shake off—first and foremost the messianic idea.

Hence, the June 1967 victory dramatically changed the basic political awareness of important segments in the society. While messianic and irrational beliefs had been penetrating deep into the consciousness of many right-wing seculars, among the religious communities, a more risky phenomenon developed; faith in democracy has firmly receded, and the aspiration to impose religious legal codes on the state has gained strength. Those laws, known as the halakha, view God and his emissaries on earth, the rabbis, as the sovereign. The fundamentalist call for a halakhic state is sounded loud and clear in public. Sociologists have estimated that this extreme messianic idea unites between one fifth and one quarter of Israeli Jews, whose goal is to radically alter the definition of the Jewish state. Instead of a democracy, they want to establish a theocracy, or in their words, a halakhic state.

Following the 1967 war, elements that originated in messianic thought affixed themselves onto secular Israeli life, as if they were a natural, systemic part of the historical process that the Jewish people was undergoing. Take for example, God's mentioned promise to Abraham the Patriarch in the Book of Genesis: "Unto thy seed will I give this land." All of a sudden, people who were remote from the Orthodox viewpoint, including intellectuals and politicians known as liberals, began relating to the divine undertaking not as a myth but as a valid and applicable political principle. The myth that was based on the biblical promise provided political justification for the seizure of the occupied territories as well as dictating the attitude toward the Palestinians. Anyone familiar with the sensible vision of the authentic Zionist pioneers and the calculated and balanced manner in which leaders of political Zionism—Theodor Herzl, Max Nordau, Chaim Weizmann, and many others—obtained international guarantees and the political rights that formed the basis for the establishment of the Zionist state can only tear his or her hair. Where did things go wrong? How can it be that the people who defiantly brandish the divine promise in the world's face, those false Zionists, have seized control of the entire Zionist enterprise? Reality, it transpires, has cheated the vision.

4

The Original Sin

FROM EARLY IN the twentieth century, during the era known by the Zionists as Shivat Zion—the return to Zion—an exceptionally interesting Jewish population gathered in what was Palestine until 1948 and then the State of Israel. It was a classical country of immigration, a miniature replica of the United States of America, with a culture of pioneers conquering the frontier and encroaching upon the land of the indigenous population; with the formation of a wide variety of institutions and the establishment of towns and cities, starting from scratch; with the entry of huge waves of immigrants when it became clear to the Jewish masses that their life in the Diaspora was untenable and that the pioneers had founded a society that was worth joining.[1] And everything was in effect based on the idea of a melting pot, with immigrants of various types thrown in one side and coming out on the other as the fulfillers of the Zionist dream. In North America, however, the melting pot worked and is still working in more or less the way that the founding fathers had intended it to, whereas the fire under the Israeli furnace turned cold. It was incapable of melting down the bodies tossed into it and shaping them into new, uniform, and hardened material. The Israeli melting pot that the pioneers built only worked properly during the first half of the twentieth century, as long as the Land of Israel was attracting avant-gardists, idealists, and revolutionaries, but it failed during the second half after the mass migrations began. More than a melting pot, the reality that has taken shape in Israel since the 1950s is like a tortuous maze, and whoever enters it is doomed to roam its corridors forever. There may be a way out, but so far no one has managed to locate it.

It is a state of extreme paradoxes, with the most prominent of these being the gap between the impressive performances of talented individuals and the way society works as a whole. The then CEO of the giant generic drugs firm Teva, Shlomo Yanai, said in a TV interview in 2010, after presenting the company's five year plan, "There is in Israel a vast number of capabilities. Nowhere in the world is there as much brainpower as in Israel."

Indeed, there is a great deal of admiration for Israeli society in the world, not because it has managed to establish a democratic state in a troublesome region—that's why it was admired in the 1950s—but because it has become a breeding ground for scientific and technological talents (including six Nobel Prize laureates from 2002 through 2011) who do not fear taking risks and who have produced amazing results.

There's no doubt that the Israelis are a relatively smart people, talented and resourceful, but the sum total of the share of wisdom with which they are endowed as individuals does not add up to a surplus of brainpower, but rather the opposite. The sum is less than the parts. The entire collective, when it acts as a group, is not capable of behaving effectively and creates a political and social reality that precludes an orderly existence. It is a reality that is almost always on the brink of an existential crisis that exists within an oppressive and depressing atmosphere, and functions as a kind of perpetuum mobile that leads from one dead end to another.

True, Israel is a strong country in military and economic terms, but there is a basic weakness at its heart, a lack of social coherence. Compared to developed societies, it lacks civil discipline and tends to anarchy. Its most salient blemish is divisiveness that rips the social fabric into little shreds of political parties, each striving to achieve a different goal. This divisiveness is so extreme that in a few years' time, if the rate of natural growth of the various communities that make up the whole does not change, almost half the population will belong to groups whose ideologies negate the fundamental values that the state's founding fathers bequeathed it.

There is a paradox within the very definition of the essence of the Israeli state as a "Jewish and democratic state." This is a contradiction in terms. There is no separation of state and religion in Israel. The state delegated to the Orthodox rabbinate the authority to apply the halakha to all matters of personal status. This is an archaic legal code that manifestly discriminates against women and gentiles.

From his birth to his death, the Jewish male is favored by the halakha over females and over gentiles. In a normal state functioning in accordance with egalitarian and democratic values an anachronistic, antiquated system would not be given the status of arbiter, unless it first underwent thorough reforms. In the terms of the U.S. Constitution, almost every political, social, and religious function that Orthodox Judaism is entitled to carry out in Israel would be barred under either the First or the Fourteenth Amendment.

The state granted the Orthodox preferential status, and to a certain extent it forces the population to behave according to its ideology in public, especially on the Sabbath and religious festivals. This is also true in matters having to do with personal status, from birth to death; of defining who is a Jew for the purposes of immigration and admission to schools; of the conduct of official ceremonies; and in many other spheres. The Orthodox sectors have set up political parties that generally are in a position to determine whether the Left or the Right will form the coalition government and therefore able to pry concessions and privileges out of the larger parties. The Reform and Conservative communities are very small and lack any real influence.

This situation, in which religion is so deeply involved in the conduct of the state, was forced upon the founding fathers against their will. Whoever is familiar with their political philosophy or has studied the ideas that they bequeathed in writing knows that they planned a state in which a pluralistic democracy would be in full control of public life, whereas religion—god and the rabbis and the dogma they represent—would have no standing in the government. As the founders of the Zionist movement were clearly the products of the Enlightenment and were well aware of the processes that Europe had undergone in the seventeenth and eighteenth centuries, when secularity triumphed in the clash between political liberty and religious coercion, they were certain that a similar process would take place in the Zionist society that would arise in the Land of Israel; just as the Europeans and the Americans (including most of the Jews there) had done, the Israelis would cast off the straitjacket of religious authoritarianism and raise the banner of equal rights. Religion in the Jewish state was supposed to serve the confessional and ritual requirements of the individual, each according to his or her own lights. Can anyone imagine that in Europe it would be possible to reconstruct a situation in which the Catholic Church and its institutions control governmental matters? The Zionist forefathers believed that this could not happen in a Jewish state. From their point of view, the entire religious sphere referred to a cultural and historical heritage and by no means whatsoever to the imposition of a system of religious principles and customs upon the citizenry. In their eyes, the Orthodox have narrowed the definition of Judaism (as does the state now). For them, Judaism meant more than a religion. Primarily it represented human values: the Ten Commandments and the heritage of the Prophets, not the sacrifice lows and the menstruation orders of the Torah; liberty and equality, not female enslavement to the order of "fruitful and multiply." Sooner or later, Israel's forefathers believed, the sovereign Jewish nation would be turned from an exiled ethnic-religious community into a free "State of All its Citizens," where individual and group rights are recognized.

If they could have done so, some of the leading founding fathers would have used the term "Hebrew" (or "Hebraic") instead of "Jewish." That way, the objectionable parts of the European Diaspora's heritage would have been wiped out, and the national narrative would have been built around the name of an ancient Middle Eastern tribe that the outside, non-Jewish world had generally related to in a positive way, unlike the term "Jewish." This is why the early Zionists were so deeply hated by the Orthodox faithful. First, as we have already pointed out, Zionism clashed with the belief that God, by means of the messiah, had exclusive rights over the redemption of the Jews and their return to Zion. Second, the Zionists aspired to established a civil state, and the rabbis who one hundred years earlier had rejected the Enlightenment movement because it threatened religion knew that a state that would be labeled secular and liberal would leave them without a flock of believers.

Why did the founders refrain from explicitly separating the state from religion? They erred because in the early years of the state, they were confident that secular Zionism had triumphed and that Orthodox Judaism had no chance of attaining the status it had achieved in the Diaspora, where in many places it dominated the Jewish masses. The early Zionists had an expression that summed up the revolution they had carried out: "We have not only taken the Jew out of the Diaspora, we have also taken the Diaspora out of the Jew." The new Jew shattered the image of the Diaspora Jew. That is what Israel looked like when I was a youth—the late 1950s and the 1960s, up until 1967. It looked then as if the antimodern, narrow-minded, Orthodox worldview, which discriminated against women and advocated separation from the gentile foreigners, had been defeated by secular Zionism. And in truth, in those years secular sociologists declared that the generation of the founders had to a large extent succeeded in creating a normal nation with a democratic government, a rational economy, a modern educational system, and a new Hebrew culture. In this landscape of the young state, the old Jew—pious, puritanical, and passive, with his old-fashioned black attire and bizarre customs—looked like a curiosity, a museum piece, a relic of an age that vanished for good.

The pioneers made a single gesture, a token of good will toward the rabbis, apparently out of a desire to preserve an iota of authentic Judaism in memory of their parents, most of whom had remained in Europe and perished in the Holocaust. If we allow the handful of Orthodox Jews in the country to observe the Sabbath in their neighborhoods by letting them keep traffic out, and by keeping kosher at all governmental premises, they'll kiss our hands in gratitude, the founders said, and in their haste they waived the vitally important principle of separation of religion and state.

In addition, a short time after the state was created leaders of the religious parties requested Ben-Gurion to exempt four hundred exceptionally gifted yeshiva students from military service so that they might continue their Torah studies without interruption. In 1968, the government increased their number to eight hundred. Following the general election of 1977, the bargaining ability of the ultra-Orthodox political parties increased. As a consequence, the new government that was formed by a conservative majority removed all limitations on the numbers of the exempted yeshiva students. Since then, persistently from year to year, their numbers have mounted. In 2011, around six thousand eighteen-year-old yeshiva students were exempted.

True, back in the 1940s and the 1950s, the rabbis never showed any signs of wanting to make the government subservient to Judaic law and did not constitute a threat to the aspiration of establishing a civil state. In the young Israel, the Jews who wore those black suits were few, most of the males among them worked for a living, and their wives bore reasonable numbers of children. In no way whatsoever did the founders anticipate that the result of their indulgence would be a monster that would rise up against its creator. This was the original sin, and its outcome was fraught with disaster.

For their part, among themselves the heads of the Orthodox community were convinced that in the long term the secular Zionist vision had no chance of succeeding. The Zionist state would be a transient episode, the rabbis told the followers who remained loyal to the faith, and they promised that in the coming generations the children of the atheistic pioneers, those arrogant Zionists who had rejected the tenets of Judaism and become secular, would seek their roots and find their way back to authentic Jewishness. At least in my own family, several Orthodox relatives voiced that opinion over and over again, and as a youth I used to respond with a dismissive smile. It is still too early to say who will be proved right—that's a matter for a separate discussion—but certainly the forty years during which Israel has ruled the West Bank have demonstrated that the founders did make at least a tactical error in not basing their vision on a binding constitution that entrenched the separation of government and religion.

The messiah, as we have seen, made a big-time comeback. Since the victory in the 1967 war, in a large part of the community of the faithful in Israel, the messianic trend gathered strength, and simultaneously, the support for the democratic system waned. Within this community there is a sect that does not even identify with the state as an entity whose existence is justified. This is the homogenous and resolute ultra-Orthodox, or Haredi, community, which comprises about a tenth of the population.[2]

The Haredim bestow sovereignty upon God, and in effect they aspire to the abolishment of the institution of the state, so that the rabbis will be able to enforce the halakha. In other words, the Haredim aspire to live in an Iranian-style theocracy where the actual control is in the hands of a council of sages that does not have to stand for election. It's doubtful that this goal can ever be realized, and they will therefore be satisfied with flushing the classical Zionist values out of the definition of the state and wresting the ability to rule from its elected institutions.

Surprisingly, however, although the democratic system is still in force in Israel, the ultra-Orthodox sects enjoy a far-reaching autonomy that few countries, if any, have been prepared to grant their minorities. They are exempt from taking part in the defense of the country, as they steadfastly refuse to enlist in the army. (There is compulsory conscription in Israel for both men and women, but it is not applied to either Haredim or Arabs.) They have their own separate, archaic school system, in which the core subjects of the secular curriculum such as English and most sciences and humanities are not taught; Torah is all their children study, day in and day out. They settle disputes in an autonomous legal system known as Din Torah (Jewish law), and most of them do not work for a living. Most of male Haredim study at religious seminaries, known as yeshivot, and the state grants them living allowances. In fact, every year, thousands of Haredi males are unable or unwilling to participate in wider Israeli society, learn a trade, and join the work force.[3]

Such a situation, in which a tenth of the population is blatantly estranging itself from the state, rejects democracy, and refuses to study nonreligious subjects, raises so many crucial problems that in many cases, life then becomes intolerable. Some examples: their refusal to join the army, which creates a distinction between the value of Haredi life and secular life; the fact they are not prepared to give their children a secular education and a large part of their livelihood is borne by the state budget; the harsh discrimination that they practice in their marital laws against females; their belief in the "be fruitful and multiply" precept, which burdens their women with impossible loads of pregnancies and births that in many cases are tantamount to enslavement; and their conduct as a closed mystical sect. These are things that a democratic state should not have to countenance, and we are speaking here of a state that, apart from a constant existential threat, also has to cope with a social structure that creates immeasurably severe complications and stresses.

The efforts to consolidate a Jewish democracy might have succeeded if Orthodox Judaism had been prepared to forgo the nondemocratic elements in its ideology, but the rabbis insist on applying the halakha literally, in its original and conservative form, and are not prepared to adapt it to the modern era, as has been done by the Conservative Jews to a certain extent, and by the Reform movements to a large degree. Because of this, the relations between the ultra-Orthodox community and the state are on a collision course.

In effect, it is the productive secular and Modern Orthodox part of society that carries the economic existence and the security of the Haredi community on its back. In the 1970s, when the Haredi flocks made up 4 to 5 percent of the population, this was an undesirable situation, but the secular Israelis tended to ignore it because the extra burden was relatively light. Today, with the Haredi communities making up 10 percent of the population, the secular citizens are complaining that the burden is insufferable. In the future, as the percentage increases, they will refuse to carry it or will choose to emigrate to the United States or other Western countries.

With a natural annual rate of increase of 5 percent, the ultra-Orthodox community doubles in size approximately every sixteen years, whereas the average rate for the Jewish population as a whole is only 1 percent.[4] The number of Haredi youths who are exempt from military service grows accordingly, and today they account for some 15 percent of conscription-age males. As already indicated, the mass draft dodging of the Haredim has already produced a severe problem of discrimination between those who are ready or who are obligated to give their lives for the country and those who are not. The anticipated increase in their proportion of the population will create a severe problem of national security—the military will be short of soldiers.

What is more, if the current rate of growth of the Haredi continues, by the end of the third decade of this century they will comprise 20 percent of the population, and by 2050, an estimated 37 percent. As most of the males in their community do not join the work force but occupy themselves with religious study, the secular population will have to bear a large part of the cost of the livelihood of the Haredi families. Can one conceive of a state in which one-fifth of the males refuse to acquire a trade and to go to work? According to official data published in June 2010, the employment rate among Haredi males was 36 percent and among Haredi females 49 percent (among non-Haredi 75 percent and 69 percent, respectively). Because of the small employment rate and the low level of education, the income gap between Haredi and non-Haredi families is enormous. An average Haredi family earns 50 percent less than an average non-Haredi family.

Although the natural increase of the Haredi population casts doubt on Israel's future as a democracy and is able to tear at the fabric of the country in order to trample its secular lifestyle, there is nevertheless a fairly simple solution that could return things to where they stood before. It would weaken the ultra-Orthodox elements in the Israeli society and strengthen the secular side, but ironically, the solution is closely connected to the chances of achieving peace with the Arab world. In other words, resolving the conflict with the Palestinians could beget a chance to dramatically decrease the Haredi political bargaining power.

Seculars from all political sides (Left, Center, and Right) should unite and make a strong coalition for the salvation of the original Zionist dream. This unity of the seculars would certainly acquire enough political power for eliminating parts of the Haredi's far-reaching autonomy, mainly their exemption from army service and the release of their children from studying the core, secular part of the customary curriculum.

How could a unity of the seculars be reached and solve the nation's most considerable problems that have emanated from and will yet be exacerbated by the Haredi dogma and way of life? Until now, the future of the territories—withdrawal from the West Bank versus de facto annexation—was the main disputed matter, starkly dividing the secular mass and enabling the Haredi rabbis to perfectly utilize their bargaining power.

Solving the occupied territories' dispute through a compromise with the Palestinians would yield not only peace with the Arabs but also a matrimonial reconciliation among the bloc of seculars. Hence, the new political situation—a majority of seculars voting in the Knesset against the Haredi's isolationist intentions—would undoubtedly nullify the bargaining advantages of the ultra-Orthodox and force the rabbis to make the necessary modifications to the process of integrating their communities into the general society.

5

"Jewish and Democratic" or "State of All Its Citizens"

THE HAREDI MINORITY is positioned on one problematic flank. The Israeli Arabs are on yet another flank, no less problematic. These are the Arabs who were not driven out of Palestine or who did not run away when the state was founded in 1948, and their descendants. They currently constitute about a fifth of the total population, and as long as the regional dispute is not resolved, it is doubtful that they will have a chance of being extricated from the dead end in which they are in effect imprisoned.[1] The definition of the state as "Jewish and democratic" does not jibe with the way they see things, and they are unable to identify with the primary ideological basis of the state: the Jewish return to Zion. When so large a group of citizens cannot connect to the idea that has shaped the country, it is doubtful that society as a whole can live in tranquility. Apparently, a majority of the liberal wing of Israeli society would agree to redefine the country as a state of all its citizens, like any normal democracy, but in the country as a whole, the alliance that the religious political parties have formed with the secular conservatives enjoys a solid majority on this matter to date.

This situation is still further complicated because the Israeli Arab minority, by virtue of its being Arab, cannot repudiate the aspirations of the neighboring Arab states, some of which have been in a state of war with Israel since it was established. There have been similar circumstances in history, but in today's world in the democratic West, there is no such a situation. Ostensibly, the enemy across the border has an enormous number of supporters living within the boundaries of the state. This is the main reason for the discrimination that the Jewish majority practices against the Arab minority and for the manifest alienation between the two communities. The Jews see the Arab citizens as representing a potential existential danger and are not prepared to accept them as equal partners. Some of the conservative elements in Israeli society adopt an openly racist stance towards the Arabs.

The discrimination practiced by the government and the legal system against the Arab minority are in blatant violation of democratic principles. In recent years, reports on racism published by the Mossawa Center—an Arab-Israeli NGO that promotes equality for the Arab citizens of Israel—stated that the number of discriminatory measures curtailing Arab citizens' basic rights have dramatically increased. The current Knesset and the previous one are responsible for a 75 percent increase in the number of bills that contained discriminatory measures. The reports document twenty-seven racist remarks uttered by Jewish public figures against the Arab community and not investigated by the state prosecution. One of the quotations was attributed to the foreign minister in the Netanyahu government, Avigdor Lieberman, head of the Yisrael Beiteinu ("Israel Our Home") party, which is supported chiefly by immigrants from the former Soviet Union. In a speech in the Knesset plenum in 2006, Lieberman implied that Arab members of the Knesset should be "taken care of" in the same way as Nazi collaborators who were sentenced to death by the Nuremberg tribunals.[2] Several times Lieberman has repeated his demand that the Arabs should be expelled from Israel. In one case, he said, "Let them take their baggage and go to hell." Lieberman is one of the right-wing politicians who frequently propose measures that would restrict the movement of Arabs and deprive them of their rights if they refuse to swear allegiance to Zionist "state values."

Another member of the Knesset, Yisrael Katz from the Likud party, the minister of transportation in Netanyahu's cabinet, submitted a bill with the aim of altering all the signposts in the country to give only the Hebrew names of all settlements, including those of Arab communities.

Two significantly discriminatory bills were enacted by the Knesset at the beginning of 2011. One, informally called the Naqba Bill, rules that anyone publishing "matter that causes contempt for or disloyalty toward the state" would be sentenced to a year in prison. The other empowers acceptance committees in Jewish communities to bar Arab citizens from purchasing land within their boundaries.

If the Knesset approves another seemingly inoffensive bill, the status of Israel's Arabs as equal citizens will be further harmed. The bill is aimed at making an explicit definition of Israel as "a Jewish state and a democracy" in Basic Law (part of a future constitution, still under construction), which is a self-evident proposition, interpreting one of the basic principals in Israel's declaration of independence: "The State of Israel is the national home of the Jewish people for its self-determination according to its cultural and historical tradition." Nevertheless, the draft contains a few traps. In paragraph 4, the status of the Arabic language as Israel's second official language would be canceled; paragraph 9 permits the state "to allow a community, including one made up of one fate or national origin, to sustain separate communities"—again, a clear attempt to void a Supreme Court ruling prohibiting discrimination against non-Jews by the Israel Land Administration.

Racist activities against Arab citizens reached an unprecedented level at the end of 2010, when dozens of Orthodox and ultra-Orthodox rabbis, many of them municipal chief rabbis and heads of rabbinical academies, signed a religious ban on Jews selling or renting apartments to non-Jews and Arabs. The ban ordered neighbors and acquaintances of Jews who sell or rent apartments to gentiles and Arabs "to distance themselves from the Jewish landlord, refrain from doing business with him, deny him the right to read from the Torah [at synagogues' rituals] and banish him until he retracts this harmful deed." Among the signers were two leading national-religious rabbis: Shlomo Aviner and Yaakov Yosef, the son of the Shas party spiritual leader Ovadia Yosef. The top Ashkenazi Haredi leader at that time, the late Rabbi Yosef Shalom Elyashiv, rebuked the ban signers.

Arab men and women find it difficult to get jobs in public and private organizations, even in those that are only in a very indirect way connected to national security. The Israel Security Agency (Shin Bet) supervises the appointment of Arabs to public positions. Generally, public institutions will not employ an Arab if the appointment is not endorsed by the Shin Bet. Private companies owned by Jews also are not eager to employ Arabs, even if they have excellent qualifications.[3] The only professional field in which Israeli Arabs have been able to integrate is medicine—8 percent of all the doctors in Israel are Arabs, many of them in senior posts. But young Arabs who have obtained university degrees in engineering and technological areas as a rule must seek employment as teachers in schools within their communities. This is the reason why the income of the average Arab household is only 57 percent of its Jewish counterpart, and over one half of Arab families in Israel are classified as poor. While at the end of 2009 the average per capita gross domestic product (GDP) came to $28,000, in the Arab sector it was a mere $10,000.[4] The state has failed to utilize the economic potential of the Arabs, and they are unable to derive benefit from the state's economic and technological potential. The rate of Arab participation in the labor market is very low—only 40 percent for men and 20 percent for women, the result being that a fifth of the population contributes only 8 percent to the gross national product (GNP). This is an egregiously intolerable situation, and its solution depends on the establishment of peace in the Middle East.

Nevertheless, it is possible that an unexpected, important shift has been under way within the Arab minority in recent years. There are increasing indications that a critical mass of Israeli Arabs is prepared to move ahead to accept the existence of Israel as a reality. The fact that it is a democracy makes Israel different from the Arab states, and in the eyes of the majority of its Arab minority, this distinction makes it more attractive, even though almost all of the state's composite elements have been adapted to suit the Jewish majority. From the point of view of Israel's Arabs, support for the continued existence of the state of Israel, with all its advantages and disadvantages, is apparently the option of choice if they wish to preserve a maximum amount of liberty, equality, and economic welfare for themselves, in comparison to the citizens of Muslim neighboring countries. This is apparently the prevalent opinion, and in the final analysis, the pragmatic viewpoint will ultimately triumph. This is why the belief that the current right-wing, religious majority in Israeli politics is likely to be replaced in the not-too-distant future by a majority that will represent a combination of secular Jews and pragmatic Arabs is not unrealistic. Classical Zionism, ironically, needs the support of the Arabs in order to overcome the false, messianic-nationalistic Zionism. In the future, a liberal and reconciliatory Jewish-Arab coalition will have a chance of putting Israel back onto its original Zionist course.

But this turnaround on the part of the Arabs has not yet occurred, and so far, a little less than one third of the Israeli nation (some 20 percent Arabs and 10 percent Haredim) is not able to identify with the definition of the state or its goals, and it is precisely this third that is multiplying much faster than the other two thirds who can accept the definition of the state, its character, and its aims.

The Haredim are multiplying particularly rapidly, and while the Arabs are a little less vigorous, they too are increasing at a quicker rate than secular Jews. Among Israeli Arabs (as well as the Palestinians in the occupied areas), the rate of natural increase is among the highest in the world—some 3.5 percent per annum. The Arab population is very young as compared to the Jews, and its mean age is 20, whereas that of the Jews is 31. There is an average of 4.8 members in Arab families, and 3.5 in Jewish ones.[5] According to official demographic forecasts, if the natural rate of increase among Israeli Arabs does not change, in less than twenty years, one in every four Israelis will be an Arab.[6] Taken together with the Haredim, who according to statistical forecasts will make up some 25 percent of the population (on the assumption that their rate of increase does not change), a majority of Israel's citizens will not agree with the definition and the goals of the state. In theory, a coalition of the ultra-Orthodox and the Arabs will be able to abolish the Knesset and empty the state of the values on the basis of which it was founded—Zionism and democracy.

Perhaps an accurate observer would point out that in the future, the Arab minority will have the option to decide whether to make alliance with the secular part of the Jewish majority and put back the state on its liberal Zionist course or join a coalition with the ultra-Orthodox and put an end to the entire Zionist dream.

Ostensibly, such scenarios seem totally unreasonable, but in practice these options are already here. Official state statistics, published in the government's statistical yearbook, present the numbers of students in schools for the next five years according to their communal groups. This is not a forecast but a real, existing fact, because those students have already been born and at age six will enter the school system in first grade. The figures show that in the 2009–2010 school year, 47.5 percent of first graders were either Arabs or Haredim, and in 2010–2011, children from those two sectors constituted a small majority of first graders. In subsequent years, the Arab-Haredi majority in the school system will increase steadily. Already, according to the fundamental basic outlook of their parents, most of the younger generation in Israel is not raised and educated according to the Zionist forefathers' values. If anyone had dared publish a forecast with these figures when I was a young man four or five decades ago, people would have laughed at him and called him an idiot. It would be as impossible for the majority of Americans to become communists, they would have told him, for the majority of Israelis to be non-Zionists. But that is the situation. The data point to so grave a problem, one that is so fundamental and even existential, that clearly a drastic solution must be found soon, and if not, it will be impossible to prolong the life of the same democratic state of Israel that was established in 1948.

Here again, the obvious questions should arise with a definite emphasis: If today secular voters still have an absolute majority, why don't they arrange things in a way that would put an end to the dangers faced by their fundamental values? Why don't they force a separation between the state and religion and nullify the option of creating a theocratic state based on halakha? Why don't they oblige the Haredim to learn secular subjects and join the workforce? Why are they, the secular majority, prepared to maintain the tens of thousands of Haredim who study in yeshivot and their families? Why don't they have the Haredim conscripted into the armed forces and do away with the situation in which only the secular and national religious must be ready to serve and sacrifice their lives? What about the possibility that in the future the army will be short of soldiers? And why don't they advance the Arab minority and open up employment opportunities for them, especially Arab women, to enable them to integrate into the state so that their birthrate will drop to the level of secular Jews? And why don't they act vigorously in order to reach peace with Israel's neighbors in order to avoid alienation between the state and its Arab citizens?

For many years, the secular majority has been evading the issues arising from the need to coexist with these two large, alienated minorities—the ultra-Orthodox Haredim and the Israeli Arabs; this is a predicament that can be likened to that of a small fishing boat that has hooked two whales threatening to capsize it. In the course of those years, the problems have only become greater, and the divisions can no longer be ignored. They are menacing the state's very existence.

What are the origins of this anomalous situation that has led Israel into a dead end? Since the victory of 1967, the occupied territories have been at the top of the national camp's order of priorities. In order to maintain the occupation, to colonize the territories with settlers, and to overcome the Left's tendency to compromise, the secular Right resorted to enlisting the support of the religious camp and vice versa, and these two sectors have forged an alliance through which they have pushed their agenda forward.

This alliance was not created out of naiveté. The secular right-wingers were not unaware of the fact that the enormous investment in the settlement enterprise came at the expense of the weaker strata of Israeli society and the still struggling "development towns," established in the 1950s to absorb the waves of immigrants, as did the huge bribes they were forced to pay the ultra-Orthodox rabbis in the form of subsidies to yeshiva students in exchange for their political support. It was certainly clear to the secular Right that the situation taking root in Israeli society was abnormal; that the settlements were a violation of international law; that dangerous nationalistic, messianic, and belligerent cells were multiplying in the territories; that the alliance with the ultra-Orthodox was corrupt because it legitimized Haredi draft dodging, and because it handed a part of the national budget over to a community that balks at contributing to the building of society and that produces almost nothing. Nonetheless, the secular Right has been incapable of cutting itself off from the Whole Land of Israel heritage because of its stubborn cleaving to the archaic nationalistic principles, which have been a lateral branch of the Zionist thinking from the outset and early into the twentieth century but are no longer relevant.

Indeed, the key to the solution of all of these problems lies in the occupied territories. The majority of people, which is secular, sane, and democratic in Israel, is not capable of tackling these acute problems it has with itself as long as the occupation is dividing it into two adversarial camps.[7] Of course, the ultra-Orthodox community is exploiting the division among the seculars to the maximum. Their leaders, the great rabbis, are superbly manipulating both secular camps, the national and the liberal, and that is the primary reason for the absence of peace.

For more than forty years, this was Israel's reality. Its preoccupation with the occupation had sapped the strength of the state and taken over its agenda, confused its elites and camouflaged its existential essence, and sabotaged its fundamental Zionist principals and deterred the option of peace. Israel as it looks today is a far cry from what the founding fathers envisaged. Moreover, there has been an erosion in its basic ethical values, attesting to an extreme attenuation in self-awareness and awareness of the surrounding environment.

But this reality is changing now. In recent years, slowly and gradually, among the secular citizens—those who are not fanatical or extremist and whose behavior and attitudes are normal in western terms—there is growing understanding that the settlement movement is not bringing redemption to Israel but rather a calamity, and that giving up territory could well engender a process through which dismantling some of the obstacles that are proving so onerous to the state could be dismantled. With the consolidation of globalization, rationality has surrendered to myth as the leadership of the moderate Right began extricating itself from the mental paralysis that had gripped it in the wake of the tremendous excitement over the conquest of the territories in 1967. Swinging its camp toward the Center, and then leftward, many of the earlier Great Israel believers took up the antimessianic positions that the left had supported for the past thirty or forty years, during which the notion of giving up territory was anathema to the majority of Israeli Jews.

PART II

As Arabs Push for a Settlement, Israel Plays for Time

6

War and Peace

NOW ZIONISM IS once again being called upon to make a critical decision in the face of the same dilemma that has preoccupied it since the Palestinian national movement first began organizing in order to eject the Jewish pioneers in the early part of the twentieth century. Is it ready for a territorial compromise?

In 1947, when the United Nations decided to partition Palestine on more or less demographic lines, the Zionist movement reacted positively. Because there were few Jewish settlers in the territory allocated for an Arab state, the decision to agree to the partition did not cost them much. Moreover, because there were hundreds of thousands of Holocaust survivors languishing in displaced persons camps in Europe, the Zionist movement was under enormous pressure to fulfill the mandate for which it had been established and to bring those refugees safely to a Jewish state, however imperfect the borders were. But twenty years later, in 1967, when the dust of the Six-Day War settled, it emerged that Israeli interests had changed. Now, the country was in firm military control of the whole of Palestine, from the Mediterranean Sea to the Jordan River, and when it was called upon to honor its historical commitment to territorial compromise, it opted to sit on the fence.

So why is it that this situation cannot last, with Israel's military strength not in decline but actually growing? From year to year, Israel has accumulated more and more economic and military power, while the Palestinians are growing weaker and weaker, especially since they split into two rival camps, Fatah and Hamas, and effectively partitioned the territory that they do control into two separate entities at loggerheads with each other, the West Bank and the Gaza Strip. But there are two reasons why the Israeli advantage is misleading. The first one is internal: if the Israelis want to maintain a democratic state with a Jewish majority, they must separate themselves from the Palestinians.

Second, Israel has consistently refrained from taking any initiative regarding the West Bank. This has been the policy adopted by the governments of Israel for forty years, from that headed by Golda Meir (1969–1974) up until now, except during the brief period from 1992 to 1995, during which Yitzhak Rabin was prime minister for the second time. His government sincerely and earnestly negotiated a settlement with the Palestinians. All other governments abstained from taking significant decisions on the future of the West Bank, always presenting a factitious desire for peace in order to minimize the damage. It was an undeclared agenda, but the world has seen through the deception, and because of this, in recent years the management of the conflict has shifted into foreign hands, specifically American and European. The foreign involvement is to the advantage of the camp that seeks a compromise. Even the Bush-Cheney administration, whose Middle East agenda was based on the use of force against Muslims, was incapable of helping the Israeli Right keep the conflict in the deep freeze. In fact, the opposite occurred. Although its policies went hand in glove with the Right in Israel, it was still the first American administration to officially recognize the necessity for the establishment of an independent Palestinian state and to create the model of "two states for two peoples." The Obama government dispensed with the force-based agenda of its predecessor and, by means of expediting talks between the Israelis and Palestinians, tempered Muslim anger. The European Union was one step ahead of the Obama administration and was planning to recognize a Palestinian state even before Israel and the Palestinians signed an agreement. This means that the management of the conflict by international factors is depriving the settlers and their supporters of their edge. Although the chauvinists in Israel have succeeded in taking control of the country's politics and in effect paralyzing it, their chances of repeating this feat in the United States and Europe are apparently zero.

This would not be the first time that external intervention will have overcome Israeli nay-saying. Some forty years ago, a sagacious Egyptian leader, Anwar Sadat, realized that Israeli leaders' protestations of peace were hypocritical, and that if he did not take the initiative, the deadlock would go on forever. Sadat wanted to get back for Egypt the lands that Israel had conquered from it in the 1967 war, and he proposed a peace agreement. Israel wanted to hold on to the territory and was ready to forgo peace. Sadat was forced to go to war.

In the early 1970s, after he had succeeded Gamal Abdel Nasser and consolidated his position as president, Sadat suggested to the government of Golda Meir that they launch a diplomatic move aimed at ending the conflict between the two countries. He demanded that the Israeli army withdraw a few kilometers eastward from the Suez Canal in order to separate the military forces of the two sides and to create an atmosphere of normalization. In exchange, he undertook to open the canal to shipping and to negotiate the terms of an agreement with Israel. Meir rejected his proposals. Behind her back, people used to call her "the only he-man in the government," and the macho Meir believed it was within Israel's ability to hold on to the territories conquered in 1967 and to treat the enemy with scorn. She never thought that Egypt had the strength to breach the status quo. Her minister of defense, Moshe Dayan, tried to persuade her to accept the Egyptian proposal by analyzing the relative advantages and disadvantages of Sadat's offer: retreat from Israel's fortresses along the canal, known as the Bar Lev Line, in exchange for the chance of reaching an agreement. But Meir was obdurate, and Dayan did not persist. Israel's lesson was a harsh one. Two years later, in the October War of 1973, more than 2,500 Israeli soldiers were killed, many thousands wounded, and hundreds taken prisoner, and the country's economy entered a crisis from which it began to recover only 12 years later. What he had tried to obtain through negotiations Sadat was forced to achieve on the battlefield. He had publicly vowed to regain every grain of sand that Egypt had lost in 1967, and he kept his promise.

Ironically, the October War in 1973 that the Israelis call the Yom Kippur War and the Arabs call the Ramadan War marked the beginning of an era of peace between Arabs and Jews. After the war both sides negotiated a disengagement agreement. It was the first time since the aftermath of the 1948 war that Arab and Israeli officials met for direct public discussions.

Both developments—the startling attack of Egyptian troops on the Suez Canal on October 6, 1973, and Egypt's readiness for direct negotiations that started twenty-two days later—were huge surprises. Nobody could have imagined that this ferocious conflict would set in motion a process that would change the course of relations between Arabs and Jews in the Middle East. In the distant future, when historians examine the events that set out the long and tense process that brought Israel to the position of being accepted by the Arab countries as a legitimate neighbor, they will start on that Saturday, October 6, with President Sadat commanding his generals to attack Israel's positions on the east side of the Suez Canal.

For me, the amazing epoch began on October 7, at a remote speck on the map of the Middle East called Baluza. It's in the northwestern corner of the Sinai Peninsula, twenty-eight kilometers (seventeen miles) east of the Suez Canal. The place is so remote that the local Bedouin call it *sifr,* which means "nothing." Six years earlier, in the 1967 Six-Day War, Israel had taken Sinai from Egypt and set up the Bar Lev Line, a chain of thirty-one highly fortified positions strung along the eastern bank of the canal to stop the Egyptians if they ever tried to launch an attack across the waterway. The headquarters for the brigade holding the northern section of the line was at Baluza.

The day before I arrived, on October 6 (Yom Kippur, or the Day of Atonement, the holiest day in the Hebrew calendar), the Egyptian army had invaded the east bank and conquered the Bar Lev Line. Israel was caught napping. A third of their fortresses were completely unmanned, and in the others there were only small numbers of troops, about five hundred altogether. Half of the armored units that, according to the plan, were supposed to rush to the defense of the positions in the event of an attack had been withdrawn to their bases in the rear several weeks beforehand.

All this happened despite the fact that in the ten days prior to the Yom Kippur offensive, intelligence reports had shown that the Egyptians were concentrating forces in the Canal Zone. Nevertheless, army intelligence assured the government that there was only a low probability of an assault on the Bar Lev Line. Therefore, most of the tanks were far from the front, and the fortresses on the line were undermanned. This gigantic blunder enabled ten Egyptian brigades—comprising some twenty-five thousand troops—to cross the canal in rubber dinghies, deploy rapidly in bridgeheads, and conquer most of the fortresses within twenty-four hours. Hundreds of Israeli officers and men were killed, and roughly a hundred were taken prisoner.

While the Egyptians assaulted the Israelis in the Sinai, the Syrian Army simultaneously attacked the Israel-held Golan Heights in the north. Thus, the Yom Kippur War began, and the Middle East became a completely different place.

The day after the Egyptians' initial assault, I arrived at Baluza to cover the war for Israel's public radio station, Kol Yisrael, the Voice of Israel. I had left Tel Aviv the evening before on a special bus that the army provided for the media. We traveled south and then west all night, traversing the hundreds of miles of barren desert along with convoys of buses loaded with reserve soldiers moving toward the front. At dawn, we were nearing the Suez Canal, and at each one of the army camps, the bus stopped and dropped off correspondents. Baluza was the last stop. I was assigned to report on the battles of the northern armored division, commanded by Maj. Gen. Avraham Adan, nicknamed "Bren." Most of the division's units were still stuck in massive traffic jams of military vehicles trying to reach Baluza. They would get there that night, and Adan would launch a counterattack the next morning.

I learned how grave the situation was soon after arriving at the small base. The Bar Lev Line had virtually collapsed during the night, which meant there was no substantial obstacle between the Egyptian forces that had crossed the canal and the State of Israel. Some of the canal-side fortresses had already surrendered, and all the others were encircled. I listened to the incoming radio signals and heard officers and men in the fortresses that were still fighting pleading for reinforcements and air support. Some of the voices still ring in my ears: "They're moving in on us. They're climbing over the fence. . . . We need immediate reinforcements," an officer in one of the fortresses implored. But most of the reserves were still far to the rear, and the Israel Air Force had been ordered to give priority to blocking the advance of the Syrians in the north, where the situation was even direr. The Syrians had made deep inroads across the Golan and were on the verge of crossing the Jordan River into the State of Israel.

At nightfall, the camp came under artillery attack, and orders came over the loudspeakers for everyone not posted to defensive emplacements to go down into the underground shelter. Together with dozens of both male and female soldiers, I entered the cavernous shelter, but after a few minutes I slipped out. I was eager to see some action and went outside, but the blacked-out camp was empty. It looked like a deserted mining town in an old western movie. The clear skies were strewn with stars, the desert air was warm and balmy, and in the breaks between the sporadic Egyptian artillery fire, the silence was almost absolute. Every now and again an illumination flare was sent up, and for about a minute it lit up the rows of barracks and military structures, some of them covered with camouflage netting. The Egyptian fire was not accurate. At almost regular intervals of two to three minutes, a shell would land on the low sand hills beyond the fence and explode with a dull, reverberating blast.

I decided to try to find a phone. Heading back into the headquarters building, I went from one empty room to another until I found a phone with a direct line out, one that was not routed through the headquarters' switchboard. (Cellular phones had not yet been invented, and at that time only American TV networks had satellite telephones.)

I dialed my station's Tel Aviv studio and delivered my first report from the front. The Egyptian army had conquered a large section of Bar Lev Line, I said, and in the last hours helicopter-borne Egyptian commando forces had landed at a road junction nearby.

Then I phoned my mother in Jerusalem. She had been widowed years before and lived on her own, and I knew that hearing my voice would cheer her up. We were very close. I used to call her by her first name, Tziporah. At the age of eighteen, in 1937, she had left her parents' home in Lodz, Poland, and immigrated to Palestine on her own. Religious relatives who had settled in the Holy Land at the turn of the century welcomed her warmly. Two years later, in 1939, her mother took ill, and Tziporah returned to Lodz just before the Germans invaded Poland. For months she was imprisoned in the ghetto with her parents, and for a while she was even employed in forced labor. Twice she had managed to escape at the last minute from SS *aktzias* (roundups of Jews to be murdered).

One morning in the winter of 1940, Tziporah was standing in a line in a bank near her parents' home. She was wearing a white coat that flattered her figure. She had bought it in Tel Aviv before leaving for Poland. A young man, a total stranger, was standing behind her. He said that he had seen a white coat exactly like hers in a shop window in Tel Aviv. She smiled and told him that surely this was that very coat. His name was Jozek, and like her he had come on a visit from Palestine and been stranded in Lodz. He asked her if she had a Palestinian passport, and she said that she did. He said that it was possible that the Germans would allow holders of foreign passports to leave Poland. A small group was organizing, and she could join if she wanted. Although she was determined to stay at first, her parents insisted that she go. They parted in tears at the train station.

Three weeks later, a passenger ship docked at Tel Aviv, the last to sail to Palestine from Europe before the route was canceled due to the war. Tziporah was on board.

After the war, my mother learned that her parents and her two brothers had been killed by the Nazis. The traumas of parting from them and their subsequent deaths accompanied my mother throughout her life until she passed away in 2005.

Tziporah was a strong woman. In 1948, during Israel's War of Independence, when Jerusalem was under siege by the Jordanian Arab Legion and food and water were rationed, she served as an escort to a water truck and supervised the distribution of the water. In 1958, when my father was killed in a road accident, she was left alone with three small children to raise. She managed to overcome the difficulties, hardly ever complained, and like most young Israelis of the day was generally optimistic.

But the sirens heralding the surprise attack of the Egyptians on Yom Kippur 1973 and the news of the grave situation on both fronts aroused the sense of anxiety that had prevailed during her parting from her parents at the Lodz station. "The Nazis are going to slaughter us," she told me on the phone. I tried to calm her. "Tziporah, these are Egyptians, not Nazis, and I am speaking to you from four hundred kilometers away. This is where the war is, far from you." My mother was not placated. "This time it's the end," she said in a trembling voice. "This time it's all over."

When I put the receiver down, I had tears in my eyes.

For years after that, I would mull over that conversation, and each time my conclusion was strengthened: if there is one thing that guides the patterns of behavior of the Israelis, it is the fear of annihilation. I doubt that there are any other citizens of the western world who have the fear of physical destruction imprinted on their psyches the way Israelis do. With the Israelis, their existential fear, which is sometimes realistic and sometimes irrational, dovetails with the collective trauma that is engraved so deeply in the Jewish soul. Is this a hereditary defect? A genetic deficiency? Is it rational to believe that a community will continue to behave in a specific way because of a trauma undergone by its antecedents two or three generations previously? It seems clear to me that a permanent posttraumatic condition is the common denominator that, more than any other factor, reflects life in Israel. And this continues, despite the fact that over half a century has gone by since the Holocaust and that the Jews have established a state of their own with a powerful army.

Back in Baluza, the next day—October 8, 1973—was even gloomier. At around five o'clock in the morning, General Adan's division set out to block the Egyptians who had crossed the Suez Canal. Three armored brigades, composed of 183 tanks, began advancing from Baluza in a southwesterly direction toward the canal. At first, the going was swift and the formation did not encounter any substantial Egyptian resistance.

At eleven o'clock, the divisional HQ was set up on a sand hill dubbed Zrakor (Hebrew for "Spotlight") on the coded maps. The sky was clear, and visibility was excellent. From a distance of about two miles, we could see the El Ferdan Bridge over the canal. On the other side of the bridge, standing out on the horizon, were green smudges the intelligence officer told us were the orchards surrounding the Egyptian city of Ismailia.

I asked for an interview with Adan, and the general agreed. He was in a buoyant mood. He pointed west, in the direction of the bridge, and said that the two lead brigades were advancing swiftly. "Our forces are crushing the Egyptians," he said into my microphone, and added, "Soon the first tanks will reach the bridge, and they may cross it."

I wanted to get this news to my editor but lacked means of direct communication with my news room. A lieutenant I knew offered me help. He was in charge of the division's signals-equipment unit that was positioned above us on the hill. The lieutenant would put at my disposal a communications line to the underground war room in the General

Staff HQ in Tel Aviv, and from there the line would be linked to my radio station's newsroom. The links were made, and a minute or two later I was dictating a detailed report to the duty editor on the progress of the battle. The counterattack was proceeding according to plan, I said, and Israeli forces were approaching the canal. Then I hooked up my tape recorder to the phone and transmitted the interview with General Adan to the studio.

At that exact moment, the Egyptians launched a heavy artillery bombardment of the hill where we were located. The shellfire was concentrated and accurate, and the crews of the armored personnel carriers rapidly closed their hatches and beat a quick retreat, leaving plumes of sand in their wake. The signals-equipment vehicle also withdrew and was soon far away from me. I managed to jump into the last retreating armored personnel carrier that hastily drew away from the shelled hill.

A few hours later we learned that while we were being shelled, the first armored brigade nearing the Ferdan Bridge was ambushed by Egyptian infantry units dug in close to the canal. These troops were equipped with Soviet-made Sagger anti-tank missiles. This was a new weapon in the arena, and Israeli intelligence had not warned the army about it. The Egyptian troops had been well trained, and in a short time, dozens of tanks had been hit and were in flames. In the lead battalion, thirty-two tank crew members were killed, and four were taken prisoner, including the battalion commander. Adan's counterattack had been blocked. Its tank brigades withdrew, and the Egyptians broadened their bridgehead on the east bank of the canal.

About an hour later, the divisional HQ stopped to regroup a few kilometers to the east. Radio receivers in the vehicles were tuned to Kol Yisrael. The news signature tune echoed over the desert, and the announcer told the nervous nation that the tide of the battle had turned. "'Our forces are crushing the Egyptians,' General Adan told our correspondent," the announcer continued. "'Soon the first tanks will reach the bridge, and they may cross it.'" Officers and men stood around me, eyeing me with disdain, and I felt like burying myself in the sand.

In Tel Aviv that evening, Dayan gave a briefing to newspaper editors and diplomatic correspondents. In the south, he told them, except for one single fortress, the entire Bar Lev Line had fallen to the enemy. The counterattack had failed. In the north, Dayan added, 180

Israeli tanks faced off against approximately 1,300 Syrian tanks. The Syrian army took the main Israeli stronghold, which had a variety of surveillance equipment, and was close to conquering the most important crossroads on the Golan Heights. Should the Heights fall, he said, the Syrians could easily advance towards the cities of Tiberias, Haifa, and Tel Aviv.

A note of hysteria marred the aura of heroism that usually surrounded Dayan, with the black patch covering his empty right eye socket. The way he depicted the situation, it was so grave that the end of the State of Israel was a logical possibility. "We are standing before the destruction of the Third Commonwealth," he told the stunned journalists, using a phrase that to Jews means an extreme national disaster and the loss of nationhood and liberty (The first and second commonwealths ended with the destruction of the Temples of Solomon and Herod in Jerusalem in 586 BCE and 70 CE respectively, when the Jewish sovereign states ceased to exist and the nation went into exile). This was an extraordinary statement, and indeed, Meir saw his desperation and stopped him from appearing on television where he had planned to report to the nation on the dire situation. She feared that his appearance would harm the Israelis' fighting spirit. Their mood was already lower than it had ever been before. This was not only the worst day of the war; the Israeli nation had not suffered so hard a blow since the establishment of the state. That evening, Meir herself contemplated suicide.

In retrospect, it is clear that most of Dayan's judgments both before the war broke out and during its early course were wrong. In the months leading up to the war, Dayan never realized that the diplomatic deadlock between Israel and Egypt would force Sadat into war. And after the hostilities began, he failed to identify the strategic objectives of the Egyptian war plan. He was seized by panic and despondency during the first days of the fighting because of the magnitude of the surprise, the large numbers of Israeli casualties and prisoners, and the failure of the counteroffensive of October 8, which led him to interpret the events on the battlefield in an extremely erroneous manner. Dayan felt that all was lost, when in fact, on that day in October 1973, the situation on the two war fronts was tough, perhaps even grave, but far from disastrous. One could compare the situation to the difference between the damage suffered by the United States from the Japanese attack on Pearl Harbor in December 1941 and the total annihilation of the United States.

Moreover, today we know with certainty that Sadat's war plan was a limited one.[1] His aim was to conquer a narrow strip of land along the eastern bank of the Suez Canal and to stop his forces there, without advancing toward the Israeli border. His overarching goal was to break the deadlock and force Israel into negotiations on withdrawal from Sinai. In this he succeeded. By inflicting a limited defeat on the Israelis, Sadat tilted the course of events in the Middle East from war to peace. Everything that has happened between the Jewish state and its Arab neighbors since then was a consequence of Sadat's decision in October 1973 to wage war in order to gain peace.

Sadat's strategy was carefully calculated and very clever. He was aware of the limits that Israel's nuclear capability placed upon his power, and with great skill he exploited the impact of surprise, and the panic and instability that it sowed in the enemy's camp, in order to achieve a diplomatic objective without going so far as to provoke Israel into using its ultimate defense. We don't know whether Sadat was aware of the fears of another Holocaust that are so deeply engraved in the souls of the Israelis, though it certainly worked in his favor. However, the Egyptian president was keeping the promise he had made to his nation when he inherited his predecessor's mantle: to return to Egyptian control every grain of sand that had been lost in 1967.

At the time, Dayan, Meir and others could not see beyond their fear that the Egyptian and Syrian victories meant the end of the Israeli nation. Would Dayan have used so loaded an expression as "the destruction of the Third Commonwealth" and the prime minister have considered taking her own life were it not for the heavy historical burden of the Holocaust? This awful memory trumped the common sense and logic of these two leaders. Both were known for their rich political experience and toughness, but their ability to function was impaired. In their minds, the survivors of the Holocaust demanded explanations from them. "You are the leaders. How is it that you endangered the very existence of the Jewish state after we had pledged together, 'Never Again'?"

On that day, the prime minister and the defense minister seemed to be taking responsibility for having allowed the shattering of the defining element of the Israeli ethos: protecting the Jewish people from annihilation. This is the foundation of Zionist ideology and the most basic component of the collective consciousness of the Israelis. The establishment of a national home for the Jewish people in the Land of Israel is the only way to put an end to the hardship and suffering of exile, the history of persecution, expulsion, inquisition, and pogroms that they had undergone for two millennia. If the Israelis could not defend themselves and prevent another holocaust, then Zionism had failed.

Indeed, in those difficult days there wasn't an Israeli whose memories or associations of the Nazi Holocaust did not emerge from the nooks and crannies of his or her subconscious. Although the fear of extermination was not justified, it was as tangible as the pictures screened on television of Egyptian soldiers dancing on the ruins of the Bar Lev Line and displaying rows of Israeli prisoners with their hands raised over their heads. In the collective Israeli memory the background to the scenes of the soldiers surrendering and being led into captivity was the famous photograph of the little boy in the Warsaw ghetto with his hands up as a Nazi soldier points a gun at him. This overwhelming sense of impending doom—the fear of a new Holocaust—continues to underline the thinking of all Israelis today. Understanding this reality and its powerful influence is critical for comprehending the complications of the Middle East peace process and its aperiodic vague turns. Anxiety over destruction is a fixed part of the Israeli consciousness, and each time there is severe tension over security, despair and despondency took hold of the Israeli public and anxiety over another holocaust played the leading role. That sense of an approaching catastrophe dominated Israel's society during the three weeks that preceded the break out of the war on June 1967, when Sadat's predecessor, Gamal Abdel Nasser, blocked the Straits of Tiran in the Red Sea to Israeli shipping, kicked the UN peace forces out of Sinai, and threatened to attack Israel and destroy it. During this period, words like destruction, liquidation, and annihilation pervaded the public discourse, and accounts of the death camps reverberated in the collective memory and fertilized it. And later, when the Six-Day War was over and the enormity of the Israeli victory became clear, the opposite spirit enveloped the Israelis, a feeling of redemption.

Another point in time in which the Holocaust memories played a role occurred during the Gulf War in 1991, when for six weeks the Iraqi dictator, Saddam Hussein, attacked Israel with ballistic missiles. Associations with the Holocaust echoed in every home. Frightened families—wearing gas masks because the authorities feared the missiles might be armed with chemical warheads—huddled in sealed rooms in their apartments, feeling the helplessness that had characterized the Jews in Europe during World War II. In fact, the actual physical harm done by the Scud missiles was minimal. Only thirty-nine fell in Israel, causing damage to several dozen buildings, and one man died of a heart attack when one exploded near his home. But the effect on the morale of the population was huge. "The Holocaust is in our bloodstream," a young Israeli writer declared around the time of Saddam's missiles. "It is like a conditioned reflex."

Indeed, for Israelis the Holocaust is not a matter of history—it is current, in the background of their lives all the time, accompanying the citizenry in everyday life, ever-present in political discourse, dictating behavior, forming responses. This enormous tragedy imposes a constant emotional burden on the Israelis. Their literature, poetry, and theater rest upon a hefty component of pain and remembrance connected to the Holocaust, as does the television, the press, and the Internet. Sad and happy occasions, disasters and achievements, wars, terrorist atrocities, almost any remarkable event is tied up with the Holocaust, even the assassination of Prime Minister Yitzhak Rabin in 1995. Two months before Rabin's murder, Likud party leader Benjamin Netanyahu made a speech at a mass rally in Jerusalem against the Oslo Accords. A poster was then circulated in which Rabin's head was superimposed on a picture of SS commander Heinrich Himmler in full regalia. Rabin's opponents proclaimed that his cooperation with PLO chairman Yasser Arafat was no different than the cooperation of the Judenraete with the Nazis. In both cases, they said, Jews were helping their enemies.

The memory of the Holocaust and its lessons are cultivated intensively by each and every political and social establishment in Israel in a variety of ways. In the army, which serves as a melting pot for immigrants from many countries and an effective instrument of social mobility, the Holocaust has a prominent ideological presence. If the Jews had had their own army during World War II, the Holocaust would not have happened—that, in essence, is the concept that the military command conveys to the troops.

The most powerful tool that the establishment possesses to inculcate the connection between the Holocaust and the need to defend the state of Israel against destruction is the educational system. The Holocaust and the lessons to be learned from it are a significant part of the syllabi in Israeli schools, and high school students eventually travel to the death camps in Poland. In the last fifteen years, tens of thousands of students have taken part in these pilgrimages. They are led by guides especially trained to teach the history of antisemitism, and the students are accompanied by survivors who tell their personal tales at the places where they were imprisoned and tortured.

These visits to Poland are, of course, far more effective in concretizing the meaning of the Holocaust than a lesson in a classroom or a visit to the Yad Vashem Holocaust History Museum in Jerusalem. At the Auschwitz concentration camp, the seventeen-year-old Israelis stand in front of the "*Arbeit macht frei*" ("Work liberates") archway and see the gas chambers and the crematoria, along with the heaps of shoes, hair, and teeth. Then they take part in memorial ceremonies where memorial candles are kindled, victims' and survivors' testimonies are read out, and collective vows of "Never Again" are made.

Participants say that the experience is totally overwhelming. Many of the youths return in highly emotional states. Sometimes, the feelings that the journey arouses in them change their attitudes to life and their behavioral patterns. But educators and psychologists have warned that these pilgrimages and ceremonies can nourish a victim's complex. In Poland the youths are subjected to such heavy doses of anxiety, some experts say, that a kind of siege mentality, a sense that "the whole world is against us" overcomes them. Militaristic tendencies possibly grow as a result of this.

The trips to Poland strengthen the Israeli and Jewish identities of the youngsters, but there are some circles who exploit them to instill certain nationalistic and religious narratives. Liberal Israelis feel that the journeys affect the students' attitudes to the confrontation with the Palestinians. The visits and the ceremonies at the sites of destruction, they believe, bolster the tendencies of the young people to see force as a solution. Identifying as the victim could make them belittle the suffering of others. These circles, who constantly advocate in the name of normality that the preoccupation with the Holocaust be moderated, are condemned by conservatives as saboteurs of the national historical consciousness of the Israelis. The remembrance of the Holocaust, the conservatives insist, should be tied to God's covenant with his Chosen People, a covenant that signifies a promise of eternal existence of the Jews as a separate national entity. The liberals reply that the conservatives are trying to sanctify the Holocaust and remove the political discourse from the realm of the rational.

It is clear that the intense preoccupation with the Holocaust causes the Israelis to exacerbate their own anxieties. They reproduce the trauma in times of stress, and that strengthens the sense of shock, which in turn reproduces the trauma, and that increases the anxiety, and so on. Ironically, during the early years of the Israeli state, when it was truly facing imminent extinction, the victims' complex did not figure prominently. However, the farther in time that Israel moves from its establishment, and as any real doubts about its continued existence fade away, the effects of the Holocaust trauma, strangely, exert a tighter grip on its consciousness. As a consequence, it is imperative that any initiative for peace between Arabs and Jews be based on the premise that Arabs fully accept the existence of Israel as a legitimate neighbor and thus cease threatening Israel with extermination.

Back on the Egyptian side, in October 1973, national trauma also played a significant role. This was the humiliating defeat they had suffered in 1967's Six-Day War. This defeat badly hurt the Arab psyche, particularly that of the Egyptians. With the 1973 Egyptian victories on the battlefield—the conquest of the Bar Lev Line, the killing of more than 2,600 Israeli soldiers, and the taking of 230 prisoners—Egyptian self-respect and confidence was restored, and this allowed the Egyptian leadership to shift from total rejection of the Jewish state to being reconciled with its existence.

By the same token Israel, intoxicated by its 1967 triumph, was forced to recognize the limitations of its power. In this way, Sadat's war initiative changed the course of history. By achieving equilibrium in the warlike confrontation between the two enemies, Egypt's president made it possible for both sides to overcome the barriers to peace that lay deep in their respective psyches.

I never discussed with Tziporah the dread that she expressed when I phoned her from the small army base in Sinai on that tense autumn evening. I never described to her the shock that gripped me when she told me the Nazis had returned to slaughter the Jews and that this time it was all over for us. Did the years after the Yom Kippur War dull the edge of her existential angst? Was her fear assuaged by the peace agreements that Israel signed with Egypt and the Kingdom of Jordan or the technological power that Israel had built up in the final decades of the twentieth century or the strong strategic alliance with the United States? Nevertheless, even without mentioning that phone conversation again, my mother didn't spare me her deep anxieties. The older she grew, the weaker her faith became in the ability of the Jewish ship to remain securely anchored in the sea of the surrounding Arab lands. She was an active member of the social-democratic Labor Party and always kept up to date with current affairs. We talked a lot about politics, and as time went by, I noticed how her views changed. The optimistic and somewhat naïve worldview that had led the eighteen-year-old Tziporah to leave her parents' home in Poland and migrate to Palestine in order to share in the building of an independent Jewish homeland had been replaced in her old age by a nagging pessimism. The national existence of the Jews in the Land of Israel was, in her eyes, no longer to be taken for granted.

My mother was not alone in this view. The stronger Israel becomes militarily and economically, the more its citizens lose their confidence. There are many reasons for this. One important reason was certainly the fact that the bonds of social solidarity that had held Israelis together during the early years of the state have grown looser. As a young nation, Israel had an egalitarian social system that helped to unite the majority of Israelis behind a common interest. Over time, rampant capitalism and excessive individualism produced a widening social gap, debilitating the solidarity and societal strength and threatening to enervate the national psyche. But even more important has been the psychological impact of the suicide terrorism that struck Israel so hard in recent years, harder than any other western society. When suicide bombing became routine and the media analyzed scenarios of nuclear, chemical, and biological terror, the term "a second Holocaust" again penetrated into public consciousness.

Outside of Israel, few have managed to decipher the genetic code of Israeli consciousness. The impression projected by the Israeli spirit—arrogance, reliance on force, audacity, and boldness—covers up the weakness that the Holocaust's PTSD expresses more accurately. Certainly, the

Arab side is not at all open to the roots of the Israelis' trauma and its decisive influence over the way that they think and behave. Only a few Arabs know about the scope and the destruction that the Holocaust wreaked on the Jews. Children are not exposed to the Holocaust at schools, and the entire cultural environment in the Arab world—media, academia, literature, and theater—ignores the fathomless Jewish trauma. Western Holocaust literature is seldom translated into Arabic.

Moreover, today, influential Arab leaders deny or minimize the Holocaust. Hezbollah leader Hassan Nasrallah recently declared to his supporters that "Jews invented the legend of the Holocaust." Syrian president Bashar al-Assad, when asked by an interviewer about the Holocaust's effect on Israel, said that he doesn't have "any clue how [Jews] were killed or how many were killed." In the summer of 2006, Iran's president, Mahmoud Ahmadinejad, hosted in Teheran a Holocaust denial conference, where he repeatedly referred to the Holocaust as a myth and criticized European laws against Holocaust denial: "They [parliaments in Europe] have created a myth in the name of Holocaust and consider it to be above God, religion, and the prophets."

7

"They Had Learned Nothing from History"

EARLY IN MAY 1974, about six months after the end of the Yom Kippur War, I covered a dramatic meeting of the Labor Party's central committee for Kol Yisrael at the Cinerama Auditorium in Tel Aviv. Golda Meir had summoned the central committee of her party in order to approve the agreement between Israel and Syria for separation of forces on the Golan Heights.[1]

During the second week of the war, the Syrian army had been pushed back and out of the territory it had seized earlier on, and the IDF had captured a "bulge" of about four hundred additional square kilometers of Syrian territory east of the former Golan Heights frontier. The eastern end of the bulge was only about forty kilometers (twenty-five miles) from the Syrian capital, Damascus. Straight after a cease-fire had taken effect, the UN Security Council demanded that both sides withdraw their forces to the positions they had held before the October war. U.S. secretary of state Henry Kissinger conducted negotiations between the two sides, shuttling between Jerusalem and Damascus.

The talks began in late February 1974, and in early May the draft agreement was brought before the ruling party's main body for its approval. The debate was stormy. The inhabitants of the agricultural settlements that Israel had established on the Golan Heights after conquering the area in the 1967 war were Labor Party supporters, and many of them were strenuously opposed to withdrawal from the bulge. Unlike the settlers in the West Bank, most of the settlers on the Golan were not religious but secular left-wingers. They did not see the Golan as part of God's promise to Abraham, as the West Bank was to the settlers there, but a border area suitable for pioneering settlement. The left-wing governments encouraged them to settle there and allocated them land and budgets. "Why give the Syrians a reward," their representatives yelled from the podium, "when they had attacked us?" Some of the more hawkish party leaders backed the settlers, and the doves had to mobilize powerful reasons to justify the retreat. At its climax, the debate focused on a hundred-odd acres of land in the southern part of the bulge that one of the Israeli settlements had annexed and where they had planted an apple orchard. The Golan farmers had agreed that the bulge should be restored to Syria but were demanding that Israel retain control of the orchard.

I was sitting next to one of the old-time leaders of the party, Pinchas Sapir, finance minister in Meir's cabinet at that time, a lily-white dove, and an inveterate pragmatist. His hefty body slumped in his seat, and his eyes closed; he napped intermittently, awakening only when startled by some shout from the podium. As the debate reached fever pitch, Sapir leaned over toward me and said, "They want to kill each other over a hundred acres of apple orchards. Imagine what will go on when we have to give back everything we conquered in 1967 in the West Bank."

Since then, thirty-eight years have gone by. Sapir has passed on, as has Golda Meir, and their once magnificent movement has lost its way and become a marginal party, but the West Bank and the Golan Heights are still occupied by Israel. If I were to meet Sapir today, I'd say to him, "You have no idea how right you were. They are still at each other's throats, and the withdrawal is no nearer."

Ten prime ministers—Meir, Rabin, Levi Eshkol, Begin, Yitzhak Shamir, Shimon Peres, Netanyahu, Ehud Barak, Sharon, and Ehud Olmert—have, with the help of their advisers and aides (including Moshe Dayan, Yigal Allon, Yisrael Galili, and many other worthies) over a period of more than forty years, rejected, postponed, and held up the withdrawal from the West Bank by every method only they could devise. Did they truly and honestly imagine that it was possible to build settlements on Arab land and annex them to Israel? And that the Palestinians would surrender their land and not rebel? And that the Arab world would react with indifference? And that the whole world would remain silent? And that, in some wondrous manner, in the course of time things would somehow settle down, the land would become the

Jewish settlers' land, and the Palestinians would become accustomed to this reality, disappear from the territories, or be driven off? Did they truly and honestly believe this would happen?

Is it possible that they had learned nothing from history? That a conquest that lasts longer than the conquered can swallow must end up in corrupting the conqueror, prolonging his agony, and intensifying his pain? And how did they not grasp that the immense investment in the territories would be lost forever? And that in order to dislodge the settlers and return things to the way they were before, the state would have to wield massive power against them and their supporters and pay billions in compensation for the property they left behind in the evacuated territories? If they had only studied British history and learned from the experiences of those who had possessed an empire upon which the sun never went down, but who were forced to give most of it up.

And in the last decade, when it had already been made clear to Israel's leaders that they would have to surrender the West Bank, why did they still go on building settlements and expanding many of the existing ones? And even when the last four prime ministers—Barak, Sharon, Olmert, and Netanyahu—declared to the world that Israel was ready to make "painful concessions" and withdraw from most of the occupied territory, why did they nonetheless carry on expanding the settlements and inhabiting them with more Israelis?

The history of the occupation shows that, as in Greek tragedy, hubris trumps reason. There is no shortage of examples. The most salient one occurred in early 1971 when defense minister Moshe Dayan was asked to respond to the declaration by the president of Egypt that in exchange for a peace treaty, Israel would have to withdraw from the entire Sinai. Dayan's comment: "Better Sharm el-Sheikh without peace than peace without Sharm el-Sheikh."

Sharm is close to the southernmost point of the Sinai Peninsula, the apex of an inverted triangle. Some 150 miles (250 kilometers) from the Israeli border, it is also close to the point on the Sinai coast that controls the Straits of Tiran at the southern entrance to the Gulf of Aqaba (or the Gulf of Eilat, as the Israelis call this arm of the Red Sea). Israel conquered Sharm in June 1967 and established a military base and airfield at this remote spot, as well as a civilian settlement called Ofira, after the Biblical Ophir, an African land where gold was mined. The settlement contained a residential area, hotels, and tourism attractions, including a diving facility close to the world-famous coral reefs. Almost the entire financial investment in Ofira was funded by Israeli taxpayers. The township at the southern tip of the Israeli empire expanded rapidly, and a well-known songwriter composed a patriotic song in its praise: "O Sharm el-Sheikh! We have returned to you, you are in our heart, our heart forever." It was aired frequently on Israel Radio.

Dayan's statement was accepted, without questioning, as the Law from Sinai. Israeli public opinion was unanimous: even in exchange for a peace treaty, the strategic point in southern Sinai could not be surrendered. Only after Egypt launched its offensive on Yom Kippur and conquered the Bar Lev Line (and Israel lost more than twenty-six hundred soldiers) did reason return to triumph over the arrogance imprinted on the Israeli personality. It was Dayan himself, this time as foreign minister in the Begin government, who negotiated with Egypt over the terms of the pact: in exchange for an Egyptian declaration of peace, Israel surrendered the whole of Sinai, including Sharm and Ofira. After the October War, it was clear to most Israelis that peace without Sharm was better than Sharm without peace, and therefore when the terms for the withdrawal from Sinai were being discussed, the matter of that remote spot's strategic value was pushed aside.

Prime Ministers Rabin, Barak, and Olmert declared, each during his term, that Israel would never withdraw from the Golan Heights, but all three negotiated with Syria while fully aware that the Syrians would make the return of that entire region to their sovereignty a condition of any peace agreement.

Ariel Sharon, when he was in the opposition, used to say that Israeli settlements in the Gaza Strip had the same status as Tel Aviv. Would anyone ask Israel to give up Tel Aviv? But when Sharon was sitting on the prime minister's seat in Jerusalem and responsibility for the future of the state lay upon his shoulders, the former oppositionist was forced to consider the constraints of reality. And the upshot is well known: it was Sharon who decided to evacuate all the Israeli settlements in the Gaza Strip in 2005.

In the beginning, the sweet daydream, the illusion that the conquered territories would remain in Israel's hands forever, was not created by the right wing of the political spectrum but by the ostensibly pragmatic left.

Shortly after the June 1967 victory, Yigal Allon, an esteemed leader of one of the factions that had formed the Labor Party and a senior minister in Levi Eshkol's cabinet, assisted a group of rabbis and their followers in setting up a Jewish settlement in the heart of the Palestinian city of Hebron, in the southern part of the West Bank. The prime minister did not oppose Allon's initiative. In March 1968, Eshkol replied to a journalist's question: "If there is someone intending to start a Jewish settlement in Hebron without dispossessing anyone, I see no sin in it . . . and there is reason to believe that the Hebronites, or the notable citizens of Hebron, would not be opposed to it."[2]

The shrewd Eshkol certainly didn't believe that the Arabs of Hebron were longing for Jews to settle in their midst, but nevertheless the prime minister of Israel preferred to lead himself up the garden path and to make a foolish statement over fighting the hawks in his government who were forcing him to establish a settlement in the worst place imaginable from the point of view of anyone who wanted to reach a peace agreement. At the same time, some of Eshkol's dovish colleagues in the party leadership were sitting on the fence and watching events in silence. Driving a Jewish stake into the heart of Arab territory was not something they liked, but they did nothing to prevent it.

In January 1968, U.S. president Lyndon B. Johnson hosted Prime Minister Eshkol at Johnson's ranch in Texas. They discussed the conditions for achieving peace in the Middle East after the June victory. Johnson asked Eshkol, "What kind of Israel do you want?" He expected Eshkol to draw the border that Israel preferred, but the prime minister evaded replying, and in effect Israel to this day has not given a clear reply to the president's question.

Today it is commonly thought that it was the right wing that sowed the seeds for the hundreds of settlements in the territories, but this is not correct. The principles according to which settlement in the territories was permitted were set by governments of the Left. The Right did not change the principles; it increased the volume of settlement. Several years before the late leader of the Likud party, Menachem Begin, won the elections and formed the first right-wing government in Israel's history, in June 1977, the territories were bustling with settlement activity. Influential intellectuals and academics from the moderate Left were encouraging it.[3] These were people who were proud of their liberal outlook, and they served as the emblem and the model of moderation and tolerance for the pioneering society that had built the state. During my own youth, these figures taught my generation that humanism and solidarity (usually of class, not nation) were the most important criteria for judging a society's values. At the hardest times of the 1948–1949 war, these mentors of their generation preached "purity of arms," rebuked military commanders for harming Arab civilians, and set limits for them. The flight and expulsion of 1948's Palestinian refugees bothered their consciences, or at least that is what they said. And now, less than twenty years later, these guardians of morality had changed their spots and were inspiring the morally deficient.

The most prominent intellectual among these new zealots for a Greater Land of Israel was the poet and columnist Nathan Alterman, who at that time was considered the unofficial national poet of Israel. He was something of an ascetic but also drank a lot and tended to be moody, but his influence over the country's leaders and public opinion was enormous. For the Labor movement Alterman was an educator, moral guide, and ideologue. Ben-Gurion admired him. Straight after the 1967 victory, Alterman took the lead in initiating a lobby against territorial concessions. "There is no nation that will retreat from the excavations of its life, and whoever returns these parts of the Land will first have to write another Bible" is one of the lines that the rightists like to quote from his writings. Forty years on, the nationalist ardor that captured the poet's soul seems rather whimsical. Before the 1967 war, Alterman was not an advocate of expansionism, and his poems did not express a yearning for Hebron or Nablus, but as soon as the guns stopped roaring and the enormity of the victory became clear, the muses spoke up and told him to start urging the government to annex the conquered territory. The 1947 Partition Plan, he wrote, had lost its validity when the Arabs rejected it and had attacked the newly born state with the intent of wiping it out. He declared that there was not and never had been a Palestinian nation (something that Golda Meir also stated frequently during the 1970s) and that if the Israelis recognized it, the justification for Zionism would be lost and terrorism boosted. "If there is a profound meaning, human and national, to the Return to Zion, then it is here, in the West Bank, that it receives its highest content," he summed up in somewhat messianic terms.

Alterman was a true representative of the zeitgeist. He represented two ideologies that were alien to rational, pragmatic, political Zionists—chauvinism and messianism. The first had been pushed out of public consciousness during the first fifty years of the Zionist revolution due to a sense of shame over the necessity of taking over Arab land; the second expressed the deep chasm between the feeling of anxiety over impending destruction before the 1967 war and the feeling that a miracle had occurred after the victory, which had been truly and honestly difficult to comprehend. Five days after the end of the war, in a column headed "Facing a unique reality," Alterman wrote:

> The significance of this victory is not only that it returned to the Jews the most ancient and exalted of its holy places, those that are engraved on its memory and the depths of its history more than any others. The significance of this victory is that it in effect has erased the difference between the State of Israel and the Land of Israel. For the first time since the destruction of the Second Temple the Land of Israel is in our hands. The State and the Land are from now on one essence, and from this time on this historic amalgamation is lacking only the People of Israel in order to weave, together with what has been achieved, the triple cord[4] that will never be snapped.[5]

In a number of his political poems and columns Alterman presented the options that the state leadership had to weigh regarding the future of the territories. Obviously, the demographic problem (annexing the territories would endanger the Jewish majority) bothered the advocates of annexation. The option of expulsion of the Palestinians from the West Bank did not come up for serious discussion because these ideologues related to themselves as liberal and humane. If the territories were annexed but the Palestinians not ejected, as the far Right demanded, the result would inevitably be a binational state. If a binational state arose, two groups would constitute the Arab population of Israel: those who had remained in the country after the war in 1949, and the Palestinians of the areas conquered in 1967. If this were to happen, the Jews would face two options: denying the Palestinians civil rights, which would mean an apartheid regime, or giving them equal rights. Because the birthrate of the Arabs is much higher than that of the Jews, clearly the Jewish majority would shrink, and eventually the Jews would become the minority. How did these left-wing intellectuals solve this demographic conundrum? They didn't. Like the politicians, the ideologues vacillated. They expected a miracle would somehow make the Arab majority vanish.

The left-wing boosters of settlement in the occupied territories were experienced and well versed in history and politics and generally were capable of weighing complex alternatives in a balanced manner. Before the establishment of the state, the left wing fought tenaciously for decades against the efforts of the nationalist camp (who were known then as the Revisionists) to persuade the Zionist movement to reject the partition of Palestine between the Arabs and the Jews.[6] The hawkish, or "activist," Revisionists insisted on demanding unrealistic borders for the Jewish state and were dubbed "secessionists" by the left, a community that refused to accept the authority of the majority. At the height of the struggle between the two camps, it was the Left that won the support of the majority, and the Right was largely marginalized. But after the 1967 war, the younger generation of these secessionists, together with a cluster of messianists, acted together on the West Bank in diametric opposition to the classical, pragmatic Zionist policy, which had produced excellent results. The left-wing establishment gave them its support.

I cannot explain the exact reasons that caused so large a number of prominent, wise, and experienced people to err in so egregious a manner for so long a time.

Perhaps I should cite here the 1841 immortal observations of the Scottish journalist Charles Mackay in his book *Extraordinary Popular Delusions and the Madness of Crowds*: "Men, it has been well said, think in herds; it will be seen that they go mad in herds, while they only recover their senses slowly, one by one." To a certain extent, as Barbara Tuchman did in her book *The March of Folly: From Troy to Vietnam*,[7] it is only possible to hypothesize why leaders make colossal blunders and afterward are unable to regain equilibrium. In order to examine such a process, a longer perspective is called for, but it is clear that Israel's leadership was influenced by the magnitude of the 1967 victory and the vastness of the conquered territories helped the frightened little country grow three times as large and become a regional power.

The person who paved the way for massive Israeli settlement in the West Bank was none other than Shimon Peres, whose name today is associated with the concepts of peace and compromise. Peres was responsible for the establishment of the very first settlement in the Samarian hills, Elon Moreh, near the city of Nablus in the very heart of Palestinian territory in the northern West Bank.

On the festival of Hanukkah in December 1975, hundreds of Greater Israel activists made their way by stealth to the defunct railway station at Sebastia in Samaria, intending to settle there. They created a media drama and agreed to leave only after Peres, who was then serving as defense minister in Yitzhak Rabin's first government, permitted them to take up temporary residence inside a nearby army base. As in many other similar cases, the temporary settlement became a permanent one over the course of time.

Before Elon Moreh, the government of Golda Meir had not allowed Jews to settle in Samaria. On seven occasions, groups had stolen into the area and tried to settle there, but the army had evicted them. On the eighth attempt, the government gave in.

The younger Peres was a hawk and sympathized with the settlers. Rabin despised the settlement movement. In his memoirs he called it "a cancer in the body of the nation." But lo and behold, a prime minister from the Labor Party who was considered a moderate once again gave in to the hawks in the party. The elderly Peres does not like to be reminded of his hawkish past. Today, from his elevated position as state president, he presents himself as a loyal soldier for peace, but the permission he gave the settlers to build communities in the hills of Samaria was a defining event: a left-wing government signaling to the nationalist camp that the entire West Bank was open to Jewish settlement.

The land upon which that first settlement was built belonged to the farmers of the Palestinian village of Rujeib, and it was confiscated from them for security purposes, ostensibly. In 1979, the villagers petitioned the Israeli Supreme Court, which ruled that private lands in the occupied territories may not be confiscated for the purpose of establishing settlements and that Elon Moreh should therefore be evacuated, but the judges hinted that if the land had not belonged to private owners, the ruling may have been different.

Now, the Right was in power, and Begin's government exploited the judgment in order to consolidate a new order in the territories. It determined that it was permitted to build settlements on any land that wasn't privately owned, and in the early 1980s Begin's minister of agriculture,

Ariel Sharon, who was in charge of the settlement in the territories, gleefully went about implementing the policy. Settlers received permission to establish their communities anywhere on the West Bank that had been defined as "state land" by the Jordanians, who ruled the area until it was conquered by Israel in 1967, or on land that was not registered as privately owned or was not cultivated and was therefore assumed to have been abandoned by its owners. "There will be many more Elon Morehs," Begin declared on his first visit to that settlement, and the Right adopted it as a slogan as most of the land in the West Bank became available for Jewish settlement.

Prominent and wise public figures had warned against prolonging the occupation and in particular against massive settlement in the occupied territories, but the majority of Israelis despised their protests, and the suffering of the Palestinians continued, and eventually they were compelled to rebel. At first they fought by throwing stones and hurling them with slingshots, and their use of violence forced the Israelis to reply in kind. Violence begets violence, and there was no courageous leader to snuff out the burning fuse; it was only after scores of Palestinian suicide bombers blew up in buses and shopping centers all across Israel, killing hundreds of Jews and wounding thousands, that Israel took stock and decided that it would be willing to negotiate on a withdrawal. However, the Israeli leaders' declarations were insincere, so the violent struggle continued at varying intensity for more than a decade. The events are still playing out, and most of the official documentation is still classified, and therefore any attempt to clarify who was responsible for each stage in the deterioration is impossible. But detailed examination is less important than the obvious and basic fact: there is an occupier, and there is a people subject to occupation. There is an oppressor and an oppressed nation, and the implications of this dichotomy were well known to all the players in the drama from scene one.

I grew up in the 1940s and 1950s, when the old-established Jewish community was small, about half a million souls altogether, and it seemed as though everyone knew everyone else. We used to know when and from where every family had arrived in the country—who had been on our equivalent of the Mayflower and who had come a little later; who came from a long line of geniuses, of important rabbis, or of intellectuals, and who was born into a simple family; who had been a capitalist in the Diaspora and who a manual worker. The community of the founders lived in three or four neighborhoods that the pioneers had built in the early twentieth century in the big cities or in farming villages established with the help of Baron Edmond James de Rothschild, or in socialist communes (kibbutzim), most of them in the northern part of the country.

My father's family moved to Palestine from Berlin in the early 1930s and lived in the Rehavia neighborhood in Jerusalem—about one mile square, inhabited by several hundred relatively affluent European, bourgeois, educated families with a pragmatic and moderate outlook. Rehavia was home to many of the pillars of the political and legal establishment of the new state, as well as the academic elite.

I grew up with children who were to become prominent figures in the left-wing, moderate camp. We went to the same elite schools, about twenty to thirty of which existed across the country, and belonged to the same youth movements. We read the same books, sang the same songs, and listened to the same radio programs. (There was no television in Israel until the later 1960s.) On our summer vacations we went to work camps at the same kibbutzim. Although they had for the most part never been laborers, our parents voted for the workers' party, Mapai, which had in fact founded the state and then won one election after another and from which today's Labor Party emerged. Our parents were in fact part of the core of the party. Some of them played key roles in it, and the others loyally followed its leaders, who honored them and led them on the way to independence in a considered and cautious manner along a winding and dangerous road. It was a leadership that advocated political realism and readiness to make far-reaching compromises on the basis of squeezing the last drop out of what was then termed "the art of the possible." Only a few of our neighbors belonged to the Revisionist secessionists, and as a rule their children also "seceded" from our society or were made to do so. A large majority of the people despised the secessionists.

What was the secret of the success of our parents' generation? Good, careful judgment and mutual support—that seems to me to have been the magic formula that guided this homogenous group of immigrants to take the right path up until 1967, a path that was far more successful than they themselves had believed it would be. Our educators and our parents understood that this was the middle way that should be chosen. They knew how to compromise; they steered clear of fanaticism the way you stay away from fire. Perhaps it was a rational conclusion drawn from the afflictions of those chapters of Jewish history when zealots had seized control of the community and led it into disaster. Or perhaps the response was instinctive, springing from a common process of socialization that stretched over a heritage that was built upon and based upon hundreds of years in the European Diaspora. Or perhaps it was a combination of both. In any case, in the neighborhoods where we grew up, our parents planned and put into practice the struggle for the achievement of a national home, using audacious and revolutionary methods (in comparison with the lack of initiative that had characterized the generation of their own parents in the Diaspora), that at the same time successfully imitated the way of life of the bourgeois middle class of central Europe. It was a remarkable and complex phenomenon, perhaps unique, and it had an inbuilt contradiction: radical action by conservative people—revolutionary pragmatism—which may have been the secret of their success.

After June 1967, the winds started blowing in a diametrically different direction in Israel. People who for half a century had been meticulously composed and collected, cautious and moderate, suddenly became arrogant and domineering. National morale was sky-high, and the printing presses didn't stop putting out triumphal albums glorifying the victors of the battlefield. Before the war, the economy had been in recession, but the victory revitalized it. The construction of army bases and airfields in the "new areas" and of the Bar Lev Line along the Suez Canal, oil pumped from the wells drilled by the Egyptians in Sinai before the Israeli occupation, and an increase in tourism boosted the economy and made it flourish. The prosperity was unprecedented. Jews from all over the world came to Israel to be intoxicated by the heady scent of the most outstanding triumph of their people in modern times. Many of the Jewish tourists were religiously observant, and they inflamed the messianic spirit that was taking root in the country. From a variety of local and external sources, slowly and persistently poisonous chauvinism was penetrating deep into the state's internal organs. A risky process had begun, imposing itself on the entire Israeli being and in the long run bearing fateful consequences.

8

Impotent Leadership

TO MY GOOD fortune, I had to breathe this phony intoxicating mountain air for only a short time. A year after the war, I went to study in the United States, after Rotary International awarded me a generous scholarship. I was offered the choice of any academic institution in the world, and I opted for studying mass communications at UCLA. It was in June 1968 when I arrived there, and two days later, Sen. Robert Kennedy was assassinated in the Ambassador Hotel. In fact, 1968 was one of the hardest and saddest years in American history. The military was bleeding in Vietnam (the number of the fallen reached thirty thousand) while at home students were burning draft papers. In April, Martin Luther King Jr. was murdered in Memphis.

That was my first sortie from Fortress Israel into the wide world, and for a twenty-three-year-old Israeli, America was like another planet. There was a gaping abyss between the austere life we led in the provincial, insular Israeli bubble, isolated from outside influences, and the power that sprang from the wealth and centrality of the United States. In Israel, for the first time, experimental black and white television broadcasts were being aired (twice a week). In the United States, the network news broadcasts brought the Vietnam War into every home. In Israel, the bank tellers hand-wrote each deposit in savings booklets. In Philadelphia, the first automated teller machine (ATM) was put into operation.

At the weekly meetings of the Westwood Village Rotary Club at Hotel Bel-Air, my hosts displayed a great interest in Israel. Only a year had passed since the swift and stunning victory in June 1967, and

Israel's image was sky high. They asked me about the war, and I asked them about American politics. Most of them were happy that Lyndon B. Johnson made do with only one term and supported Nixon for president. They despised the Black Panthers (the very thought that within our lifetime a black man would be elected to the presidency was more than unimaginable in those days; it would have been considered downright stupid) and believed that the United States must win in Vietnam, though their daughters and sons demonstrated against the war at their colleges. Twice, together with thousands of UCLA's students, I took the day off from studies to participate in demonstrations organized by the Student Mobilization Committee to End the War in Vietnam. The antiwar movement that peaked in 1968 (as a consequence of the Tet Offensive) was one of the most divisive political forces I had ever witnessed.

My encounter with American students aroused a complicated internal conflict over a matter that, until then, Israeli youngsters did not tend to agonize over: the defense policies adopted by the leadership. In the Israel of the 1960s, the concept of security was something of a sacred cow; public opinion rebelled against the leadership for the first time only after the Yom Kippur War in 1973, six years after the student uprisings in Europe and the United States. Who is a patriot, I asked myself. Is it the person who supports the establishment and enlists to fight in Vietnam, or the one who burns his draft card because he believes the war is senseless? In Israel at that time, reporting for military duty in the reserves or the regular army was a matter of course, a reflexive action, something totally natural whose validity only a very few people even contemplated questioning. After all, the enemy had openly declared his intention to destroy our state, and it therefore had to be defended, and if I don't do it, who will? But the outcome of the 1967 war had created a new reality. Now, for the first time, David had become a Goliath. The defender had become a conqueror. What would happen when this role-switch brought about another violent conflict and the occupied people rose up and demanded independence and the conqueror refused to do away with the occupation and withdraw from their land? Would the patriots be those who complied with the state's orders and went out to quell the uprising, or those who defied the orders in protest against the occupation?

In California, I often wondered if the fantastic military victory of June 1967 had not in fact sown the seeds of discord. Such soul searching was not what Israel was preoccupied with in 1969, because the euphoria had not yet subsided. It bothered me because I was far away (the only contact with my family and friends was through letters and brief, expensive phone calls twice a year, on the eve of festivals), and mainly because I was riveted by the fierce confrontation underway in American society over the war in Vietnam. As someone who had grown up in a conformist and obedient society; who had been inculcated with the habit of shouldering responsibility for the future of the state in all circumstances; who believed that the unity of purpose and of thought—in an admittedly Bolshevik manner—that Israelis had displayed to the world were authentic and justified; and who had absorbed many doses of indoctrination, the individualism that I discovered in California blew my mind. The political independence of American citizens and the option they had of doubting the purity of the establishment's motives and protesting against its activities were not common in the society that I had come from, where the individual was taught to subjugate his own aspirations to those of the tribe. The actual debate that took place among my American peers at UCLA over the justification of their "ego involvement" in wartime was a novel and peculiar thing for me. In general, the ways the American students formed their conception of reality in the late 1960s and the ways they looked at life were so different and so remote from my own that I often wondered which of us were living our lives correctly. John, a student from Dallas with whom I shared an apartment in West Hollywood, told me he was going to head north and slip across the border into Canada in order to dodge the draft. In my terms, the very thought of evading military service, particularly in wartime, was a betrayal of my country's most important principles. I asked myself if the political attitudes of the young individualists who surrounded me at the university were more sophisticated and wiser than my own naïve concepts, if they perhaps sprang from a lack of a fundamental sense of shared destiny, or if they were just plain cowardly. But nevertheless, the political discourse among the students was so serious and deep, and so great an effort was invested in organizing protests, that the dramatic debate to which I was exposed elicited doubts about the conflict at home. If the ostensible historical justice from which the Jews had benefited (in that by general agreement the world had granted them their own state by virtue of the Partition Resolution of the UN General Assembly of November 29, 1947) had been an injustice toward the Arabs, was that action in fact appropriate? And if adherence to Zionist ideology expressed a collective and an individual attempt to meet the existential threat of antisemitic persecution, why had the establishment of a Jewish state at the expense of the Arabs been historically justified, in a region in which it was doubtful that the chances of survival were any greater than they were in Europe? Was it not possible to sustain the Jewish religion freely in a state that was not Jewish? If so, why wasn't it preferable to settle in a democratic, open society with a progressive constitution like the United States of America, in which one could presume that the citizens' liberty was assured?

From the time I was exposed to the new reality, I became what is known in Israel today as a post-Zionist, a person who sees the flaws in Zionism and criticizes them. I saw the fundamental wrongs of American society, such as the gap between the poor and the rich and the sweeping permission for the possession of firearms (ostensibly for self-defense), but altogether, despite the bitter crisis gripping the country in those years, American society captivated my heart.

I was a different person when I returned to Israel. In my first conversations with my close friends, I noticed the gap. By getting rid of the occupied territories, we will avoid getting into deep trouble, I explained to my friends, but they did not hear what I was saying. The territories are a deposit to be held as a bargaining chip, I declaimed with fervor, and if the Arabs are not ready to negotiate, it may even be worthwhile to withdraw unilaterally to secure borders (as some of the moderate ideologues of the Left were advocating at the time). My friends were amazed. What has happened to him in California, this sane guy, they asked themselves. He has been infected by the hippies. After a while, I stopped pestering them. The gap separating us remained in place for a few years, and only after the October 1973 war did it begin to narrow. My friends began drawing closer to my positions by stages, and today most of them agree with my diagnosis that the treasure acquired in the 1967 victory had turned into a curse, although I doubt that many of them share my optimistic forecast regarding the prospects of peace.

The politicians were the last to acknowledge the new reality, but they weren't idiots. They acted the way that today's small-time politicians are used to acting. A statesman is someone who presents an exciting vision on the basis of which his associates build a program, and the enthused voters mobilize to ensure it is realized. But statesmen have been a rarity in recent generations, and most of the democracies have been doomed to be ruled by small-time politicians. At the outset of the twenty-first century, politicians almost everywhere do what seems to them to be most useful at that particular moment to himself, his cronies, and his party.

The people chosen by the Israelis to lead the state in recent years have presented no vision. Not one of them has emerged as an outstanding personality. They have been as clever and intelligent as most of the educated people in the population. Most of them have been experienced party politicians. Several had been outstanding soldiers, but Sharon and Barak excelled on the battlefield more than they did in the political arena. None of them were surprising, and their visions were no more far-seeing than a snapshot of any particular moment. They were guided by public opinion polls, by the media, and by holding a finger up to see which way the wind was blowing. Some of them believed that they possessed natural powers, innate instincts that enabled them to decipher reality and work out which way it was going. But the leaders of the whites in South Africa believed for decades that apartheid would last forever, and the heads of the military wing of Sinn Féin were convinced they would defeat Great Britain.

There is no doubt that the political deadlock was caused by the impotency of the leaders, but there is no reason to blame the three prime ministers of the last fifteen years—Barak, Olmert, and Netanyahu—who were genuinely representing the elite class from among the first generation of Israelis, who were raised in an independent Jewish state.[1] (Ariel Sharon is a special case and belongs to another generation of leaders.) They were not capable of doing anything more than what the politicians are ordinarily capable of doing. They are not guilty; the political culture is guilty. It is a culture that rewards irresponsibility, hypocrisy, and flattery rather than tenacity in trying to solve the country's problems, even at the price of losing support. Since Yitzhak Rabin there has been no leader capable of making daring moves. The seat of the leader in Israel has remained unoccupied.

Indeed, it has not been the leaders who have changed reality in Israel in the last twenty years, but the circumstances. Three shifts have forced some of them to examine their positions and alter them. The first was a substantial structural change. During the last quarter of the last century, the socialistic Israeli economy switched direction, became capitalistic, and joined the globalized world, and today there's no way of running a country if the world despises you. International cooperation entails listening to the voices emanating from other nations and falling in line with them. An obstinate Israel would have no chance of integrating into the global economy. And already, because of the continued occupation, wide circles view Israel as an outcast, pariah state. If this attitude spreads in the world, Israel will lose diplomatic and economic partners.

The second shift has been in the internal political sphere. The ideological right wing that rose to power in the 1970s and grew as the antithesis to the protracted hegemony of the Labor movement lost its way. Many of the followers of the populist ascetic Menachem Begin diverged from the purist heritage of their spiritual forefathers and surrounded themselves with corrupt political hacks.

The third change, as we previously mentioned, was imposed from the outside. The attacks on the United States by al Qaeda on 9/11 highlighted the link between the insecurity of the developed world and the continuation of Israel's occupation of the Palestinian territories. That connection internationalized the conflict, and its management has shifted into foreign hands, American and European. The truth is that the governments of most of the developed countries understand very well the existential threats that Israel faces due to its geographical location. They also do not hesitate to empathize with a nation that has suffered so much throughout history, but nevertheless they are losing patience. Their demand for a solution to the conflict that menaces their security is becoming more urgent.

These changes served as the yeast that has swelled the sane mass of Israelis, which is expanding and reaching the critical stage. Important lessons are crystallizing in the secular strata of society: Israeli society needs a fundamental overhaul, and the condition for carrying it out is the end of the occupation, partitioning of the land, and the signing of a peace treaty. The internalization of this principle by the majority of the Israelis has taken place at an irritatingly slow pace and in a strange manner, perhaps because of the complex political and religious structure of society, but at last it has happened. In recent years there has not been a single public opinion survey in which less than 65 percent of the population expressed support for partition of the land into two states. This is a strange finding; in most of the topics heading the political agenda, Israelis tend to the right, but even so, they want a territorial compromise. This paradox is an apparent sign of cleverness. They tend to the right because the Middle East is a tough neighborhood, and people living there and desiring to control their own destiny must show strength. And they want a compromise because they realize that a state that wants to participate in globalization must listen to what the world is saying. Between toughness and conciliatoriness, fine tuning in order to find the precise tone is not easy and demands a substantial degree of sophistication, but it is apparent that the unaffiliated, secular public is capable of finding that right tone. Moreover, the members of the moderate and silent majority have shown a tenacity no weaker than that of the vociferous and aggressive settlers when it stood up successfully to the Palestinian suicide bombers, biting their lips, devising complex defense mechanisms, and most importantly internalizing the lesson that should have been self-evident: the benefit that the state would derive from a compromise is greater than the benefit that would arise from holding on to all the land. And therefore, all that remains of the ideology of the Greater Land of Israel zealots is a dim echo. The figures who led the settlement enterprise have grown old and tired, and the streamlined machinery they set up is gradually falling to pieces. On the ground, they have been replaced by leaders of local cults, extremists, some of whom are not acceptable to many of the settlers themselves.

Throughout the process, the leaders of the state have lagged behind public opinion. For several years, while average Israelis have wanted to see a compromise, their leaders have not known how to translate this aspiration into reality. The gap is especially salient when it comes to the land grabs perpetrated by the settlers. Although most Israelis already resent the settlers because they are perceived as a divisive force that is liable to thwart a peace agreement and to attenuate the strategic alliance between Israel and the United States, generation after generation of leaders have nevertheless pushed the settlement enterprise forward.

Over time, pragmatism would overcome politics. Ideology would not decide the fate of the region, and neither would messianism, chauvinism, fanaticism, or fundamentalist radicalism. The deciding factor would be sound, practical, and productive logic. The general consensus among the majority of the citizens is going to defeat the paralysis that has gripped the politicians. The practical implementation of this change is being delayed only because Israel's current leader, Benjamin Netanyahu, is still proving incapable of mustering sufficient mental strength to make the decisive final turn and break away from the archaic ideologies that he was nurtured on. Netanyahu is the last of the dissenters' Mohicans. Most if not all of his national camp's influential political associates have moved to the left, joining the opposite camp of the compromisers.

9

Secular Messianism

THE SURRENDER OF ideological principles that right-wing politicians like Netanyahu are being asked to carry out is by no means a simple matter. The change from their point of view is primarily spiritual or psychological. For them, "the Whole Land of Israel" is no mere election slogan, nor a transient whim or a passing fashion. The pact they have forged with the land is an authentic expression of their worldview. Fundamentally, this is an ideology that can be defined as secular messianism, based on a sincere faith in three national ideas to be found at the hub of their lives: "You have chosen us," "the eternity of Israel," and "the divine promise." To religious nationalists, the meaning of this "holy trinity" is that God has chosen us from all the nations and has bestowed upon us special powers as individuals and as a group, as well as a pledge that our people will exist forever. He has also promised us the Land of Israel with extensive borders, some of which we achieved in June 1967. But in the eyes of the secular messianists, the "you" who chose and promised is not necessarily God, but rather Jewish destiny and its special history, heritage, and imperatives handed down by the ancient forefathers—spiritual symbols and myths that combine to form an illusory ideological system of thought that can be presented in secular terms and upon the basis of which the hard core of Netanyahu's political supporters was educated.

In the twenty-first century, in a democratic country that boasts of being a high-tech power, should this pseudoreligious mishmash serve as a political platform? Of course not, and we have already seen that the myth has nothing in common with classical Zionism. But it is the reality of those remaining in the ideological core that keeps the faith with the wholeness of the land, and in their eyes a leader who dares to depart from its principles will be considered a traitor.

Since the signing of the peace treaty with Egypt on the White House lawn in March 1979, the extreme Right has applied the label "traitor" to a large number of leaders who had in the past been considered Whole Land of Israel zealots. In effect, any leader who advocated a compromise with the Palestinians was merited such abuse, and they have included Menachem Begin, when he ordered the total destruction of the settlements Israel had established in Northern Sinai prior to the return of the area to Egypt (the order was given to Ariel Sharon, Begin's minister of agriculture, who carried it out very skillfully); Yitzhak Shamir, when he agreed to Israel's participation in the Madrid Peace Conference in October 1991; Netanyahu himself, when he signed the Wye Plantation agreement in October 1998 and agreed to hand part of the West Bank over to the PA; Sharon, in 2005 when he ordered the disengagement from the Gaza Strip and the evacuation of the settlements that had been established there, and now Netanyahu once again, after he declared his support for the two-state solution and temporarily froze building in West Bank settlements. Each one of them deliberated and agonized, tore their hair out in sorrow, crossed the Five Stages of Grief—or at least that's what they told their electorate—and ultimately decided to work toward a compromise and surrender a strip of territory. One thin slice after another, the salami is being sliced. Each prime minister delayed handing territory to the Arabs for as long as possible, and when all hope was finally lost, when it seemed that the Americans and the Europeans were losing their patience, each has agreed to make the concession so that he would be able to look as if he were presenting his own initiative or at least making some movement toward a solution. Some prime ministers did make substantial territorial concessions. Rabin gave up control of the large cities in the West Bank and Gaza; Netanyahu gave up most of the area of Hebron; Sharon, in 2002, decided to build the separation barrier ("the Wall"), intending it to be the border between Israel and Palestine, and then, in 2005, he gave up the entire Gaza Strip and some settlements in the northern West Bank. Prime ministers have also made "virtual" concessions, launching public relations campaigns to declare their willingness to compromise. Barak said he was prepared to withdraw to the lines of June 4, 1967, with slight adjustments, and Olmert said he supported a return to the 1967 borders and the division of Jerusalem, but beyond the statements, they never actually gave up any actual land. Israeli governments have become accustomed to using double-talk. Netanyahu has been particularly outstanding in this regard, in both of his terms as prime minister.

If these Israeli prime ministers had only been prepared to take risks for the sake of a better future for their neighbors and themselves, then the process of withdrawal from the territories could have been carried out in one step, saving both sides thousands of dead, maimed, and wounded, as well as vast amounts of money that have simply gone down the drain. Imagine what would have happened if Rabin had not been assassinated and his initiative had proceeded, and the opposition that fought against him in the 1990s—mainly Sharon, Netanyahu, and Olmert, who only a few years later offered the Palestinians precisely the same peace plan that Rabin and Arafat hammered out—had mobilized to resolve the conflict. The investment in the construction of new settlements on the West Bank could have also been saved—the infrastructures, roads, crossing-points, lockups and prisons, expenditure on the military, the police and Border Police, the security services, and the compensation that has already been doled out to the settlers who were evacuated from Gaza and is yet to be paid to those who will leave the West Bank. At a conservative estimate, since 1967, the economic cost of the occupation reached the total of at least $90 billion, including security and civilian expenses, construction and maintenance of the settlements, construction of the security barrier, and potential loss of gross domestic product mainly during the two long periods of the Palestinian revolt, or intifada. According to this estimation, the average cost of each year of the West Bank's occupation is around $2 billion. (In 2010, Israel's GDP was $220 billion, and its GDP per capita was $29,800; the state budget was $87 billion.) In short, Israel's occupation of the territories has been the single largest expenditure in the country's history.[1]

The Israelis underwent a similar process of awakening during the last five or six years of their occupation of South Lebanon. It was a long, agonizing process, replete with casualties, and it is worth examining because the time that has passed by since then enables us to place it in perspective. The First Lebanon War was Israel's Vietnam War. The latter dragged on for fifteen years, and the former for eighteen. In Lebanon, 1,216 Israeli soldiers were killed, whereas in Vietnam, there were 58,200 American fatalities. Relative to the populations of the two countries, the numbers are very similar. (The population of Israel at the time was around six million, or one fiftieth of America's 300 million.)

Israel invaded Lebanon early in July 1982 in order to remove Yasser Arafat's militias from the border area and to protect the Galilee. The operation—known today as the First Lebanon War—was a success. The Lebanese population, mostly Shi'ites, welcomed the IDF units with flowers and handfuls of rice, for the invasion served their own purpose in stopping the Palestinian militias from doing as they pleased in Lebanon. In August, Arafat was forced to withdraw from that country with most of his armed forces, finding refuge in Tunis.

The IDF had apparently accomplished its mission, and it should therefore have withdrawn from the occupied territory and returned to Israel. However, the political echelon decided on an interim solution. In order to create a buffer between the Palestinian militiamen who had remained in Lebanon and Israel's northern border, the IDF forces pulled back only partially and redeployed inside Lebanese territory, south of the Litani River. A more limited area therefore remained under their control, but an occupation is an occupation, and like all others, this one too aroused local resistance that got ever stronger with time. Soon Israeli troops were having to protect themselves from a new Lebanese organization, Hezbollah, whose aim was to drive out the invaders and who mounted an effective guerrilla campaign to this end. Hezbollah militias initiated attacks, and the IDF units found themselves mostly protecting their own movements within the security zone. The price Israel paid was high. Funerals were held for fallen soldiers almost every day, the national mood was dismal, and Begin fell into a deep depression from which he never recovered. He had to resign, and he became a recluse in a small rented apartment in Jerusalem for nine full years until he passed away.

Already by the end of the 1980s it was clear that the IDF was bleeding in Lebanon, and that its continued presence there was only strengthening and hardening Hezbollah. Why then did Israel not pull out of that country ten or fifteen years before it actually withdrew? Because of conceptual rigidity. When Hezbollah was waging an offensive and the number of IDF casualties rose, Israel refrained from withdrawal so as not to demonstrate weakness, and later, after the arena was quiet for a time, Israel ostensibly had no reason to withdraw, and so on repeatedly, time after time. The leadership did not dare to break this vicious cycle, and unlike American society during the Vietnam War, for years the Israelis did not exert any significant pressure on their government to put an end to this protracted military adventure. In general, one may say that Israelis reveal remarkable strength when they are pressed and do not reveal much wisdom when times are quiet. In almost all the important and complicated trials of strength—the War of Independence, the October 1973 war, and the suicide-terror intifada—the entire society, civilians and soldiers, functioned effectively and showed solidarity. But in the lulls between wars, when there was a need to take steps to stabilize the region and to avert the next violent confrontation, the leadership was overcome by paralysis. Generally, during wartime the leaders took great risks and displayed capability, but most of them did not have the wisdom to take risks for peace. In 1970, when the War of Attrition was over, Meir refused to comply with Sadat's proposal to act to calm down the front along the Suez Canal. Israel was asked to draw its forces back a few kilometers east of the waterway, to enable it to be opened to shipping, and in this way to advance a process of dialogue. Meir said no, and the upshot was the surprise offensive of October 1973.

In southern Lebanon, the entire system was based on a strategic error, because the security zone south of the Litani River was too narrow to prevent the firing of Katyusha rocket launchers into the Galilee, and at the same time, the longer the occupation continued, the stronger the Hezbollah militias grew, and the more casualties were inflicted on the IDF units serving in Lebanon. In effect, the Lebanese resistance to the Israeli presence—resistance that was guided by Syria—managed to maneuver the IDF into a situation in which it was a double loser: the security zone did not provide security for Galilee, and the units in southern Lebanon were bleeding.

In his election campaign in 1999, Barak promised that if he became prime minister, he would pull the army out of Lebanon within one year, and indeed a little over a year went by between the time that he entered the prime minister's office and the operation when in a single night all of the IDF's units withdrew from Lebanese territory. This was Barak's most successful action as prime minister. "Eighteen years of wallowing in the Lebanese quagmire have ended," Barak told me. "I am proud of my decision and I am proud of its result." On only two other occasions did Israeli prime ministers take the bull by the horns and make strategic moves that bolstered stability and peace during periods of calm: Yitzhak Rabin when he signed the Oslo Accords after the first intifada, and Ariel Sharon when he pulled out of Gaza after the second intifada (despite the fact that for the thirty preceding years Sharon had caused Israel grave damage by inspiriting the settlement movement and later by building settlements).

It is of course impossible to ascertain how different modes of conduct would have worked under similar circumstances, but the leadership of the Labor movement in its pragmatic era would have worked for a rapid solution. Men like Ben-Gurion, Weizmann, Sapir, Prime Minister Moshe Sharett,[2] and perhaps even Dayan toward the end of his life would have tried to end the vicious cycle of attack, retaliation, another attack, another retaliation and so on, month after month, year after year. Certainly, Begin and Shamir were psychologically incapable of giving up the West Bank, but it is possible that if in the early 1990s the pragmatist Sharon had mobilized to help Rabin's peace moves and thrown his weight behind the withdrawal initiative, as he did only ten years later in the Gaza Strip, it would have been possible to achieve substantial progress toward an agreement. But Sharon aspired to become prime minister himself. His personal ambition blurred his grasp of reality, and it was only after he settled into the prime minister's office in 2002 that his worldview metamorphosed after he internalized the gravity of the demographic threat on the internal front and the vital need to preserve American support externally. Sharon drew the conclusions and in 2005 evacuated all the Jewish settlements in the Gaza Strip and began evacuating settlements on the West Bank as well. But his health betrayed him, and he suffered a stroke in 2006 and has been in a persistent vegetative state since then.

When Sharon proposed the disengagement from Gaza, the Knesset supported him,[3] as did public opinion. If Netanyahu were to decide to take a dramatic step vis à vis the Palestinians, and perhaps the Syrians too before the upheaval there started, a significant majority of the Israeli public would undoubtedly back him. Even in the present Knesset, which had been dispersed when the official campaign for the January

2013 elections started, there is a clear majority in favor of a territorial compromise with the Palestinians.[4]

The about-face in Sharon's positions proved that the advantage is on the side of the pragmatists and that as time goes by the ideological core of the right grows smaller, and today it is close to vanishing. The fanatics are still vociferous and term any moves toward compromise on Netanyahu's part (such as his "Two states for two peoples" speech at Bar-Ilan University on July 14, 2009) a disgrace and threaten his life, but nevertheless the circumstances that prevailed in Israel in November 1995 and made the assassination of Rabin possible no longer exist. If Netanyahu decides to hand most of the occupied territories over to the Palestinians, his life would not be in danger, simply because the stronger political elements on the right—the ones that gave support to the fanatics who were fighting Rabin and the Oslo Accords—have crossed over to the other side.[5]

And this is why, fifteen years after the assassination, there are no political figures of stature and influence standing behind the fanatics who threaten to bring down any leader who promotes a compromise. Their absence stood out on three occasions: first, when settlers and extremists incited against Sharon after he ordered the disengagement from Gaza[6]; second, when Netanyahu accepted the idea of a Palestinian state, and third, when Netanyahu ordered a temporary construction freeze in the West Bank settlements. In each of these cases, the organizers of incitement campaigns were Knesset members from the backbenches, nameless functionaries and intellectuals and publicists lacking in actual influence. None of them had the charisma or the authority that Sharon and Netanyahu had when they incited against Rabin.

In Israel, over the last twenty years, a political situation has arisen that is apparently without precedent anywhere in the world. The classical Left has all but vanished, but the nationalistic Right has not gotten any stronger. After the 1967 war, there was much movement from the center toward the extremes, but in recent years the movement has been in the opposite direction, and the congestion in the center has therefore grown. A large number of right-wingers have gone over to the camp that is interested in reaching a territorial compromise. First came the authoritative leader Begin, who surrendered the whole of Sinai, including the cluster of settlements that Israel had built in the northern part of the peninsula.[7] Next came Shamir, who agreed to negotiate a territorial compromise. Third was Sharon, who gave up the Gaza Strip and all twenty settlements there with some twelve thousand settlers, who were evacuated in the summer of 2005. Next was Olmert, who offered to divide Jerusalem. Then Netanyahu undertook to recognize a Palestinian state on the West Bank. Each one of them quit the Whole Land of Israel camp with a group of followers, and over time the once rigid and frightening nationalist camp was left flaccid and unimposing. Occasionally, far-right extremists are causing turmoil, although the patriotic coterie encouraging them is limited in number and lacks substantial political power.

10

The Demographic Threat

THE ANNEXATION OF the West Bank to Israel, whether de jure or de facto, will engender a binational state with an Arab majority. On this issue, intelligent people in Israel are undivided.

In a binational state, it would be impossible not to give the Palestinians citizenship and the vote. On this too, intelligent and decent people agree.

And, nevertheless, for a long period of time, these basic truths did not seep into the consciousness of the Jews in Israel and were not internalized. Why? Because interested parties succeeded in marketing the image of an illusory reality, in which two nations live side by side, one in its own independent state and the second in an occupied territory, and with everything carrying on perfectly normally.

In mid-June 1967, when the fighting was over, the Green Line—which separated Israel from the Jordanian-controlled West Bank and the Egyptian-controlled Gaza Strip on maps—was erased, and traffic flowed freely between Israeli territory and the conquered areas, in both directions. Israelis went on excursions into the West Bank, ate in restaurants in Jericho and Ramallah, and made purchases in the markets of Qalqilya and Nablus, and Palestinians too could freely cross what had previously been the border and visit Israel. In Jerusalem, movement between the two parts of the city was both free and safe. For the Israelis, it was convenient to imagine that this situation could last forever. But as the settlers broadened their project, seized control of more land, and built more settlements, the bitterness of the inhabitants of the land deepened until it reached the point where it boiled over and broke out in violent resistance. At the first stage, in the first intifada, they threw stones and discharged firearms, and when these conventional methods did not persuade the Israelis to end the occupation, the violence was intensified in the suicide bombers' intifada. The result was immediately evident on the ground: the free movement ended with the Israelis keeping away from the West Bank, the Palestinians being refused permission to work in Israel, and the Green Line becoming a border once again. In recent years, the only people still moving regularly between Israeli territory and the West Bank are settlers leaving and returning to their homes, generally secured by military units.

The suicide offensive forced the Israelis to internalize the fact that a political determination must be made. It turned out that the Palestinian aspiration for an independent state was resolute. If Israel wished to rule over the occupied territories and to retain the settlement project, it would have to pay a price: to sustain more suicide attacks and to be constantly at odds with the world, or alternatively to establish a binational state in which, within a few years, there would no longer be a Jewish majority. For the first time since 1967, the Israelis were being pushed against the wall by the demand that they take a decision about the fate of the territories. Their decision was clear-cut: no to a binational state, yes to partition, and two states for two peoples.

Thus, after thirty years of being misled by their illusions, the Israelis grasped that if they insisted on remaining in the occupied territories, the demographic threat would become reality. Between the sea and the river, there would be more Arabs than Jews, and the Jews would lose not only the majority but also the power to control their own destiny. In recent years, all the governments of Israel (apart from the first Netanyahu administration in 1996–1999) have defined the demographic forecast as an existential threat.

This was the most important revolution that most Israelis have undergone in the last generation. Secular liberals recognized the imperative arising out of reality, as did conservatives and nationalists, for whom the vision of the Whole Land of Israel had been an essential part of their worldview. Most of them remained loyal to the moderate Right and to their conservative views. But nevertheless, they were fundamentally realistic and understood that it would be possible to maintain a democratic state with a Jewish majority only if Israel would withdraw from the West Bank and enable the Palestinians to establish their own independent state.

To be accurate on the matter of motivation, most Israelis support the two-state solution not out of any acknowledgement of the legitimate rights of the Palestinians, but rather out of necessity and urgency—the necessity to separate and break off contact in order to block the entry of suicide bombers into Israel, and the urgency of preserving the Jewish demographic majority. The national aspirations of the Palestinians are of no interest to the average Israeli. From the moral standpoint, the fact that the Israelis still are not willing to recognize the injustice that Zionism has inflicted upon the Palestinian people proves that what we are witnessing is not a reconciliation, but nonetheless, the practical outcome is what matters.

The question therefore is not whether Israel will give up the territories, but whether it is able to do so. In other words, have the concrete facts that the governments and the settlers have planted in the ground struck such deep roots that removing them is no longer possible?

The notion that the territories have already been annexed and it would be impossible to separate them from the State of Israel has its supporters not only among the right-wingers and the settlers, but also on the radical Left; the latter is the political home of an Israeli thinker who has since the 1980s been developing and publicizing a hypothesis to that effect. He is Meron Benvenisti, who in the 1970s served as deputy to the mayor of Jerusalem, Teddy Kollek, and is familiar with the Arabs and fully conversant with the history of the conflict and has spent recent years researching and writing.

The annexation of the territories is a fait accompli, Benvenisti contends:

> Sometime in the late 1980s, the settlements crossed the critical threshold, beyond which continued demographic and urban growth [of Jewish colonization] were ensured. Settler leaders succeeded in setting up a powerful lobby on both sides of the Green Line, establishing a legal and physical infrastructure that actualized the de facto annexation of the territories to the State of Israel. Since then the number of settlements and even the size of their population became irrelevant due to the fact that Israel's ruling instruments were perfected

> to such a degree that made the distinction between Israel proper and the occupied territories—and between settlements in the West Bank and Jewish communities inside Israel—completely vague. In a similar manner, the takeover of land ceased to serve as an apparatus designed for settlement construction and became a means of restricting the movements of the Palestinian population and of appropriating their physical space.

Benvenisti believes that the interdependence between the Arab and Jewish communities cannot be disentangled without paying a heavy price. The dovish camp pretends that the situation in the territories is temporary, he writes, and adds that Israeli doves are aware that this "temporariness" is Israel's chief means of annexing the territories in order to establish Jewish domination there absolutely. It is a sold game. Under the false slogan of impermanence, permanently and persistently the settlement's enterprise is being expanded by the authorities.

On the Palestinian side, Benvenisti's twin is Ali Abunimah, an American journalist whose parents were born in British Palestine. In his book *One Country: A Bold Proposal to End the Israeli-Palestinian Impasse,* Abunimah tries to convince that Israel and Palestine are by now geographically and economically intertwined in a way that would prevent separation. The two-state solution, he wrote, has been replaced by a de facto binational state. He supports the formation of a single democratic state "based on the equality of citizens and taking into account the legitimate concerns of Israel's Jewish population."

Abunimah represents quite a significant trend. More than a few important Arab thinkers have enthusiastically espoused the binational state solution. After all, there is no doubt that the most effective way of reducing Jewish influence between the Mediterranean and the Jordan River is simply to step up the Palestinian birthrate and to wait patiently. The Jews' ability to maintain their rule in their state depends on one factor: their proportion in the population. If they lose the majority, they will also lose control.

Yasser Abed Rabbo, a moderate Palestinian leader and a former close adviser to Yasser Arafat, told me, "The idea of the bi-national state is gaining momentum in the Palestinian streets. Its underlying rationale is that only in a state covering the whole area between the Jordan

River and the Mediterranean will the Palestinians have a majority and sooner or later will be able to truly rectify what they see as the injustice of 1948."

Rabbo cited a well-known Christian-Arab intellectual, Cecil Hourani. Two months after the Arabs were defeated in 1967, Hourani published a self-critical analysis in the Lebanese newspaper *A-Nahar*,[1] which started a heated argument in the Arab world. Its title was "The Moment of Truth: Towards a Middle East Dialogue," and the Israelis were so excited about it that the army's chief of staff ordered the distribution of a Hebrew translation of it among intelligence officers.

Hourani's article criticized the Arabs for their habit of pretending that occurrences that don't suit them do not exist and always comprehending reality too late. He called on the Arabs to accept the existence of the State of Israel within the 1949 Armistice Lines (pre–June 1967 Borders) and advised the Arabs that if Israel annexed the occupied territories, they should patiently build their majority. It seems as though Hourani realized back then what would create a deep rift among Israelis many years later. "By incorporating the Gaza Strip and the West Bank into her, the proportion of Arabs to Jews will be radically changed," Al Hourani wrote on August 1967. He concluded, "If the Israeli government accepts the Arabs within the territories she controls as full Israeli citizens, with equal civil and political rights, Israel will no longer be a Jewish state. . . . It will become a Jewish-Arab state."

Another intellectual, Ahmad Samih Khalidi of St. Antony's College in Oxford, an adviser to the PA, said that if Israel refused to vacate all of the land it conquered in 1967, the Palestinians will evoke the Jews' worst nightmare and demand a solution based upon "mutual respect, equality and mutuality, and a sense of genuine partnership in sharing the land."[2]

But the scenario that provides for the creation of a binational state has no chance whatsoever of happening. The Arab intellectuals cited previously are expressing their heartfelt desires, no more, and Meron Benvenisti is wrong. He underestimates the common sense of the Jews, to put it mildly. Why should the Jews agree to give up control of their destiny and become a minority once again, as they had been in the Diaspora for two thousand years? After building a state for themselves, are they now going to abolish it with their own hands? Only absolute fools could accept such a solution. If they were forced to live in a country ruled by others, most of the Jewish Israelis would prefer to immigrate to Europe or America.

The idea of uniting the two peoples in one state has hovered in and out of Zionist thought since the 1930s, but it was always harbored either by an idealistic ultra-liberal minority or by messianic extremists, both misled by their unrealistic imaginations. The majority rejected them, and reality proved that the idea was a recipe for catastrophe. It is enough to take a glance at binational states not far from Israel: Lebanon, Cyprus, and the new states that emerged after Yugoslavia broke up—they have all seen civil wars. There is absolutely no chance that the Israelis will voluntarily commit suicide, and we should therefore acknowledge that on the matter of the occupied territories, the die has already been cast, and the future will see two states for two people. In the history of Zionism, when it comes to policy, pragmatism prevails.

11

A Bulldozer That Built and Destroyed

THE LAST PERSON you would have expected to surrender land and order the abandonment and destruction of Jewish settlements was Ariel Sharon, the retired general who ran around the West Bank and the Gaza Strip for decades like a man possessed, hopping from hilltop to hilltop and marking the new settlements he planned to build on a map covered in transparent plastic. Sharon earned the title "the father of Jewish settlements in the territories." He used to take important visitors from abroad to a dominating hill in the West Bank to show them how close it was to Tel Aviv. With a lone mortar located here, he would say, it would be possible to paralyze Ben-Gurion International Airport. "Sharon's Lookout," they used to call that site, and he himself was nicknamed "the Bulldozer" because there was no stopping him when he decided to establish a settlement. He filled his map with red dots and the land with settlements, and the settlers idolized him. He insisted on building settlements in the most sensitive locations, in areas where the Palestinian population was the most dense. Sharon was the ugly Israeli, an arrogant and domineering get-things-done man: brutal, resolute, and obstinate.

But it was the very same Sharon who wiped settlements off the map. Why did the Bulldozer order the army to clear all the settlers and settlements out of Gaza, as well as some isolated settlements in the northern West Bank, thereby marking the beginning of the destruction of his life's work?

Towards the end of his career and his active life, after reaching the apex of his aspirations and being elected prime minister, this cunning warrior, who was admired by both secular and religious Israelis (although he was a nonbeliever who devoured pork with gusto) and who made the settlement project his obsession, realized that there was no greater constraint than reality. In the face of Palestinian determination and international pressure, Sharon was forced to give in. But did he ever admit that he had been wrong? Did he regret that he had deceived his disciples, built up an illusion for years, and squandered huge resources in constructing settlements and infrastructures that would end up as heaps of rubble? In Israel's short history, very few politicians have ever owned up to making an error.

The second intifada ate away at Sharon's stamina. It broke out during the term of his predecessor as prime minister, Ehud Barak, whose Labor Party was in power opposite Sharon's Likud party. On September 28, 2000, Sharon set out to make a political demonstration by visiting the highly sensitive site in the Old City of Jerusalem that the Jews call Temple Mount because twice in ancient times their forefathers had built their temples there only to have them destroyed by their enemies. It is known by the Arabs as Haram al-Sharif, or the Noble Sanctuary, and since the eighth century the Al-Aqsa Mosque, the third holiest place in Islam after Mecca and Medina, has stood there. Sharon's visit was a transparent provocation aimed at irritating the Palestinians by showing that the Jews controlled the site, and it achieved its goal.

Sharon arrived on Temple Mount with a group of Likud Knesset members. In the forecourt of the mosque, hundreds of Palestinians were waiting for them, and they confronted the police who surrounded them. A veritable battle ensued. The Arabs threw stones, and the police fired rubber bullets and tear gas canisters. In the end ten Palestinians and twenty police officers were hurt. That evening, the national police chief declared, "It was our duty as the police to make the visit possible. If we had thought it was dangerous, we would not have allowed it. It is the duty of policemen to protect themselves." Sharon stated, "They [the Palestinian demonstrators] are inciters. The Temple Mount is in our hands." PA chairman Yasser Arafat defined the act as "a dangerous step intended to threaten and to harm the Muslim holy places in Jerusalem."

The next day, the Muslim day of prayer, thousands of Palestinians protested in the Old City of Jerusalem and on the Mount of Olives, which overlooks it. They hurled rocks and gasoline bombs, and the police and the military responded with tear gas and rubber bullets. In the coming five days, violent demonstrations broke out in other cities in the territories, and the army and the police killed forty-seven Palestinians and wounded almost two thousand.

The Oslo Accords were on the verge of collapsing. Two months earlier, in July 2000, the summit conference that President Bill Clinton had convened at Camp David had failed, and Arafat and Barak had gone home without an agreement, with each blaming the other. It is possible that the failure of the summit led Arafat to instigate a violent uprising—that is the accepted explanation in Israel, but there is no conclusive proof of it.[1] But it is clear that Sharon's visit to the disputed site was the spark that ignited the flames. Barak had approved the visit. During his term, the settlements in the West Bank had been enlarged by at least three thousand new housing units. That was the worst mistake made by Barak and his government—land grabbing and settlement sprawl in the midst of peace negotiations. Arafat protested, but Barak argued that the Oslo Accords did not bar building inside existing settlements.

In the first week of October the demonstrations gained strength and spread into Israel itself. Arab citizens of Israel expressing solidarity with their Palestinian brethren faced off against police near their homes in northern Israel. Groups of protesters blocked roads and threw stones and gasoline bombs at vehicles. A main highway connecting the north with central Israel was blocked. The police reacted with great force and gunfire, killing thirteen Arab citizens. In response, the Israeli Arab sector declared a general strike.

On October 12, a Palestinian mob lynched two Israeli reserve soldiers who had driven into Ramallah by mistake. The scenes were broadcast on television and shocked Israelis.

In January 2001, Barak and Arafat launched another attempt at dialogue, under Egyptian auspices, at Taba, on the Gulf of Aqaba, but no headway was made. Barak resigned, and the Knesset decided on new elections. In February, Sharon roundly defeated Barak and set up a national unity government. The conflict with the Palestinians escalated, and Sharon's government abolished the security coordination apparatus between the sides. The Oslo Accords had collapsed.

Unlike the first intifada, which was, generally speaking, a popular uprising and largely limited to the use of stones and Molotov cocktails by the Palestinians and batons and arrests by the Israelis, the second one saw both sides using all the power at their disposal in terms of fighting in built-up areas. The Palestinians dispatched suicide bombers into Israel, which responded with targeted assassinations from the air. The Palestinians fired primitive rockets and mortar bombs from the Gaza Strip at the Israeli town of Sderot and nearby communities, and in response Israel used artillery and aircraft to bombard targets in the Strip. One suicide bomber after another crossed the unprotected border between the West Bank and Israel to blow themselves up at crowded sites, and Israel's response was to conquer the hub of the Palestinian fighters' activity in a refugee camp in the West Bank city of Jenin and lay siege to a group of Palestinian fighters and their commanders hiding out in the Church of the Nativity in Bethlehem.

In May 2002 another attempt was made to salvage the peace negotiations, leading up to a speech made by President George W. Bush on June 24 in Washington, D.C., in which for the first time the U.S. government had undertaken to support an independent Palestine.

In his speech, the president introduced the Road Map to Peace, a plan proposed by the Middle East Quartet—the United States, the European Union, the United Nations, and Russia. "The Road Map represents a starting point toward achieving the vision of two states, a secure State of Israel and a viable, peaceful, democratic Palestine," Bush said, and added, "It is the framework for progress towards lasting peace and security in the Middle East."

The plan precisely details the obligations to be undertaken by the two sides. First, the Palestinians would abandon terrorism in exchange for a freeze on Israeli settlement activity, and then would come negotiations on the core issues: borders, settlements, Jerusalem, and refugees, with the aim of concluding a treaty defining the permanent borders between Israel and Palestine and reaching a comprehensive solution of the conflict by 2005.

The Israeli cabinet accepted the plan, with twelve ministers voting for it, seven against, and four abstentions. This was a historical decision, because for the first time ever, an Israeli government had agreed to the establishment of a Palestinian state. On May 26, at a meeting with senior Likud party members, Sharon stunned his supporters with a statement that expressed the implications of the change in policy: "I think the idea that it is possible to continue keeping 3.5 million Palestinians under occupation—yes it is occupation, you might not like this word, but what is happening is occupation—is bad for Israel, and bad for the Palestinians, and bad for the Israeli economy. Controlling 3.5 million Palestinians cannot go on forever. Do you want to remain in Jenin, Nablus, Ramallah and Bethlehem? I don't think it is right."

The settlers felt betrayed and were dumbfounded. Was this their partner and comrade Sharon speaking, or an activist of the Peace Now movement that Sharon had always held in contempt? How could Sharon use the word "occupation," which since 1967 had been the term employed by the Arab side to describe the situation? The heads of the political and security establishments in Israel had never dared to utter it in this context. From the point of view of Israeli officialdom, the territories belonged to the Land of Israel and had not been "occupied" but liberated and returned to their rightful owners. And now, this was not a left-winger turning things upside down and depicting the liberation as an occupation—*kibush* in Hebrew—but the darling of the Right, and this was no inadvertent slip of the tongue, but a conscious statement. Sharon uttered the word three times in one sentence and erased the taboo that the nationalist camp had imposed on its use. In effect, Sharon had announced that the dream of ruling the West Bank was at an end.

And it happened during the same week that a coalition government headed by the Right decided to support the establishment of a Palestinian state. It was a sudden and drastic change that on the one hand attested to Sharon being a pragmatic and realistic leader and on the other hand revealed how wrong and distorted his previous political worldview had been until then. On the same day, a public opinion survey was published in Israel in which a representative sample of 593 citizens was asked, "How do you relate to an end to the Israeli occupation of the territories?" 62 percent responded positively, 32 percent negatively, and 6 percent expressed no opinion.

When Sharon crossed over from the Right to the center, he was seventy-five years old. He had correctly interpreted the public's position. If five years earlier someone had predicted that Sharon would do what he did, that someone would have been pronounced delusional. Now, Sharon's actions and statements accurately reflected the immense change in his view of the world.

Thus, the world—in the form of the Quartet—had forced a right-wing government in Israel to carry out an about-face, and the upshot was that the volume of the dispute between the Left and the Right was significantly reduced. The fanatics had lost out. This was a substantial change, no less important than the act of signing the Oslo Accords by Rabin and Arafat on the White House lawn in the summer of 1993. The Oslo Accords reflected a position that was supported by about half of the citizens of Israel. Nine years later, in May 2002, the proportion of the population that supported an independent Palestine had grown to about two thirds, because together with Sharon, a hefty part of the Right had joined with the Left, the same Right that in the mid-1990s had conducted a crude and violent campaign of incitement against Yitzhak Rabin. The principles of the Oslo agreement that Rabin had signed were identical to those laid out in the Road Map by the Quartet. Could the parameters of a solution change? No, because there's only one solution—a territorial compromise. But human beings can and do change.

Indeed, the Sharon government's shift in direction was uniquely important, but to the same degree it is clear that the chances of implementing the Road Map at that time were not great. Neither side was ripe for so substantial a sea change, particularly the leaders. The more Arafat demonstrated his determination to survive, the greater the revulsion that Sharon felt toward him. The Israeli army surrounded the PA's governmental precinct in Ramallah, isolating the chairman from his people, and waited for him to surrender. The war was waged at a low intensity, with normal life continuing as usual on the surface, but with violence and terror building up to an unprecedented extent and having a devastating effect on both societies. An interesting situation had arisen, with a right-wing government in Israel headed by Sharon the hawk having drawn the correct conclusions and acknowledging the necessity of carrying out a strategic reversal of its policies on the territories. But there was a fly in the ointment: Sharon was incapable of implementing the new policies in cooperation with Arafat. "That man is the greatest obstacle to peace. Therefore, Israel is determined to bring about his removal from the international arena." This was the message Sharon repeated several times in various formulations until "that man" was gone.

In September 2003, the Sharon government approved the construction of a barrier to separate the West Bank and Israel in order to prevent the entry of suicide bombers.[2] Officially, Israel calls the barrier the separation fence. The Palestinians and most of the international media call it the separation wall. Actually, it consists of stretches of seven- to nine-meter (twenty-three- to thirty-foot) concrete slabs surrounded by a sixty-meter (two-hundred-foot) wide exclusion area, with a patrol road on the Israeli side along the entire length.

The idea of creating a physical barrier between the Israeli and Palestinian populations was first proposed by the late Yitzhak Rabin. "We have to decide on separation as a philosophy. There has to be a clear border," Rabin said in 1994, and from his opposition bench in the Knesset, Sharon turned up his nose. Now, sitting on Rabin's chair at the prime ministry office, rightist Sharon was compelled to implement his leftist predecessor's separation idea, and for the first time ever, Israel was defining a geographical border between the two communities. This was no mere empty declaration of Israel's readiness "to make painful concessions," as Israeli prime ministers constantly assert, but the construction of a physical barrier separating the two sides.

In practice, the path along which the fence/wall has been built actually delineates the border that Israel would like to see between itself and the Palestinian entity on the West Bank. Upon completion, the barrier's total length will be 760 kilometers (470 miles) and will be entirely inside the West Bank east of the pre-1967 Green Line border.[3] In some places, the deviation from the Green Line is minimal, but in others the encroachment is far deeper. The amount of West Bank territory left on the Israeli side cannot be calculated accurately, because some changes to the path are still being considered, but a rough estimate is 10 percent of the West Bank, an area inhabited by 30,000 Palestinians who are being cut off from their country. If the areas that the fence slices off the West Bank inside Jerusalem's city limit are added, that number rises to some 200,000 Palestinians. Israeli settlements located near the Green Line have been left on the western, Israeli side of the barrier, while settlements deeper inside Palestinian territory are on the eastern side. In some locations, the barrier cuts Palestinian farmers off from the land that they cultivate. One of these Palestinian villages is Naalin. During the course of the last five years, its inhabitants, together with Israeli peace activists and international backers, have been conducting a tough legal and physical struggle to remove the fence westward of the Green Line. Naalin has become a symbol for the Palestinians' battle against the construction of the barrier. Each Friday protest has become a kind of ritual, usually involving a mix of marching, chanting, and throwing rocks at Israeli troops.

The construction of the barrier was a unilateral move, but it indicated the willingness of the Sharon government to carry out a substantial withdrawal as a first step toward giving up most of the West Bank and a large number of settlements.[4]

Sharon carried out his most significant step in February 2004, when he published his withdrawal plan, dubbing it "disengagement." Again, it totally contradicted all of the declarations he made before he was elected prime minister: Israel would evacuate all of its military bases and settlements in the Gaza Strip and withdraw to the Green Line. At the same time, Israel would pull out of several isolated settlements in the northern West Bank.

The withdrawal plan came as a surprise. The previous year, when the Labor Party proposed that Israel withdraw from the Gaza Strip, Sharon reacted with a statement reminiscent of Dayan's declaration of his preference for Sharm over peace: "What applies to Tel Aviv applies to Netzarim," said Sharon. Netzarim was an isolated settlement in the heart of the Gaza Strip, a Jewish enclave surrounded by Palestinian neighborhoods that the army had to spend much time and effort defending. The settlers adopted Sharon's statement as a slogan, but it was reality—the military burden and demographic concerns—that tipped the scale and led a majority of Knesset members to support Sharon's plan, as did most citizens. (The vote in the Knesset was sixty-seven for, forty-five against, and seven abstentions.) The twelve thousand or so Jews who had settled in the Gaza Strip were surrounded by a million-and-a-half Palestinians, including hundreds of thousands of refugees from the 1948 war and their descendants, many of whom were wretchedly poor and lived in crowded refugee camps.

Naturally, the adherents of the Whole Land of Israel camp were infuriated by the withdrawal decision and vowed to fight it with all their power, whereas the Left applauded Sharon. But when the confrontation was stripped of ideology and only strategy was being discussed, both sides came up with valid arguments. Those opposed to the pullout contended that it would be interpreted as surrender to terror and would bolster the extremists and the Hamas movement; those in favor claimed that the day-to-day friction with the Palestinians in the overcrowded and explosive Strip should be avoided, and it would be better to combat the extremists from inside Israel. The fundamental flaw in Sharon's plan lay in the fact that it was unilateral. Making the PA a partner in the move may have leveraged the withdrawal from Gaza into becoming a comprehensive settlement.

Sharon was not inclined to publicly discuss why he had deviated from the principles he had so vigorously espoused throughout his political career, but a close associate of his, Dov Weissglas expounded on the reasons in a newspaper interview:

> In the autumn of 2003 everything was stuck and time was not on our side. There was international erosion, internal erosion. Domestically, in the meantime, everything was collapsing. The economy was stagnant, and the Geneva Initiative had gained broad support. And then we were hit with the letters of officers and letters of pilots and letters of commandos [refusing to serve in the territories]. These were not weird kids with green ponytails and a ring in their nose with a strong odor of grass. These were people like Spector's group [Yiftah Spector, a renowned Air Force pilot who signed the pilot's letter], really our finest young people.[5]

In his book *Sharon: The Life of a Leader,* Sharon's son Gilad wrote that he was the one who initiated his father's plan for Israel's unilateral withdrawal from Gaza. "It was impossible any longer to protect the Jewish settlers in the Strip appropriately," Gilad said to his father, and added that the majority of Israelis had no desire to continue paying the price for preserving the settlements in the vicinity of Gaza.

The Palestinians were not enthusiastic about Sharon's disengagement from Gaza, because it was partial and unilateral. Most of the influential Palestinian spokespersons regarded it as an Israeli attempt to separate the solution for the Gaza Strip from the solution for the West Bank. Dr. Hanan Ashrawi, a member of the Palestinian Legislative Council (PLC), also known as the Palestinian parliament who regularly interprets the Palestinian cause for the world media, told me that leaving Gaza is a small price to pay for Israel if it gives that country a free hand to tighten its grip on the West Bank. "The Gaza Strip was a demographic and security burden for Israel," said Ashrawi. "By withdrawing from it unilaterally, Sharon is turning Gaza into a large prison and imposes on the Palestinians a long transition period."

But Ashrawi was wrong. It was not the withdrawal that Sharon initiated that cut the Gaza Strip off from the West Bank, but the results of the elections for the Palestinian parliament in May 2006 in which Fatah lost to Hamas. Precisely at the time when supporters of compromise were on the ascendancy in Israel, the Palestinians gave their votes to extremists. This was a development unparalleled in its tragic implications, and it was the administration of George W. Bush that bore most of the responsibility for it.

The final decision on the issue of Hamas's right to participate in the elections was made in Washington, in the office of Secretary of State Condoleezza Rice.[6] The administration was ostensibly acting in the name of democratic values, and Rice stated that the election results were an expression of peaceful political change. But similar to its conduct on the eve of going to war in Iraq, Washington's reading of the way Middle Eastern sects function was completely wrong. The mistake was made by CIA analysts who persuaded the State Department that Fatah would win. On this matter, in Israel the agencies were divided. Mossad's opinion was that Hamas's chances of winning were good. Shin Bet and military intelligence made the opposite estimation. They gave Fatah better chances. All three agency heads, separately and during personal meetings, gave their prognostication to the U.S. ambassador in Tel Aviv at that time, Richard Jones.

The meeting between Jones and the head of military intelligence, Amos Yadlin, took place in the beginning of June 2007, following violent clashes between Fatah and Hamas in the Gaza and a few hours before Hamas took control on the strip. According to State Department cables (revealed by WikiLeaks in December 2010), Yadlin told the ambassador that a Hamas takeover of the Gaza Strip would be a positive step, because Israel would then be able to declare Gaza as a hostile entity. If that happens, said Yadlin, "I would be happy." The American ambassador noted that if Fatah loses control of the Strip, Abbas would be urged to form a separate government in the West Bank, and Yadlin said that Israel would be able to cooperate with a Fatah-controlled West Bank. It may well be that the IDF's command and Prime Minister Sharon engineered Hamas's takeover of Gaza, because as Yadlin told the ambassador, Israel prepared a Hamas victory. Either way, if the United States had not given the green light to Hamas participation in the vote, the organization would not have achieved control, and the separation of the Gaza Strip and the West Bank would not have happened.

Israel's unilateral withdrawal from the Gaza Strip was well prepared and carried out in exemplary order. The plan was set in motion on August 15, 2005, and the evacuation was completed in eight days. The seven years that have gone by since then have proved that the advocates of withdrawal were right. The military burden is lighter, the number of casualties is down, and it is clear that combating Hamas and other violent movements is more effective when carried out from inside Israeli territory. It was a bold decision by the cabinet that demonstrated long-term political judgment, and it was implemented out of a sense of confidence in the soundness of Israeli democracy. Despite the tough, tenacious resistance displayed by all of Great Israel's factions, the full realization of the disengagement plan transpired that however acrimonious the differences of opinion between political rivals, they cannot thwart the fulfillment of democratic decisions. The occupation of the Gaza Strip entailed deployment of a large military contingent and cost Israel a high price in blood, and the evacuation was therefore a necessity.

The successful disengagement exposed a deep rift within the Likud party. Bejamin Netanyahu resigned from his post as finance minister in Sharon's government, proclaiming that the disengagement "endangered the safety of Israeli citizens." Following Netanyahu's resignation, the Central Committee of the Likud refused to approve Sharon's candidate for the evacuated post, Ehud Olmert. Sharon's reaction was perfectly planned in advance and carried out rapidly. Together with a significant number of Likud's moderate leaders—including Olmert and Tzipi Livni—Sharon quitted the party that he helped to found in 1973 to establish a new centrist, liberal party named Kadima ("forward" in Hebrew).

At the same time, a split divided the Labor Party when a group of leaders headed by Shimon Peres left the party and united with Kadima. For the first time since Yitzhak Rabin was assassinated, peaceniks observed Israel's political arena optimistically. With Peres on his side, Sharon planned to keep fulfilling his disengagement plan in the West Bank by removing more isolated settlements and defining a new border line between Israel and the future Palestinian state.

In January 2006 the Bulldozer collapsed. The former general suffered a severe stroke and since then he has been permanently incapacitated.

Shakespeare's description of Henry V suits this fidgety warrior, a "callous but sentimental, inspiring but flawed king."

Sharon was succeeded by Olmert, another unquestioning adherent of the Whole Land camp who had gradually become a moderate in recent years until he ultimately fully adopted the Left's positions.

Olmert described the disengagement as an action that could not have been avoided. In September 2009, in testimony before a state commission of inquiry into the treatment of the evacuated Gaza settlers, Olmert said, "Sharon brought about one of the most important achievements for the future of the State of Israel, his timing was correct, he deserves to be admired for his courage and I am proud that I had the great privilege of acting as his partner in this matter."

When Sharon, Olmert, Livni, and many of their supporters broke up the Likud party over the disengagement, shifted toward the center, and set up Kadima, the Netanyahu camp stayed on the right. Since his "two states for two peoples" declaration (at Bar-Ilan University in June 2009), he and a small group of former Whole Land advocates have been making their way toward the center, ostensibly biting the bullet, but with a wink that is intended to convey a deceptive spin, as if the concessions are merely verbal and will not be carried out. But the outside world has taken the prime minister at his word, and Netanyahu and his supporters are going through the motions to save their dignity. In fact, they too are leaning leftward, and as the next elections approach, it will become clear that the Greater Israel camp today comprises only a handful of zealots, devoid of practical influence.

PART III

Palestinian Pragmatism: Instead of Terror, Passive Civil Resistance

12

Two Palestines

AS OFFICIAL ISRAEL was changing course and taking the first steps toward relieving them of the yoke of occupation, the Palestinians were only beginning the process of deciding what solution to the conflict they were aiming for. Like the Jews, Palestinians in favor of compromise faced off with their opponents, this time in the forms of Fatah and Hamas.

Fatah, an Arabic expression denoting victory, is the largest and most influential Palestinian political faction. Five activists headed by Yasser Arafat founded it in Libya in 1954 when they declared the start of an armed struggle aimed at eliminating the State of Israel. From the beginning, Fatah espoused a revolutionary, secular ideology.

In 1967, the movement officially joined the PLO, a federation of parties that had been formed three years earlier to secure "the liberation of Palestine through armed struggle." Under the chairmanship of Arafat, Fatah became the PLO's driving force.

In the late 1960s Israel forced the PLO leadership and most of its militia fighters to cross into Jordan and ask King Hussein for asylum. In 1970, after the Black September crisis (which saw the Palestinians trying to topple the Hashemite dynasty, with the assistance of Syria) Yasser Arafat and most of his fighters were forced into exile in Lebanon. At the height of Israel's invasion of Lebanon in the mid-1980s, Israel ejected the PLO's fighting units from Lebanon as well, and they were forced to seek shelter in Tunis, far from their homeland and completely cut off from the PLO's cells in the occupied territories, who carried out the struggle against Israel independently and at a low level of intensity.

The first meaningful Palestinian rebellion against the occupation, the 1987–1991 intifada, did not take place because of some program created by Chairman Arafat. It was a spontaneous popular uprising that sprang up on December 1987, first in the Gaza Strip and then the West Bank. So low was Israeli intelligence's estimation of the Palestinian ability to defy Israeli rule that the defense minister at the time, Yitzhak Rabin, who was abroad when the first disturbance occurred, refused to cut his working trip short. He told his associates that the uprising would die out even before his scheduled return to Israel. But his plans were disrupted. For the first time since 1967, Israel became aware that in the first two decades of occupation, a great deal of frustration had accumulated in the territories, and because of this the uprising gained momentum.

In the midst of the Palestinian rebellion, in their Tunisian exile, in October 1988, the PLO leaders revised their plan of action. Instead of an independent state on all of the territory of historical Palestine, which would entail the liquidation of Israel, the movement agreed on a goal of establishing a state in the West Bank and the Gaza Strip. Arafat presented this significant change in Geneva. "The PLO," stated the chairman, "would support a solution of the conflict based on UN Resolutions 242 and 338." It was an effective (if not completely official) recognition of Israel's right to exist within pre-1967 borders, with the understanding that the Palestinians would be allowed to set up their own state in the West Bank and Gaza. The United States had recognized this change of policy and allowed diplomatic contacts with PLO officials. Israel ignored it.

Meanwhile, in the occupied territories, the intifada gained momentum. Setting up a daily routine in dozens of locations, small groups of Palestinian youngsters were fighting IDF's soldiers with stones, knives, and gasoline bombs, while adults arranged general strikes, boycotts on Israeli products, and in some communities a general refusal to pay taxes. From the Israeli side the outcome had lingered until the authority in Jerusalem changed hands from Right to Left. In the summer of 1993, now led by Rabin, Israel had taken the most decisive turn since June 1967, recognizing the PLO as a legitimate political entity and starting negotiations with its leaders over their demands.

On the eve of the signing of the Oslo Accords, the PLO recognized the existence of the State of Israel and accepted UN Resolutions 242 and 338. In effect, the PLO under Arafat both recognized the principle of two states for two peoples and restricted its territorial demands to the June 1967 borders.

This significant turn in the official course of the PLO stimulated internal opposition. One of the important figures undermining Arafat's turn into moderation was the pious ideologist Sheikh Ahmed Yassin, who at the start of the first intifada founded Hamas (an acronym for the Arabic phrase "Islamic Resistance Movement"). Hamas is a fundamentalist religious movement affiliated with the Muslim Brotherhood, and its declared goal is establishing a theocratic Islamic state in the entire territory of Palestine. According to the Hamas Charter of 1988, the conflict between the Palestinians and Israel is a religious one between Islam and the "infidels." The territory of Palestine, the charter declares, is sacred Muslim land, and no one has the right to give any part of it up, a mirror image of the Jewish messianic ideology of the "Whole Land of Israel." Apparently, the establishment of Hamas was encouraged by official Israel, bent upon carrying out a policy of divide and rule.

From its start Hamas had activated an affective civilian arm, dealing mainly with education and welfare. Then, in the mid-1990s, following the massacre that Baruch Goldstein perpetrated in the Cave of the Patriarchs in the city of Hebron, Hamas created a military arm, waging war against Israel. On February 9, 1994, that year's holiday of Purim, Baruch Goldstein, a Brooklyn-born Jewish physician from the settlement Kiryat Arba, entered a crowded room in the Cave of Patriarchs wearing his military reserve uniform and opened fire with an M-16 rifle, killing 29 Muslims at prayer and wounding another 150. Angry mobs began rioting in the aftermath of the massacre, which led to the deaths of 26 more Palestinians and 9 Israelis. The shocking event in Hebron was a crucial turning point. Before the massacre, as a rule, Hamas was attacking military targets, not civilians. In retaliation for the slaughter, the movement launched a series of suicide bombings inside Israel, killing dozens of civilians. Responding to Hamas's suicide bombings, the rightist political camp designed and perpetrated an extremely bold and nasty inciting campaign against Rabin and his government. The prime minister and his peace camp were desperate. With the perspective of seventeen years, it is absolutely evident now that Goldstein's massacre destroyed Rabin's peace initiative. A year and a half later, backed by zealots and leaning on radical rabbis, the religious fanatic student Yigal Amir fired three pistol bullets into the prime minister's back and killed him at a peace rally in Tel Aviv on November 4, 1995.

After the assassination, half a decade went by until the Palestinians realized that Israel was playing for time by delaying its withdrawal, and in 2000 they launched a second intifada, which lasted until 2005. This time they used extreme violence. Some 150 suicide bombers blew themselves up in buses and shopping centers and at busy intersections, killing over 500 Israelis and wounding 3,500. Now for the first time Israel's silent majority began internalizing the occupation's grave consequences. The damage caused to the state and its citizens in terms of the loss of life and limb was enormous, the diplomatic harm was no less serious, and the huge investment of state funds in the occupied territories was a dead waste. Only then did the settlers realize that there was a rupture in relations with the general public, and their leaders were compelled to admit that the settlement enterprise in the occupied territories had not succeeded in conquering the hearts of the Israelis.

As long as Arafat ruled the roost in Ramallah, the two Palestinian systems existed side by side. In one room the chairman was negotiating peace, and in another room he signaled to the heads of his militias to carry on the armed struggle against Israel. He refused to discard his pathos-laden khaki uniform and to don the suit of a statesman. As long as there was tension in his relations with Israel, the security apparatuses that he set up in order to protect himself and his organization were tasked with waging war against Israel.

Late in 2004, the seventy-five-year-old Arafat's health deteriorated. He was admitted to a hospital in Paris and died a few days later. Some Palestinians believe Israel had a hand in his death, either by poisoning his food or infecting him with a disease, but there is no evidence for this.

The chairman's death marked the start of the decisive confrontation between Fatah and Hamas. Throughout 2005, both camps readied themselves for the PA election, and in early 2006 Fatah lost its majority, and Hamas took over. Against the backdrop of exposés of corruption in the Fatah leadership, including the late Arafat himself and his wife, Suha (who had been living apart from him in Paris with the couple's only daughter),[1] Hamas won a majority in the PLC. This outcome created a disastrous situation, because in effect the government was divided between two organizations separated by an ideological abyss: the parliament and the prime minister's office were now in the hands of Hamas, while the presidency and the various security apparatuses remained under Fatah control. The tension between the two organizations broke out into violent confrontations that increased in intensity until an open civil war erupted, vicious and bloody. It ended in June 2007 with Hamas seizing control of the Gaza Strip and most of the senior Fatah officials there having to leave their homes and relocate to the West Bank. A number of Fatah activists were brutally murdered.

Since then, the Palestinians have been divided in two. The PA, recognized by the enlightened world (including Israel) as the official representative body of the Palestinian people, controls the West Bank and is headed by the president, Mahmoud Abbas (Abu Mazen), and the prime minister, Salam Fayyad. The Gaza Strip is ruled by Hamas and is treated like a pariah by Israel and most of the world. It has its own prime minister, Ismail Haniyeh, whose government since its creation was controlled from Damascus by the recently retired head of the movement, Khaled Mashal, who was supported by Syrian president Bashar al-Assad. Following the uprising in Syria and the revolution in Egypt, Hamas's leaders turned their back on Assad and abandoned their political bureau in Damascus. Presently Hamas is guided by the leadership of the Muslim Brothers in Cairo.

With international assistance, Fatah has started building a secular, democratic, and liberal Palestinian state in the West Bank. Its security system is being set up under American guidance. At the very same time, Hamas has established a theocratic Palestinian state in the Gaza Strip based on Islamic sharia law and is stockpiling weapons in preparation for a coming round in the conflict with Israel.

Attempts were made occasionally to bring the heads of the two factions together for reconciliation, but with no success until the Arab Spring's gigantic upheaval forced Hamas to make a significant change in strategy. In November 2011 in Cairo, under the auspices of Egyptian intelligence, Abbas and Mashal agreed in principle to form a unity government, which would prepare Palestinian elections to go ahead.

Not less important was Mashal's unprecedented and clear announcement that Hamas supports a Palestinian state in the West Bank, Gaza Strip, and East Jerusalem. "Fatah and we have political differences,"

Mashal said, "but the common ground is agreement on a state within the 1967 borders." Still, Hamas's new strategy doesn't represent a formal political recognition of Israel's existence, nor is it an acceptance of the Oslo Accords. It is a simple consent to a Palestinian state within the 1967 borders, which is a very important change in itself.

Netanyahu's government has seen the Fatah-Hamas reconciliation as an advantage, for as long as the United States classifies Hamas as an outlawed organization, Israel has an excuse to reject making concessions to Abbas. Nevertheless, Washington and the other Quartet members are aware of the fact that reconciliation among the Palestinians is a prerequisite for the relaunch of direct negotiations between Israel and the Palestinians. A lasting agreement with Israel could be achieved only when the two Palestinian parties speak with one voice. Would the Obama administration promote negotiations with a group of Palestinians sworn to Israel's destruction? Not under any circumstance. Still, at the finish, realism changes even the most stubborn. Awareness of reality compelled Hamas's leadership to approve the two-state solution based on a territorial partition, which is de facto the same two-state solution that the Fatah had approved, minus a handshake with the enemy.

13

Softening the Hardest

THE ISRAELI OPPONENTS of a territorial compromise would like to perpetuate the split between Fatah and Hamas. It weakens the Palestinians and makes an agreement with them more remote. Israeli doves, on the other hand, would like to see a united Palestine, because making peace with half of a nation and waging war against the other half is inconceivable. In effect, as long as Hamas continues to deny Israel's right to exist, there is no chance whatsoever of ending the conflict, but it is doubtful that this extremist organization is capable of holding on to its rule over the Gaza Strip for long under existing conditions. It has failed, and as we have mentioned, most of the world's nations treat it as an outcast. Since its separation from the West Bank, the suffering of the population of Gaza has increased dramatically.

On the battlefield, too, Hamas has failed. Its leaders have realized that they are incapable of threatening Israel's existence. It is true that in its Operation Cast Lead against Hamas in Gaza from December 2008 to January 2009, Israel used excessive force, but there was no small degree of hypocrisy in the criticism leveled at a state that had been attacked by rockets—albeit primitive, but still lethal and destructive—and mortar bombs for eight years, and most of the time had restrained itself. In this respect, the report from the United Nations inquiry headed by Judge Richard Goldstone was not balanced. Goldstone presented his report to the Human Rights Council in Geneva on September 29, 2009.

The Goldstone report found that both the Israeli government and Hamas were at fault. The planners of the military operation, the report claimed, had not intended to strike only at the missile launchers and thereby exercise their right to defend themselves, but Israel also had another target: the whole population of Gaza. "The operations were in furtherance of an overall policy aimed at punishing the Gaza population for its resilience and for its apparent support for Hamas," Goldstone wrote. "It was a deliberately disproportionate attack designed to punish, humiliate and terrorize a civilian population, radically diminish its local economic capacity, both to work and to provide for itself, and to force upon it an ever increasing sense of dependency and vulnerability."

Although the inquiry panel did show understanding for the reasons for Israel's attack on Hamas and the difficulty of identifying armed Hamas fighters when they took cover among civilians, it nevertheless found that the IDF had not done enough to avoid harming innocent noncombatants. In Israel, three civilians had been killed and dozens wounded by rockets fired by Hamas and other organizations, whereas in Gaza hundreds of civilians were killed, the report stated. Israel had failed to distinguish between combatants and civilians as required by the laws of warfare. The report called on both sides to investigate their own operations and recommended that in the absence of adequate investigations, the persons suspected of breaching the Geneva Convention should be prosecuted at the International Criminal Court in The Hague.

Official Israel did not cooperate with the Goldstone inquiry and did not allow its politicians or military personnel to testify before it. Israeli public opinion suspected that the panel had first marked its targets and then formulated its reasoning. Most Israelis—both hawks and doves—believed that the military operation in Gaza had been essential. The army did not order its units to commit war crimes but tried to keep its own casualties down to a minimum. Why should Israeli soldiers get killed if the enemy militias attack them while sheltering among the civilian population, in the most densely crowded territory in the world? If the enemy it is facing does not make an effort to give the civilians on its own side immunity from being harmed, why should the army expose its own troops to harm? And there was the matter of proportions in the casualty rates—if another thirty or fifty Israeli civilians and soldiers had been killed in the fighting, would the harm done to Palestinian civilians have been justified? The use of phosphorus shells was definitely wrong, as they had been fired at some targets from both air and land before the Israelis had determined whether there were civilians inside them, but there was no proof that either the political echelon or the military command had intended to harm civilians. It was possible that the objectives of the operation had not been intelligently defined. Instead of fighting a complex battle in a built-up area, killing and wounding a large number of non-combatants and risking international condemnation, Israel should have made an effort to trap the Hamas government and put an end to its rule. This would have been feasible within the framework of resources that the Israeli government allocated to the operation. (Israel's failure to seize the Hamas government is reminiscent of President George H. W. Bush's decision to stop his generals on the way to Baghdad in the first Gulf War, and missing out on the chance to eliminate Saddam Hussein twelve years before George W. Bush did so.) Was it up to Israel to decide the internal Palestinian struggle and to install Fatah rule in Gaza at the points of the IDF's bayonets? Certainly, the liquidation of the Hamas regime and handing the Strip back to Fatah is a prime interest for Israel, and moreover there is no lack of precedent in modern history for a foreign army invading a country and removing a certain political faction in order to put another one into power. If the military operation had focused on seizing the organization's leaders instead of facing off with its armed fighters in a densely populated built-up area, presumably the extensive harm done to the civilians would have been avoided and the Goldstone inquiry would not have been necessary.

What Operation Cast Lead did was to restore Israel's deterrent power vis à vis Hamas. Evidence for this came about a year later, in March 2010, when the vice president of the United States, Joe Biden, visited Israel and the PA. Just when he was about to leave his hotel to attend a private dinner given by Prime Minister Netanyahu, the news media reported that the government of Israel had approved a plan to expand a Jewish neighborhood in East Jerusalem. The vice president took offense, Washington blew its top, and the PA suspended negotiations with Israel even before they had begun. A crisis erupted in relations between Israel and the United States.

Hamas wanted to exploit the opportunity to incite the Palestinians of East Jerusalem and the West Bank to begin a third intifada. The organization's radio and TV stations in Gaza, together with the Al-Jazeera network (whose headquarters are in Doha, the capital of Qatar), fanned the flames, but only a few Palestinian youths responded to the call.

Most of the population of the West Bank did not want to endanger the achievements of the PA. Hamas had an interest in exacerbating the crisis by launching missiles into Israel, but the blow it had sustained a year before had created an effective deterrent, which lasted almost four years, up to November 2012. Then, when the deterrence became ineffective, Israel launched Operation Pillar of Defense, attacking around fifteen hundred sites in the Gaza Strip and killing Ahmed Jabary, chief of the Hamas's military wing. Hamas and local militias responded by firing fifteen hundred rockets into Israel. At least two Fajr rockets were fired toward Tel Aviv.

Hamas therefore had been given the opportunity to prove the effectiveness of the armed resistance but had failed. The outcome of Hamas's fight against Israel in operations Cast Lead and Pillar of Defense had been disastrous. In effect, the upshot of the two short battles in the Gaza Strip had dashed any hopes the Palestinians had harbored to defeat Israel by means of classical guerrilla warfare; the unilateral disengagement of Israel from the Gaza Strip initiated by Ariel Sharon in the summer of 2005 had robbed Hamas of the advantages that local militias enjoy in guerrilla warfare. In Operation Cast Lead, the IDF attacked Gaza from the outside. It had no bases inside the Strip, and there were no civilian settlements. The troops were not engaged in defense. They were on the offensive, and in the short time at their disposal, they let loose significant fire power, leaving Hamas without any recourse. Following its defeat in the Gaza fighting, on top of the failure of the suicide bombers intifada, Fatah learned that building up the infrastructure of a state in the making with western assistance and passive resistance to the opposition was the correct solution.

By the end of 2012, most Palestinians on the West Bank were clearly showing their confidence in their leader, Mahmoud Abbas, who successfully demonstrated his diplomatic abilities on the international arena. Politically and militarily, Hamas had been weakened. It failed to improve the Palestinians' life conditions in Gaza; it was compelled to adopt a policy of status quo toward Israel; and it failed to intensify the crisis and to set the West Bank alight.

Is Hamas destined to be uncompromising forever? Some experts on fanatical Islam claim that the organization will never recognize Israel. Its leaders act in accordance with the Koran's precepts, and to them the presence of infidels on Palestinian land is unacceptable. The Hamas extremists call the Israelis infidels and the sons of apes and preach their destruction, say the skeptics. But many experts on Jewish history said similar things about the Whole Land of Israel zealots, who swore never to surrender the territories that God had promised Abraham, and the ultra-Orthodox Jews, who quoted from Rashi's commentary on the Talmud: "Esau hates Jacob," which is interpreted as meaning that peace can never prevail between Jews and gentiles.[1]

But this interpretation has no grounds in history. When faced with an existential dilemma, fanatical groups have generally calculated their steps pragmatically. When the majority of Catholics in Northern Ireland were against the continuation of the armed struggle, even the most ardent IRA fighters were compelled to lay down their arms; the National Party of the Afrikaner minority in South Africa, whose leaders coined the term "apartheid" in the late 1940s, handed the government over to the black majority in an orderly fashion in 1990; and the party of Menachem Begin, which had sworn allegiance to the Whole Land of Israel, was forced to agree to the "two states for two peoples" formula. Ideologies change constantly: the communists in China, who have privatized parts of the economy; the communists in the late Soviet Union, who broke up the communist empire with their own hands; the Saudi royal family, which appointed a woman to their cabinet; and Jewish rabbis, who have trained female colleagues. There are exceptions, such as Nicolae Ceauçescu of Romania, who made a panicky escape from his palace in Bucharest but was caught and hanged; the defeated Saddam Hussein, who roamed his childhood haunts in Tikrit before being trapped in his underground lair and eventually hanged; and the "King of Kings" Mu'ammar al-Gadhafi, who was captured and killed on October 20, 2011, as the Libyan rebels conquered his hometown, Sirte. In a global world, squeezed between Egypt and Israel, Hamas is not capable of coming up with any solution for the distress of the Palestinians beyond further distress, and therefore its leaders will strive to find common ground with Fatah.

This was implied in the declarations by Khaled Mashal, mentioned at the end of the last chapter. Hamas would be prepared to cooperate with "a resolution to the Arab-Israeli conflict which included a Palestinian state based on 1967 borders," meaning that the movement accepts

1948's border line (which is pre–June 1967's lines). It's doubtful that the heads of Hamas will themselves sign a pact with Israel; at the decisive moment, when negotiations come to a successful end, they will move to the back of the stage, nod their heads from a distance, and allow the leaders of Fatah to ratify the treaty.

14

A Palestinian Easy to Like

THE SPLIT BETWEEN Hamas and Fatah has, for the first time, shown the world that there is a moderate wing in the Palestinian nation. This was sensational news. For decades the Palestinians fighting Israel were their own worst enemies, captives to a dynamic that nourished losers. Time and again, the Palestinians banged their heads against Israel's defenses and, when they were repelled, wallowed in self-pity. Their leaders initiated acts of terror against civilians (Israelis and otherwise), and this tactic also failed them. The world media often quoted Abba Eban, Israel's ambassador to the United Nations and foreign minister, who said in 1973, "The Arabs never miss an opportunity to miss an opportunity." The leaders of the Hamas state in the Gaza Strip are still doing the same, but as far as the Fatah leadership is concerned, Eban's accusation is no longer valid.

At the height of the second intifada, anyone listening closely to the voices emanating from enlightened circles within Fatah heard sharp criticism of the suicide bombing strategy. The two present leaders of the interim Palestinian state, Abbas and Fayyad, were among those critics, and they are responsible for the new direction. They are attentive to what the enlightened world is saying, they accept the conventional norms of international relations, and they avoid repeating the mistakes of the past. Instead of inciting a violent uprising, they have advocated passive civil resistance à la Mahatma Gandhi and Martin Luther King Jr. They have urged the Palestinians to make use of their right to demonstrate, boycott the products of factories in the settlements in the occupied territories, and conduct international information campaigns against the occupation. At the same time, they have busied themselves with strengthening the institutions of a Palestinian state from the foundations up in order to be ready for the declaration of their state, cooperated with Israel to preserve security and combat terror, and acted to weaken Hamas.

In August 2009, Fayyad published a plan for the unilateral establishment of a de facto Palestinian state in the West Bank and East Jerusalem within two years. He named it "Ending the Occupation, Establishing the State." Two years later the basic infrastructure for the state was founded, but the occupation continued. The failure of the Obama administration to halt settlement expansion and bring Israel to the negotiation's table forced Abbas to make a consequential policy change by challenging the United States. On September 23, 2011, Abbas stood in front of the UN General Assembly and petitioned for an independent state. His plea was based on his prime minister's plan and supported by a persuasive international recommendation, granted by the World Bank, the International Monetary Fund (IMF), and the United Nations. These three institutions confirmed that "the PA had crossed its threshold for relevance for statehood in terms of its successful institution building." In addition, Fayyad's enterprise was complimented by a special IMF announcement: "Not only is the public financial management system [of the PA] ready to support the functions of a state; it has even become a model for other developing countries."

Fayyad's fifty-four-page primary document is devoid of revolutionary rhetoric and is worded in dry technical language. It sets out how the institutions of a state, including government departments and public services, would be built up and how its existence would be official in 2011. Ever since the PLO was founded, this was the first detailed and serious public presentation of a plan for the creation of an independent Palestinian state.

The Palestinian people's commitment to reach statehood, Fayyad asserts in his foreword, is based upon the struggle of "peaceful and popular movements" in conjunction with "building a government based on the principles of justice and the rule of law, equality and tolerance, safeguarded by a clear separation of powers of the executive, the legislature and judiciary." The inspiration for Fayyad's plan was derived from the Federalist Alexander Hamilton, the first U.S. secretary of the treasury.

Fayyad's plan covers the entire area of the West Bank, from the Jordan River to the old Green Line border between that territory and Israel. The issue of the borders of a Palestinian state has not been officially discussed between the sides, and therefore from Israel's point of view Fayyad's plan does not exist. "If occupation has not ended by then [2011] and the nations of the world from China to Chile to Africa and to Australia are looking at us," Fayyad said in 2009, "they will say that the Palestinian people have a ready state on the ground. The only problem is the Israeli occupation that should end."

Fayyad's first phase plan for the development of a Palestinian state requires investment of nearly $5 billion (around $1.5 billion in 2011, $1.8 billion in 2012 and $1.6 billion in 2013). Most of the investment will come from international donors. Up to 2011, the United States and the European Union were bearing the preliminary economic burden of Fayyad's plan. The security forces had been trained according to American plans and guidance. A National Training Center was set up near Jericho, and a new base for 750 security officers has been set up outside Jenin. Some 3,000 elite troops were trained in Jordan. Headquarters for preserving security have been set up in each West Bank city, the first in Hebron. The Palestinian state will have a professional police force whose elite units have been trained in Europe, Jordan, and Egypt and has been equipped with advanced weaponry, communications systems, and vehicles.

The quiet on the West Bank has fostered economic activity. The consumption of cement has increased, indicating a revival in the building industry. Near Ramallah a new city named Rawabi, with a target population of forty thousand, is under construction. In Nablus, a shopping mall has been built, and a stock exchange has been opened. People go out to enjoy themselves. Cafés and restaurants are crowded. Most of the tourism is still internal, but there has been an increase in visits by Israeli Arabs.

This is not yet a flourishing economy. Foreign investors are not lining up, and industry is crying out for capital. There is considerable unemployment, and per capita product is very low. The West Bank is not similar to the Asian and South American undeveloped states where growth is rapid. The figures put out by the PA's statistics bureau show that most of the growth is in the real estate, communications, and services sectors, while industry has not developed at all. This pattern indicates a lack of private investment in production sectors. But if we take into account the blows sustained by the Palestinian economy in the chaotic period during which Israel was combating the suicide bombers—by closed territories, almost nightly targeted assassination raids, and tanks and armored personnel carriers in the city streets—it is clear that economic recovery must take a long time. The West Bank was a war zone, and the PA, with slow steps, is managing to extricate it from the crisis.

In both the Fatah and PA leadership there are other circles that oppose Fayyad's plan. The Western spirit that prevails over it is objectionable to Muslim conservatives, and the American inspiration for it bothers the nationalistic circles. Fayyad himself is not a Fatah man, and he was not a fighter in his youth. He is an economist who studied at the University of Texas at Austin and who served as an adviser at the World Bank. Abbas appointed this technocrat, who was born in 1952 in a small West Bank village near Tulkarm, to the post of prime minister because of his management skills and because the United States and Europe were very much in favor of him.

The opposition to the Fayyad plan succeeded to block Fayyad's election to the PLO executive committee, and therefore his authority to carry out significant political moves is in doubt. To accomplish his aims Fayyad needs strong backup not only from Abbas and Fatah's establishment but also from the more conservative Palestinian community represented by Hamas. But expecting that Hamas would encourage a plan inspired by Alexander Hamilton, established upon liberal values and Western ideas, is preposterous. Hamas is Fayyad's major opponent, expressing firm opposition to appointing him prime minister of a future Palestinian interim unity government being negotiated between Fatah and Hamas as a prelude for general election. Certainly, moderate Palestinians are convinced that Fayyad's standing abroad is an asset in ensuring the continued flow of international aid and in pursuing the bid for statehood recognition, but Hamas believes otherwise. The organization accuses Fayyad of cooperating with Israel's blockade of the Gaza Strip and causing harm to Hamas's fighters. "Fayyad shares responsibility for the arrest of Hamas members in the West Bank in recent years," Hamas spokesperson Abdul-Aziz Duwaik told me in a telephone conversation. Fayyad himself responded modestly: "I would not like to be used as a pretext for continuing the split between the factions. When Chairman Abbas will tell me to go I'll be leaving my office immediately." As long as Fayyad remains Abbas's choice for leading the PA's caretaker government, and as long as Hamas refuses to reconsider its objection to Fayyad, the making of a Palestinian unity government is in doubt.

Hamas's opposition to Fayyad's program is problematic, but it could be neutralized by Israel's support for the plan. The sad truth is that Israel doesn't know how to handle the economist who has turned weakness into power and has managed to challenge the occupier by laying down a policy that does not conform with Middle Eastern patterns. Israel has been accustomed to extremist, violent, and irrational enemies, but this moderate Arab had confused things, and the Israeli Right has not managed to link him to terrorist activity. Actually, there has been a reversal of roles. The Palestinian in the West Bank has become moderate, and the hawks in Israel have been thrown off balance. For sure, Fayyad is the most sophisticated adversary that Israel has encountered since Sadat proposed a separation of forces in the Sinai to Golda Meir in the 1970s.

So far, the PA under Abbas and Fayyad has handled the governmental challenge well. The security situation on the West Bank is reasonable. The armed gangs of youths, the *shabab,* who used to run amok on the streets of Nablus, have disappeared. In the West Bank, Hamas has largely been neutralized. In early 2009, when Israel attacked the Gaza Strip, the West Bank remained calm. The same was true after the Israeli commando raid on the Turkish aid flotilla to Gaza in May 2010.

The change in the West Bank is not a matter of image. It is a change of substance, and it springs mainly from the failure of the violent option chosen by Hamas. If Hamas had not failed, it is doubtful that such broad popular support would have formed for the policies of passive resistance shaped by Abbas and Fayyad. If no game-changing event occurs among the Palestinians, both will lead Fatah and Hamas to reunite and reach an agreement with Israel. Israel cannot expect more amenable leaders than this duo.

Abbas presented evidence of the dramatic change that has taken place in the PA's attitude to some thirty leaders of the American Jewish community at a dinner given in June 2010 by the S. Daniel Abraham Center for Middle East Peace in Washington, D.C. Several of the people involved in various stages of the negotiations between Israel and the

Palestinians attended the event, among them former national security advisers Sandy Berger and Stephen Hadley; assistant secretary of state during the 1980s, Elliot Abrams; as well as Bush's Under Secretary of Defense (Comptroller) Dov Zakheim, high-ranking members of the American Israel Public Affairs Committee (AIPAC), and representatives of important Jewish organizations.

Abbas told the gathering things that no Palestinian leader had dared to utter before him. He declared that he recognized the connection between the Jewish people and the Land of Israel and its capital, Jerusalem. He said that from the Palestinian point of view, the intifadas had been a "terrible failure." Netanyahu's demand that the Palestinian state would be unarmed was reasonable, and he would accept the 1967 borders, with territorial exchanges. He would not agree to having Israeli troops deployed on Palestinian land but was prepared to accept an international force there to prevent breaches of the security aspects of the treaties, and even an international Jewish force. "I don't need tanks, I don't want missiles, I need an internal security force," the chairman asserted. In Israel, there was only a faint echo of this meeting. It came at a time when Israel was busy dealing with the tragic outcome of the Turkish aid flotilla to Gaza, but the White House and some of the Jewish leaders were very impressed by his conciliatory remarks. In the course of 2011 and 2012, Abbas met several times in Ramallah with groups of Israeli policymakers, industrialists, and journalists, and he expressed similar viewpoints. Here too the general response in Israel was not positive because of the antagonism spread against Abbas by Netanyahu's government following his plea to the UN for an independent Palestine.

On November 29, 2012, a substantial majority of the UN's General Assembly endorsed the PA's bid for a nonpermanent observer membership, presenting a broad international consent to the establishment of an independent Palestinian state aside Israel. Official Israel was furious and immediately ordered the construction of three thousand new homes for Jews on occupied lands, most of them in East Jerusalem. This act of punishment was defined by right-wing politicians in Israel as an appropriate Zionist response; globally it was interpreted as a reckless provocation against 179 governments (138 approved the new Palestinian's status, including Spain, France, and Italy, and 41 abstained, including Germany and the UK). Many friends of Israel in the United States and Europe wonder how the Jewish state could lose its common sense. They ask where the government of Israel is heading, and isn't the current moderate Palestinian leadership worthy of a true Israeli willingness to negotiate seriously?

One of those who wondered was the U.S. secretary of defense, Leon Panetta. On December 2, 2011, at the annual gathering of the Saban Forum in Washington that brings together U.S. and Israeli officials and policymakers, Panetta called on Israelis and Palestinians to resume peace negotiations. "The problem right now is we can't get them to the damn table to at least sit down and begin to discuss their differences—you know, we all know what the pieces are here for a potential agreement," said Panetta, and added, "We've talked it out, worked through, we understand the concerns of Israel, understand the concerns of the Palestinians. If they sit at a table and work through those concerns, and the United States can be of assistance in that process, then I think you have the beginning of what could be a process that would lead to a peace agreement." The next day in Jerusalem, responding to Panetta's criticism, a spokesperson for Netanyahu blamed the Palestinian leadership for the lack of negotiations and for playing "diplomatic games." The lack of reason on the Israeli side stems from the fact that its previous government was inspired by ultranationalists and settlers. Challenging the international community throughout the entire course of Netanyahu's term as prime minister, the Whole Israel camp was stalling for time and expanding settlements and outpost in the territories. Since the end of the ten-month settlement freeze on September 26, 2010, more than eighteen thousand housing units have been constructed in settlements and outposts. Yet, slowly but persistently, the international community trends toward the Palestinian cause, accepting that an independent state is not only justified but practical and necessary. If Israel's newly elected government lingers any longer, it will miss the train.

15

The Right of Return

ISRAELIS WOULD BE astonished to discover that rules and principles that govern the relations among nations might occasionally be on their side and not just cause damage or loss. The precedent rule discussed here applies to the most complex and sensitive dispute between Palestinians and Israelis.

One question will decide the fate of negotiations between Israel and the Palestinians: whether the refugees of 1948 will have the right of return to the cities and villages that Israel conquered in its War of Independence, the events that the Palestinians call the Naqba. If the Palestinians waive the right of return, peace will be attained in the Middle East. If they insist on returning to their former homes, the conflict will continue. In all other issues, the disputes are technical. A little more land here in exchange for a little less there, a little more water here or there, another battalion of UN observers, another camera on this or that border to stop terrorist incursions. If both sides sincerely want peace and if they negotiate in mutual respect, one square kilometer of land in the Judean or Samarian Hills, or sovereignty in one or another Jerusalem block, is unlikely to prevent them from reaching a historic achievement that the whole world wants to see happen. The demarcation of the border and setting up the security arrangements are all important matters, but their solutions are technical. The right of return is a fundamental matter of principle. For the Israelis, it means survival or demise. For the Palestinians, it is a psychological obstacle whose significance and complexity can hardly be exaggerated.

From the Israeli standpoint, agreeing to the right of return would mean the end of the Zionist dream. If the hundreds of thousands of Palestinian families who fled or were expelled from Palestine were permitted to come back and live inside the Green Line, the Jewish state would simply be annihilated.

From the Palestinian standpoint, final surrender of the right of return would mean giving up their claim to the cities, villages, fields, orchards, vineyards, olive groves, cactus hedges, and, of course, parts of their historical heritage and their basic feeling of inhabiting important spheres of their homeland. Every single day they would have to see their lost property from over the border, from their tiny state of Palestine, and at most they will be able to mourn over it by reading the poems of the Palestinians' national poet, Mahmoud Darwish. It would be a terrible decision, and the person making it is not to be envied: peace (which would mean self-government, normal life, decent livelihoods, and high standards of living) against the chance to sometime drive out the invaders who had driven their forefathers out of their land—no wonder the leaders of the Palestinians have hesitated up to now.

Perhaps a landmark judgment handed down on March 1, 2010, by the European Court of Human Rights (ECHR) will make it easier for the Palestinians to give up the right of return and agree to accept compensation for the loss of their property and their suffering.[1] The court's decision was far reaching and set a new precedent: a situation that has arisen on the ground takes precedence over "family roots" when thirty-five years have gone by since a home was confiscated, so there is no longer an obligation to return it to its original owner. A bench of seventeen judges considered the issue in Strasbourg, and the majority voted in favor of the position of conquerors, who had seized property that did not belong to them, and rejected the claims of expellees, whose property had been taken from them.

The decision to this effect was handed down after hearings on a petition by seventeen Greek Cypriot refugees who had been forced to flee to the southern part of their country during the 1974 war between Greece and Turkey. Turkish Cypriots had grabbed their property—various plots of land, some of which were cultivated and some with fully furnished houses or buildings—and the Greeks had gone to the court asking their property be returned.

The judges ruled in *Demopoulos v. Turkey and 7 other cases* that a claim that a piece of property had been a person's home did not hold unless he could prove continuous possession. Thirty-five years had gone by since the petitioners had lost possession of the real estate in question, a new generation had grown up there, the local population had changed, and some of the property had changed ownership at least once through sale, donation, or inheritance. The upheavals of time are stronger than emotions, the judges stated, and there was no necessity to return to the original owners the lands and buildings from which they had been forced to flee. The rights of the present inhabitants were stronger than those of their predecessors, and the refugees would therefore have to be satisfied with financial compensation: "It cannot be within this Court's task . . . to impose an unconditional obligation on a Government to embark on the forcible eviction and rehousing of potentially large numbers of men, women and children even with the aim of vindicating the rights of victims of violations of the [European Human Rights] Convention." The implication is simple and clear, and also analogous to the Palestinian-Israeli dispute over the refugees' right of return: putting an old wrong right does not justify the creation of a new wrong.

The petitioners claimed that rejecting their plea would be tantamount to rewarding criminals and that a plot of land and a home are "roots of the family," but the court dismissed both of these arguments and declared that rights to property could be exchanged for a sum of money or an alternative property. Moreover, the highest judicial instance of the Council of Europe warned the petitioners that if they refused to accept compensation and preferred to wait generations until they could regain their property, they were liable to wake up one morning and find that the world no longer recognized their rights. According to the judges, their decision tended to favor the Turkish occupying power because they had made concerted efforts to offer fair compensation to the displaced Greeks.[2]

The judgment represented a historic precedent because until then, international law had usually ruled that refugees should be allowed to choose between getting their property back and financial compensation. Indeed, prior to this ruling, that had been the accepted interpretation of UN General Assembly Resolution 194 of 1948, which had stated that the Palestinian refugees could choose between returning to their homes in Israel or receiving monetary compensation.

Of course the European judgment is legally valid only within the states of the Council of Europe that have ratified the Convention for the Protection of Human Rights and Fundamental Freedoms (currently forty-seven states), but because of the distinguished stature of the court in Strasbourg, the large number of judges, and their reputations, their ruling will have an effect on any serious court in the free world in similar cases. It is doubtful if, from now on, refugees will be permitted to return to their homes if many years have gone by since they were forced to leave them.

However, it is doubtful that the Jewish settlers in the West Bank will be able to depend on this judgment, as the settlers have appropriated land that was not within the sovereign territory of the country of which they were citizens. In this matter, there is an Israeli legal precedent that weakens still further any claim the settlers may have to the land. In 2005, Israel's High Court of Justice rejected a petition by the settlers in Gaza against their eviction.

Beyond the legal issues, the basic question is whether the world accepts the existence of a Jewish state within the 1967 borders as a justified fact, and it is clear to me that the answer is positive. But does the world accept the outcome of the 1967 conquests and the settlements and creeping annexation? Of course not. The world was happy in the summer of 2005 when Israel disengaged from the Gaza Strip. One after the other, the leaders of important countries came to Israel, warmly embraced the Jewish state and those who headed it, and encouraged them to finish the job by withdrawing from the West Bank and assisting in the establishment of an independent Palestinian state. The fact that the warlike wing among the Palestinians, represented by Hamas, reacted to Israel's withdrawal from the Gaza Strip with an outburst of violence against it elicited a strong negative reaction across the globe. Hamas was ostracized and boycotted by the international community, and the world took steps to stop it from smuggling arms into Gaza. And when Hamas's sister organization, the Lebanese Hezbollah, attacked Israel in 2006 without any provocation, the world seemed to react harshly toward Hezbollah and took steps to limit its military power. In both Gaza and Lebanon, Israel employed military power that some important governments considered to be excessive but nevertheless supported the Jewish State. But Israel would be wrong if it interpreted that support as a license to delay reaching a comprehensive solution.

PART IV

Beyond Provinciality: Facing External Factors

16

Delayed Ignition

ALTHOUGH HE IS wont to boast of his deep familiarity with American politics, Netanyahu has not cracked the code of the phenomenon known as the Obama administration.

The Middle Eastern picture that the Obama administration presents to the world is anything but one-dimensional. The current American leadership scattered patches of grey on the black-and-white picture that the Bush administration had painted, highlighting the complexity of the conflict with the Palestinians.

Netanyahu became prime minister at about the same time that Obama became president. He had a few months at his disposal to examine the new reality in Washington and to adapt his policies to it. In early June 2009, directly after the president's famous speech in Cairo, the world became aware that the United States had chosen a new path. But the Israeli government did not.

The change introduced by Obama was not merely rhetorical. It was a strategic change, of course. Netanyahu and his people certainly listened carefully to the president's election campaign speeches, but they judged him according to the way they themselves were accustomed to acting. By their lights, a politician who makes a promise is under no obligation to honor it, and furthermore, their friends in the Republican Party encouraged them. "Who does he think he is, this Obama?" whispered leading Republicans to Netanyahu and his aides. This preachy, amateur greenhorn will soon be jolted by reality, they said. The tone of arrogance (some might say racism) that characterized certain circles in the Republican Party during Obama's first year in office was echoed in various sectors of Israeli politics and media. Imprudent figures on the Israeli Right did not hesitate to call Obama an antisemite.

Indeed, the Bush administration had pampered Israel to the point of corruption. Both Bush's and Sharon's positions toward the Islamic world were so close to each other that an observer on the sidelines had to wonder who was setting the tone—Washington or Jerusalem. Even with a little more perspective, it seems to me that a historian analyzing the first decade of the twenty-first century will find it difficult to solve the conundrum. Is it conceivable that the shock of the 9/11 attacks had so powerful an effect in Washington that Bush, Cheney, Rumsfeld, and Rice all lost their American compass and decided to adopt the over-simplified and narrow view of the conservative Right in Israel, whose essence was that Muslims understand only force?

Netanyahu boasts of having strong ties to the American Jewish community and understanding its prevalent trains of thought, but he was wrong about the Jews too. Is there anyone who doubts that the Jews who voted for Obama—almost 80 percent of the total Jewish voting population—were choosing the absolute antithesis to the Bush administration, "the friendliest that has ever occupied the White House," as the previous Republican administration was frequently labeled by politicians and pundits in Israel and in the United States? Could it be that the vast majority of American Jews did not grasp that the candidate of their choice did not back the interests of the settlers? Of course they did. The ultra-Orthodox Hasidim of New York, whose sons and daughters live in West Bank settlements, did not vote for Obama. When searching deep into their soul, is not the vast majority of American Jews differentiating between the interests of the State of Israel and the interests of the settlers? In their eyes, are these interests identical? Of course not. But the AIPAC managed to disguise this reality. Money and public relations have helped the well-oiled Jewish lobbying network implant a false image in Washington, the outlines of which were drawn in Jerusalem.

The 2011 AIPAC Policy Conference in Washington demonstrated how deeply the worldview of nationalistic Israel's right wing had penetrated into the consciousness of the American Jewish mainstream. About five thousand American Jews, the crème de la crème, were assembled in the packed convention hall of the gala banquet: men and women, old and young, upper class and middle class. Most are liberals who commonly support progressive political philosophies and Democratic candidates who pride themselves on being peace-loving people and proponents of equality, justice, and liberty. But when it comes to the future of Israel, their common sense and discernment are magically transformed, making them cheer fervently and praise nationalistic concepts. In AIPAC's worldview, critical assertions about Israel are a sort of heresy. Occupation is a four-letter word. The ugly Israeli is a legend. Indiscrimination and violence against Palestinians are nowhere to be found. One who dares to criticize Israel is not a friend. Either you are with us, or you are an enemy. When President Obama stood on the stage, bringing up his plan to base an Israeli-Palestinian peace deal on the 1967 border lines, he risked his second term. Boos were heard from the crowd, and only few applauded. "We cannot afford to wait another decade, or another two decades, or another three decades, to achieve peace. The world is moving too fast," the president said, and his subtext was corresponding with Netanyahu's maneuvers aiming at delaying the renewal of negotiations with the Palestinians. Obama could have used Panetta's words and tell Israel to get back to the "damn table," but looking at his potential November 2012 constituents, he preferred cordiality and patience: "The extraordinary challenges facing Israel will only grow. Delay will undermine Israel's security and the peace that the Israeli people deserve." A sensitive observer could feel a slight move of discomfort in the crowd. AIPAC's members had sensed that the president's tone was not identical to Jerusalem's.

How is it that a liberal community, tolerant and open minded, has surrendered its high moral standard of values to the ultraconservative, archaic, and murky sections of Judaism? Are the Israeli leaders of the nationalistic Right so capable that they succeeded in swaying the opinions of the knowledgeable and talented hundreds of thousands or even millions of American Jews? How did they hypnotize so many successful, wise people? Thus far, Israel's peace camp is unable to explain the enigma.

It was not a unique phenomenon. One year earlier, the sounds that came out from AIPAC's annual conference were even more strident. It took place in the shadow of the dispute between the United States and Israel over continued Jewish construction in the occupied section of Jerusalem. In his opening address, the new president of AIPAC, Lee

Rosenberg, stated, "The people of Israel and the democratically elected government of Israel passionately believe in peace," and drew warm applause. Among Israelis, who really believes that a right-wing Israeli government under the leadership of Netanyahu, Lieberman, and Yishai is passionately committed to peace with the Palestinians?[1] More to the point, does a large majority of American Jews—the 70 percent who identified as liberals in the last presidential election—identify with the settlement project, whose foundations are built on injustice?

Alan M. Dershowitz, a superstar American attorney, is also a highly skilled Jewish spokesperson who ignores the difference between Israel's two faces, violent chauvinism and peace-seeking liberalism. Speaking to a large public audience at the AIPAC conference, Dershowitz fired off a series of catchy sound bites in an authoritative tone. The louder his voice and the more emphatic his assertions, the more stormy the applause. Several times the convention's audience stood up to cheer on this engaged soldier of the Right. His mantra "Islamic extremists" works remarkably well on American crowds, like an incantation.

Dershowitz rejected the argument of senior American military officers that Israel's policy in the territories was making Muslims more extreme and was therefore endangering the lives of American troops fighting in Afghanistan and Iraq. "The implications of this argument are the delegitimization of Israel in the minds of Americans," said Dershowitz. "For Muslim extremists, it is not what America does, it is not what Israel does. It is what Israel is. It is what America is. Islamic extremists cannot accept the concept of secular democracy, a democracy that grants equal rights to women, equal rights to all. It is what we are that they hate. It is not what we do."

This is of course, prime nonsense. Is what Israel does really not important for extremist Muslims? The more land that Israel takes control of in the West Bank and the more it collides head-on with the Palestinian population, the greater the extremism in the Muslim world grows, spurring more moderate Muslims into becoming suicide terrorists. There is a plethora of evidence that this is so, and those who deny it are misleading themselves and their audience. It is impossible to exonerate the Israelis by simply saying that being a democracy excuses everything. Frequently and in many countries, undemocratic actions are taken under the guise of democracy.

The views of Dershowitz and his ilk in the conservative camp were appropriate for a year or two after 9/11, when al Qaeda's attacks brought Israel and the United States closer. The victims of Muslim terror radiated solidarity for each other. But later there was a complete turnaround. When the military and the Pentagon and the White House studied the factors that made an American victory more or less attainable, it became clear to them that Israeli policy in the occupied territories was liable to hamper their own interests and make winning the war harder because it led the Muslim world to intensify its resistance on the battlefield.

But beyond dealing with the political anachronism that Jewish conservatism presents, it is appropriate to give some thought to an issue of principle that is connected to the ethical worldview of American Jewry. To my eyes, the strangest thing is that the sons and daughters of the Jewish leaders who marched alongside Martin Luther King Jr. from Selma to Montgomery in Alabama fifty years ago automatically support every whim of the right wing in Israel. That was American Jewry's finest hour, to use Winston Churchill's phrase. Back then, King compared the march to the Israelites crossing the Red Sea. Together with him, in the front rows of the marchers there were politicians, trade union leaders, movie stars, and Christian and Jewish religious leaders. Rabbi Abraham Joshua Heschel of the Jewish Theological Seminary in New York was at King's side. The identification of the Jews with their struggle so captivated the black protestors that many of them wore yarmulkes. To these days memories of the march evoke inspiration; Jews, who had been persecuted and discriminated against for generations, were now at the forefront of one of the greatest struggles for equal rights in history.

The Jews of America mobilized to fight discrimination against blacks, and fifty years later they voted in droves for the first black president,[2] not only because he was the candidate of the Democratic Party but also because he represented a weak and victimized community. But strangely, when Israel oppressed the Palestinians in the occupied territories and seized a large part of their lands, those same Jews chose to nod in consent.

Observing the current situation in Israel from a Jewish American perspective is even more complicated. Is the majority of American Jewry prepared to accept a situation in which the Israeli Foreign Ministry refuses to hold meetings with a delegation of five Democratic Congress members because they came to Israel as guests of the liberal Jewish lobbying group J Street, a pro-Israel and pro-peace organization? It happened on February 17, 2010. The J Street delegation requested to meet both Foreign Minister Avigdor Lieberman and his deputy, Danny Ayalon, and never received a formal response. A few months earlier, Israeli ambassador to the United States Michael Oren refused a J Street invitation to appear at its conference. Both incidents represent in practice the Far Right's strong influence over the policy of Netanyahu's government. For a significant bulk of coalition partners, an open political debate representing a wide range of views and attitudes concerning the future of the territories is essentially prohibited.

This is only one aspect of the problem. The issue is far more complex. As we have seen, in both Israel and the United States, the most ardent supporters of the settlers are the Orthodox and the ultra-Orthodox. A large majority of American Jews does not belong to those streams, and it is difficult to understand how secular, Reform, and Conservative Jews have found themselves in the same boat as the backers of the settlers. After all, most of the delegates to AIPAC conferences are Reform or Conservative Jews to whom the nationalist and Orthodox Israeli Right refuses to grant equal religious status. The ultra-Orthodox parties in the Knesset work assiduously to break down the status quo on the "Who is a Jew?" issue and establish the monopoly of the Orthodox rabbinate over conversion to Judaism so that the Law of Return would not apply to converts processed by Reform and Conservative rabbis. Such a move would likely create a rift within world Jewry and permanently alienate the younger generation of Jews in America from the State of Israel. It would no longer be the country of all Jews. The signs of the ground of Orthodox domination over the religious sphere in Israel, sometime through violent means, are grave indeed. At the Western Wall in Jerusalem, the Haredim have used force against Reform and Conservative Jews and have beaten females trying to conduct prayer services there. The police have cooperated with them. Is it possible to come to terms with a situation in which a female Reform rabbi was arrested because she donned a prayer shawl in the Western Wall plaza? Or the humiliating obligation for women to sit separately from men in so called kosher bus lines, which go into ultra-Orthodox neighborhoods in Jerusalem?

In 2011, exclusion of women from the public domain in Jerusalem became so severe that important American leaders expressed their worry about whether the same democratic values are shared by the two states. One of them was Secretary of State Hillary Clinton. On December 3, 2011, at the Saban Forum in Washington, she spoke at length about international matters such as the Iranian nuclear program and the postponed negotiations with the Palestinians. Responding to a participant's question, Clinton said she is worried about domestic issues in Israel. "I am astonished by legislative initiatives in the Knesset, restricting left-wing NGOs." Clinton said, "and I am worried by the exclusion of women from public spaces." Clinton cited a *Washington Post* article about IDF Orthodox soldiers who were ordered by their rabbis to ban official events in which women were singing. This boycott, she told her audience, reminded her of "extremist regimes." Relating to the segregation of women on bus routes in Jerusalem, Clinton mentioned Rosa Parks, the African American who in 1955 refused to give up her bus seat to a white man. "I really cannot understand what is going on in Israel, it seems more suited to Iran than Israel," the secretary of state said.

Jews are not yet ready for such a statement, but it is accurate: Orthodoxy has forged a pact with chauvinism, and both of them oppress anyone who stands in their way, be they liberal American Jews or Palestinian Arabs in the territories. Is it permissible for American Jewry to protest against the religious coercion that Orthodox fanaticism exercises against Reform Jews and at the same time remain silent in the face of the injustice that Jewish nationalist fanaticism exercises in the occupied territories? Both harm the security and the unity of Israel. One cannot demonstrate for pluralism in Judaism and then turn a blind eye to the wrongs being perpetrated in the name of Judaism in the occupied territories.

Most American Jews are notably subservient to official Israeli policy, even when the Israeli government's position is opposed to the interests of the Jews of America. Since the establishment of the State of Israel, the organized Jewish community in the United States has followed an ostensible policy of playing a passive role. The Israeli government must determine policy independently, and we will mobilize to help it—until now this has been the declared position of American Jewry. The reasoning sounds logical: American Jews do not join the IDF to fight to protect the existence of the state, and those who are not ready to lay down their lives to defend the Jewish state should not be allowed to be involved in determining its policies. American Jewish leaders have repeated their position at meetings with Israelis. However practically, following the 1967 war, through a slow but decisive change, the Israel lobby became a vigorous player in the internal Israeli political arena. In the early 1990s, some strong Jewish lobbyists were helping the Right in Israel thwart the implementation of the Oslo Accords. Some were even inciting against Yitzhak Rabin's peace initiatives.[3] It was doubtful whether they represent the majority of American Jews, but their wealth, organizational skill, and influence over Congress overshadowed advocates of compromise. The right-wingers cooperated with Orthodox Jewish organizations who see settlement in the occupied territories as the fulfillment of a divine commandment and with fundamentalist Christians who see it as a precondition for the second coming of Jesus.

Here is the crux of the matter: The support of American Jews is a vital part of Israel's national security. The link between the two is crucial, and the government of Israel should therefore constantly monitor its strength.

When the link is strong, Israel is stronger, and if it weakens, so does Israel. From the point of view of official Israel, the problem lies with the nonobservant younger generation, most of who are liberals who voted for Obama and who are trending away from Israel and Zionist ideology.[4] If you are a young, secular American Jew, it is reasonable to assume that you are liberal, and therefore it is doubtful that AIPAC's version of Zionism—strenuous support for a right-wing Israeli government disposed to using force—will not appeal to you.[5] On the other hand, if you are an ardent Zionist who tends to support a hawkish view towards the Palestinians, it's reasonable to assume you are Orthodox. This is the spirit of the times among young American Jews, and many secular right-wing Israelis, including Netanyahu and his staff, have failed to understand it. Most young American Jews are individualists and would prefer to conduct an open conversation reserving their right to criticize Israel's policies. Their political views are dovish. Generally, they oppose the use of military force, support a compromise with the Palestinians, and want to see peace established in the Middle East. They are fanatical about human rights.

Not only did the Netanyahu government fail to grasp the spirit of the times, but it lacked a basic understanding of political ethics in

Washington. Israel told the United States that it was freezing settlement construction, but it was building settlements at the same time. They were ready to negotiate and at the same time allowing Jews to settle in Arab parts of East Jerusalem. That's why on November 7, 2011, at a G20 summit in Cannes, when the microphones were switched on, French president Nicolas Sarkozy described Netanyahu as a liar in a private exchange with Obama. "I cannot stand him. He's a liar," Sarkozy said, and the U.S. president responded by saying, "You're fed up with him? I have to deal with him every day."

Netanyahu's double-talk had no chance of being accepted by the president and his team, just as Arafat's double-talk, when he spoke of peace but plotted terrorism, was rejected by the Bush administration. For years, the Israelis had been developing sophisticated machinery for explaining its actions and positions that was based on deception. We have already seen how the nurturers of the settlement project were presenting themselves as seekers of peace, claiming that settlement in the occupied territories and peace are mutually exclusive. The fraud succeeded for decades.

And on the other side of the ocean, AIPAC fell in line with the deception and intensified it until it took root and became established as reality. The 9/11 attacks energized the disseminators of the apocalyptic myth of the war between civilizations, and the political melancholy that prevailed in Washington played into AIPAC's hands, and the lobbying organization's grip on American politics during the Bush administration grew stronger. The true seekers of peace in Israel and the United States had no address in Washington. Their silence cried out to the skies, mainly because everyone knew that AIPAC's rightward bias represented a minority. But it was impossible to break the vicious cycle. Whoever wondered out loud whether the Israeli government really wanted peace was condemned as sabotaging the unity of the camp, and because of this many chose not to speak up. Many of those who objected to AIPAC's political path preferred to avoid disputes and gave up on taking an active part, and only a few of them made the effort to express an opposing view and risk being defined at best as deviant and at worst as ridden by self-hatred by the Jewish and Israeli establishments. In the face of the wealthy and the professional Jewish organization functionaries, the chances for the critics of AIPAC to moderate the right-wing influence was meager, and it is against this backdrop that a strong alternative Jewish lobby should be set up. The concept of "love of Israel" is not supposed to provide a cover up for bad policies. One can love the Jewish people and the State of Israel and still object to the evils of the occupation. Indeed, if you love the Jews and Israel, you should object to the evils of the occupation and act to end it.

17

A State of Isolation

IF ISRAEL WERE to cease its dispossession of the Palestinians and give them the West Bank, it is possible that Muslim anger would subside, as would the danger of innocent civilians in the West being harmed by terrorist attacks. Such a notion must have occurred to many British, French, and Spanish citizens, and although it is simplistic and does not actually take into account the fanatical anti-Western ideology of al Qaeda, it does nevertheless contain a grain of reason. Bin Laden's successors and others of that ilk certainly won't stop fighting the West if Israel retreats from all the territory it conquered in 1967, but it is clear that an Israeli withdrawal would lead to a situation in which considerably fewer Muslims would support al Qaeda.

On this matter, Israel's grasp of reality has been flawed. In the years immediately following 9/11, the Israelis failed to realize that they should assist the citizens of the free world to alleviate their anxiety. Instead, they denied there was a link between the suffering that Israel was inflicting upon the Palestinians and the rise of Islamic terror across the globe. Israel paid no attention to the fact that in the eyes of Western public opinion, its conduct represented a weak link in the struggle against Muslim terrorists. Erroneously, the Israelis considered themselves a front-line bastion operating valiantly on a mission for the large democracies against the aggression of the Muslim fanatics. We are a strong and vital part of the global defensive armor, they tried to persuade everyone else. In the United States under the presidency of George W. Bush, this worked well; in Europe, not at all. Most of the leaders of Europe intimated to Israel that there was a connection between the occupation and

Islamic rage, and when Obama replaced Bush, his administration adopted the European strategy that said that solving the Israeli-Palestinian conflict would soften that rage and thereby energize the struggle against terror. In wider global circles, the inclination to rein in the rebel gathered strength, and if Israel balked at withdrawing from the occupied territories, it would suffer. Moderates still tried to conduct a dialogue with the Israelis and persuade them to comply. The less patient adopted the system that brought down the apartheid regime in South Africa and treated Israel as a leper state.

Israel's standing was eroded to the extent that some of its leaders of the first rank, including government ministers and the heads of political parties, did not dare to leave the country and to visit some of the most important states in Europe, lest they be arrested and indicted for war crimes. Israeli military officers traveling abroad, in countries considered to be friendly, are also liable to be detained. Lawsuits have been filed in British courts against politicians and officers in the names of Palestinian families who were harmed in Israeli military operations, mainly the Operation Cast Lead campaign against Hamas in Gaza in late 2008 and early 2009. The legal claims were based on the report of the UN investigation panel headed by Judge Richard Goldstone. The report had found that while both sides had apparently committed war crimes during the fighting, Israel had acted disproportionately, killing over fourteen hundred Gazans, including many civilians, among them some three hundred children. The PA and Hamas acted vigorously, though separately, to exploit the Goldstone Report, and they achieved the best results in Britain.

Until recently, British law provided the country's courts universal jurisdiction, allowing organizations and individuals to file complaints in all judicial instances against persons whom they believe have committed war crimes or crimes against humanity and to request arrest warrants against them, even if the crimes were committed outside British territory. Such universal jurisdiction was adopted in several European countries after World War II, when police forces and espionage agencies were hunting fugitive Nazi war criminals.

On September 29, 2009, Defense Minister Ehud Barak was visiting Britain when an organization representing Palestinian families harmed in the Gaza operation filed a criminal complaint against him in a London court and requested that he be detained on the grounds that he had instructed the army to commit war crimes. Barak escaped arrest by the skin of his teeth.

Three months later a court in London issued another arrest warrant, this time against Tzipi Livni, who served as foreign minister in the Olmert government and later became leader of the Kadima party and leader of the opposition in the Knesset. This time, too, the offense cited was political responsibility for the war crimes that were allegedly committed in the Gaza Strip during Operation Cast Lead. As a result, a crisis erupted in relations between Britain and Israel. The British ambassador to Israel was summoned to the Foreign Ministry in Jerusalem to hear an official protest, and the Israeli ambassador in London met with Britain's foreign secretary and demanded that the universal jurisdiction law be repealed. The minister telephoned Livni to apologize.

Then, on January 5, 2010, Israel canceled the visit of a military delegation to Britain after Her Majesty's Government notified the Israelis that it could not guarantee that the officers in the group would not be arrested. Ten months later, an Israeli cabinet member was compelled to cancel a visit to London for the same reason.

Eventually, this universal law was indeed reformulated in a way that prevents filing lawsuits in most British courts against foreign officials, but the negative attitude of the general public toward Israel was not changed. And the same happened in many other places.

On university campuses in the United States, hostility toward Israel is white-hot. Demonstrators greeted ex-prime minister Olmert with calls of "child murderer" on each campus that he visited during a lecture tour in 2009. This time, Olmert failed to put across the "Israel is the victim" message.

On February 8, 2010, students at the University of California at Irvine heckled Israeli ambassador Michael Oren with cries of "killers." And he was compelled to leave the hall. A year later the district attorney in Orange County charged eleven of the demonstrators, all members of the Muslim Student Union, with misdemeanor disturbance of a meeting. In response, a group of more than one hundred of Irvine's faculty members, among them renowned professors, many of them Jews, published a statement of support for the indicted students.

The protests weren't confined to American campuses. On the same day as the Irvine incident, a large group of vocal protestors forced Israel's deputy foreign minister to stop his lecture in Oxford, England. President Shimon Peres had to be rescued from angry demonstrators at public meetings during his visit to Brazil in late 2009. A number of trade unions and universities in Europe and South America have launched boycotts of Israel. In Scandinavia, during the summer of 2010, longshoremen refused to offload Israeli cargos. In several European states, supermarket chains refused to sell goods produced in the settlements. On October 2, 2011, in Stockholm, 218 academia professors, lecturers, and students published a petition for a Swedish academic boycott of Israel. At the beginning of November 2011, a London-based NGO, the Russell Tribunal on Palestine, held a public hearing in Cape Town on whether Israel is guilty of the crime of apartheid. One of the distinguished participants was Archbishop Desmond Tutu.

At a tennis tournament in Auckland, New Zealand, on January 5, 2010, pro-Palestinian demonstrators jeered Israel's top female player, Shahar Peer, in a match against the Slovenian Polona Hercog, chanting "Shahar, go home." After the match, Peer told the media, "It was quite difficult to concentrate at the start of the game, because I was hearing the shouts against me throughout the first set. I'm glad I managed to overcome it and win." The next day, when Peer played the Slovakian Magdalena Rybarikova in the quarterfinals, the protests continued, and the organizers had to stop the match for fifteen minutes.

In the spring and summer of 2010, international human rights organizations, together with governments that support Hamas, started dispatching flotillas of ships to try to breach Israel's blockade of the Gaza Strip. Israel stopped the vessels before they reached the shore. In one incident, when naval commandos stormed the Turkish ship *Mavi Marmara,* nine passengers were killed and dozens were injured. Some of the passengers had opposed the boarding party violently with iron bars and chains, and the troops whose lives were in danger opened fire at them.

A few days after that incident, South Korea downgraded a visit by Peres from a ceremonial state visit to a routine working one. The Foreign Ministry in Jerusalem considered calling it off, but Peres objected. "In our international situation, we cannot cancel visits of our own accord," he said. The security ring around Peres was bolstered, and the Koreans canceled a ceremony at Korea University, where Israel's president was supposed to get an honorary doctorate, for fear that the students would attack him.

In the wake of the flotilla incident, international pressure mounted against Israel, and its isolation increased, as did its mobilization against the rest of the world. Some of the ministers in Netanyahu's government and part of the media exploited the circumstances to inflame the public mood and step up the feeling that "the whole world's against us."

Israelis found it hard to understand why this was so, and many began accusing the critics of antisemitism. Mostly they were wrong. I agree with Judith Butler from the University of California at Berkeley that such accusations constitute an attempt to silence and censor legitimate political discourse and sometimes are even "a blow against academic freedom." She was responding in 2003 to then president of Harvard University Lawrence Summers's declaration that criticizing and calling on universities to divest from Israel are "actions that are anti-Semitic in their effect, if not their intent," and that European boycotts of Israel and antiglobalization rallies at which criticisms of Israel were voiced are "effectively anti-Semitic." In an article titled "No, it's not anti-semitic,"[1] Butler wrote, "If we think that to criticize Israeli violence, or to call for economic pressure to be put on the Israeli state to change its policies, is to be 'effectively anti-Semitic,' we will fail to voice our opposition for fear of being named as part of an anti-Semitic enterprise." Thus, legitimate criticism of Israel was interpreted by Jewish organizations and personalities as antisemitism, making it even harder to maintain a dialogue between Israel and its critics, including people who were not even remotely antisemitic and were even friends and supporters of Israel. In fact, Israeli politicians do not recoil from taking advantage of the reluctance of outsiders to confront Israel because they do not want to become embroiled in a dispute with a country of which a large number of its citizens were victims of the Holocaust.

The paradox is that one of the important lessons to be learned from the Holocaust is that occupation—any occupation—must be subjected to the strictest ethical scrutiny. This is why substantial changes were introduced in the way international law views war crimes during the second half of the twentieth century, after decades of violent dictatorships and their gross violations of human rights. On the one hand, the Jews were justly demanding that the world take the lessons of the Holocaust to heart so that the terrible phenomenon would never be repeated. On the other hand, when influential international judicial bodies took measures aimed at protecting human rights, and those measures constrained

Israel, the Jewish establishments rose up against them. Israelis prominent in politics and the media never grasped the significance of this change and couldn't understand the situation. Some of them spoke like Vice President Spiro Agnew when he said in response to his indictment for tax evasion in 1973, "The bastards changed the rules and didn't tell me." The right wing in Israel accused the rest of the world of hypocrisy. When the Jews were being persecuted, the world stood by in equanimity, they contended, but now that the roles were switched and the Jews were taking back the territories that history had taken away from them, once again the world had turned against them.

The Palestinian side understood the changes that were under way in the world better than the Israelis did. More than at any time in history, states are now being held accountable for their violations of human rights. For one thing, under the leadership of the Obama administration and the governments of important countries in Europe, the humanitarian aspect of international relations has been greatly strengthened. Moreover, globalization has created links between countries that were only tenuously connected to each other in the previous century. These parallel processes have made it possible to expose the myths, the chicanery, and the machinations that both the Israelis and the Palestinians have used in the protracted struggle between them. Stripping the conflict of its artificial wrappings has, for the first time, given it a realistic mold.

18

Iran—
Two Scenarios, One Realistic

SOMETIME IN THE spring of 2011, a Western partnership of intelligence agencies set in motion a shadow war against Iran's ayatollahs. Four associates—the United States, the United Kingdom, Saudi Arabia, and Israel—had established a decentralized alliance tasked with the missions of gathering secret intelligence and carrying out special assignments in Iran through a variety of sources, human and technical. It has no central authority, nor operational coordination, but this focused and efficient apparatus includes hundreds of agents who carry out sabotage missions against Iran's nuclear project and promote chaos within the Islamic Revolutionary Guards.

The operational menu includes a wide variety of highly clandestine activities, often outside of standard military protocol and resembling the Cold War's black operations: assassinations of nuclear scientists; eliminations of high-ranking members of the Revolutionary Guard; and the destruction of missile installations and vital components and devices within heavy industry's factories. The first joint operation was probably carried out on April 8, 2011, when four key gas pipelines exploded simultaneously in different locations in Qom Province.

In addition, the alliance is continuously operating drones and spreading cyberweapons like the Stuxnet computer worm—an ingenious code that had infected computers and damaged about half of Iran's centrifuges.

So far the effect is remarkable. Iran's huge nuclear enterprise has been substantially harmed, and the regime is confused. The leadership of the Islamic Revolution is currently busy defending itself, its military, and its nuclear project.

Two consequential undertakings were executed in November 2011. The first was a blast at a missile base operated by Iran's Revolutionary Guard Corps, killing Maj. Gen. Hassan Moqqadam (a senior leader of Iran's missile program) and upwards of forty other soldiers. The explosion was heard in Tehran, thirty miles to the east. Satellite photographs showed much of the base in ruins. Iran called it an "accident that occurred while weapons were being moved."

The second explosion occurred at Iran's uranium conversion facility in Isfahan, where mined uranium is transformed into uranium fluoride gas, which is then transferred to be enriched by centrifuges in the city of Natanz.

Speaking to Reuters on December 3, Barak played down speculation that Israel and the United States–led allies were waging a clandestine war on Iran. "Sanctions and the threat of military strikes were still the way to curb Iran's nuclear program," he said.

A few days later, in the city of Yazd, an explosion in a steel factory killed seven people. Then, on January 2012, in Teheran, the nuclear scientist Mostafa Ahmadi Roshan, who worked in Natanz, was killed by an explosion of a magnetic device attached to his car by a motorcycle rider. Roshan was the fifth Iranian nuclear scientist to be killed by mysterious explosions since 2007. On August 17, two high-voltage electrical lines were severed by explosions; one line connects the city of Qom to the new underground enrichment plant in nearby Fordow and the other leads to Natanz's centrifuges facility.

The covert operations are being supplemented by an array of defensive measures. The United States has spent billions of dollars installing a strong regional defense apparatus through deploying early warning radar detectors, missile interceptors, and command and communication systems on the territories of its Arab allies in the Persian Gulf and in Israel. In addition, since the beginning of 2010, in cooperation with six Arab states led by Saudi Arabia, the Pentagon had spread a fleet of battleships in Persian Gulf's strategic location.

Still, the most effective tools are economic sanctions. During 2012, the tightening sanctions imposed by the United States and the European Union had paralyzed the Iranian economy. Banning its oil and isolating its banks from the international payment system brought Iran's currency, the Rial, to collapse. The country's oil output dropped to the lowest level in twenty-three years and its revenues in foreign currency dramatically diminished. At the end of 2012, the official annual inflation rate was around 17 percent, but the true figure could be as high as 70 percent and the dollar was traded at more than double its official value (in addition, Iran's economy suffered from bad management, corruption, and a deficient subsidy policy). The combination of tough sanctions, an affective shadow war, and a reliable Western threat to use force if necessary are able to enforce Iran to give up enriching weapons-grade uranium.

On the military sphere, at least three defense establishments are engaged in planning for a potential unconcealed military action against Iran—the Pentagon, the UK Ministry of Defence, and Israel's Mossad and new "Depth Corps," aimed at extending joint IDF operations in distant locations. Western intelligence agencies believe that the window of opportunity for destroying, or at least delaying, Iran's nuclear project is slowly closing, due to the fact that the Revolutionary Guard has begun transferring essential nuclear facilities and materials, including enriched uranium, into the fortified bunkers that were constructed in the city of Qom. This concealment process was completed most probably at the beginning of 2013.

In a detailed report published on November 2, 2011, the *London Guardian* had cited Ministry of Defence officials stating that if the United States will present plans to attack Iran, the Royal Air Force would be assisting the operation with logistic aid, such as aerial refueling, surveillance capabilities, and permission to use the British island colony of Diego Garcia. Primarily, the attack will be waged from the air, with some naval involvement, using missiles such as Tomahawks, which have a range of eight hundred miles (about thirteen hundred kilometers). There are no plans for a ground invasion, the report claimed, but "a small number of special forces" may be needed on the ground, too.

Iran fired back. Details of an Iranian plot to kill the Saudi ambassador to the United States, Adel Al-Jubeir, which Attorney General Eric Holder had disclosed on October 11, 2011, demonstrated Iran's firm decision to strike back by any means. In a diplomatic cable released by WikiLeaks in 2008, Al-Jubeir cited Saudi ruler King Abdullah's request from the United States to "cut off the head of the snake," which means destroy Iran's leadership. Apparently, the plotters wished revenge. A special unit of the Revolutionary Guard, the Quds force, had planned the attack. A purported member of a Mexican drug cartel was hired to carry out the assassination by blowing up a fashionable restaurant in Georgetown, Washington, D.C., while Al-Jubeir dined there. The restaurant regularly serves politicians, diplomats, and journalists. Although the planning was clumsy, American investigators, who briefed journalists off the record, claimed that the operation was "conceived, sponsored, and directed from Tehran,"as one of the attending journalists quoted the briefing. Iran denied the allegations.

The Quds force (Quds is the name of Jerusalem in Arabic) is responsible for extraterritorial operations of the Revolutionary Guard. Its fingerprints were found in most Middle East states, including Iraq, Syria, Lebanon, and Yemen. The force's commander, Brig. Gen. Qassem Suleimani, is one of the world's leading terrorist suspects. In Iraq, Suleimani had cooperated with the Mahdi Army, the Shi'ite militia headed by the cleric Muqtada al-Sadr.[1] In Syria, Suleimani's agents are currently helping President Assad suppress antigovernment protests. In Bosnia and Afghanistan, his force was involved in setting up covert operations. Western intelligence agencies believe that Suleimani has installed sleeper cells in some large U.S. cities and European and Latin American capitals, likely to be activated if Iran is attacked.

The Quds force was most probably responsible for killing Saudi diplomat Hassan M. al-Kahtani in the Pakistani city of Karachi on May 16, 2011. Two assassins riding a motorcycle gunned down al-Kahtani. A few days earlier, unidentified assailants, probably Quds force members, had thrown hand grenades at the Saudi Consulate in Karachi, though nobody was hurt.

In December 2011 Iran's regime climbed up another step by sending students—members of the Revolutionary Guard's Basij militia—to carry out a forceful assault on the British embassy in Teheran. This storming recalled the 1979 occupation of the U.S. embassy in Teheran. The current attack was motivated by the UK government's decision to take the lead in imposing sanctions on all Iranian banks and pressing for an EU boycott of Iranian oil. Suleimani was the assault's planner and organizer. Posters with his picture were held aloft by some protestors.

At the same time, Iran had strengthened its antispy safeguards, and in December 2011 its armed forces downed an RQ-170 Sentinel, a U.S. remote-piloted spy plane. U.S. sources claimed that the drone was lost during a flight over Afghanistan and probably crashed in eastern Iran.

A few days later, Iran's Intelligence Ministry announced the arrest of a CIA analyst, an Iranian citizen, "who was trained by the U.S. Army's Military Intelligence Division in Iraq and Afghanistan" and was tasked with "carrying out a complex intelligence operation and infiltrating the Iranian intelligence apparatus."

Hezbollah had intensified its antispy safeguards as well. In a few announcements published since 2009, Hezbollah had proclaimed the capture of scores of local and foreign spies working for the United States and Israel. The CIA dismissed Hezbollah's assertions. "The agency does not, as a rule, address spurious claims from terrorist groups," a spokesperson for the CIA said. Mossad generally does not communicate with the press either. An Israeli source, who protects his anonymity because he is not authorized to distribute confidential information, told me that for a long period both the CIA's and Mossad's abilities to gather information in Lebanon were seriously damaged.

Yet, an experienced observer should be capable of anticipating the X factor—the one particularly influential agent or substance that has the ability to bring about an alteration of Iran's political environment. In my eyes, regarding the dispute between Iran and the West, the tiebreaker is Syria's president, Bashar al-Assad. His fall will mark the end of Iran's great expectations for the bomb. In fact, this was the essence of Israeli military intelligence's annual appraisal as well. On November 21, 2011, IDF's chief of staff and the head of the intelligence branch displayed the army's intelligence appraisal for 2012 to Netanyahu's cabinet members, informing them that behind the scenes, the Iranian Revolution's leaders are helping Assad in his efforts to quell the resistance. At the same time, the army's annual estimation claimed, the ayatollahs are worried that Assad's collapse will result in a retraction of the defense treaty between the two states. Syria's retreat from the Iranian connection, the generals told Israel's cabinet, would drastically weaken the ayatollahs military capabilities and shatter their strategy of extending their version of the Islamic Revolution to other Middle East countries, including Iraq. Syria is Iran's most subtle spot, the generals added, and the Obama administration should apply pressure appropriately in order to bring down Assad's oligarchy.

Iran was one of Obama's most challenging tests during his first presidential term. His foreign policy included excellent achievements: killing Osama bin Laden; assisting from the background the coalition of nations engaged in Libya's liberation so that the risks were minimized; closing the gloomy chapter of the Iraq War; and providing the precise measure of support to the Arab Spring. Obama, Secretary of State Clinton, and their national security team handled the United States' role extremely well during these important events. The end of the ayatollahs' revolution might be their finest achievement.

Here is a realistic scenario:

In the spring of 2013, six months after Barack Obama is elected to his second term, tension prevails once more in the Middle East, and armies go on the alert. In the Pentagon, the lights are burning until the early hours, and the communications lines of the U.S. Central Command are humming. The first American strike is planned to be a signal to Iran, or a kind of trial run to test responses. The United States hits two targets. Stealth aircraft knock out the defenses around the uranium enrichment centrifuges at Natanz in the Esfahan district, and missiles fired from naval vessels hit the underground site that was exposed in September 2009 near the holy city of Qom.

The Iranian command refrains from a direct response against American targets. The mullahs prefer to activate their proxies against Israel. Tehran orders Hezbollah to bombard Israel from Lebanon with missiles, and the movement's leader, Hassan Nasrallah, is eager to fight. His patron, al–Assad, has been removed from power, and the civil war's carnage in Syria continues, but nevertheless, from his bunker in the Beqa'a Valley, Nasrallah issues orders for volleys of missiles to be fired into Israel. Yet this time, unlike the Second Lebanon War in 2006, Israeli intelligence is well prepared. The Israeli military's response is very rapid and effective. Within less than twenty-four hours, the Israeli Air Force has hit most of Hezbollah's missile stockpiles and destroyed its command posts.

At a press conference in Washington, Obama notifies Iran that the international front that has formed against its nuclear project is still prepared to reach a diplomatic settlement. He gives the ayatollahs two days, telling them that if they want to talk, the coalition would be happy to do so. It would allot ten days to the negotiations, the president announces, no more than that. In Iran, confusion reigns. Across the globe, tension mounts as the hands of the clock near the deadline.

Iran opts not to respond at all, and exactly thirty minutes after the offer has expired, the United States strikes again with limited force. Missiles fired from ships hit the construction site of the nuclear reactor at Arak,[2] as well as two Revolutionary Guard bases in Tehran, causing dozens of casualties.

Within hours, the boastful threats that Ahmadinejad has made are exposed as fantasies. Iran never had a chance against the United States. The Iranian military and its Revolutionary Guard are totally at the mercy of America's spy satellites, just as Saddam Hussein's armor had been in March 2003. Stealth aircraft prove capable of destroying the entire Iranian military within a matter of days.

On the diplomatic front, Iran is isolated. Saudi Arabia and Egypt denounce it openly. Russia gives the measured attack its silent consent. Turkey and Syria do not want to become entangled, and China makes some noises of protest at the UN Security Council but remains on the sidelines, as does Venezuela, although its president, Hugo Chávez, verbally abuses the United States. As it did in the Gulf War, Washington prefers to leave Israel as an observer from the sidelines. Israeli involvement in the attack would draw objections from the moderate Arabs. Washington wants them on its side.

Of course, markets all over the world run wild. The price of oil doubles and stock prices fall, but because of the uncertainty already prevailing in the global economy, the response in the markets and the media is restrained (although the decline into yet another recession does arouse a high degree of anxiety). The United States and Europe are already in the throes of the crisis, and experts say the timing of the American attack is right. It is better when troubles come all at once, the pundits write.

Before a week goes by, the ayatollahs give in, and the crisis is at an end. Iran stops enriching uranium, and its nuclear facilities are opened to inspectors from the International Atomic Energy Agency (IAEA). Another few weeks go by, and the ayatollahs are forced to relinquish power. For a while anarchy reigns in Tehran, but within days the Green Party takes control of the situation, sets up a provisional government, and calls for elections.

Here is an alternative realistic scenario:

In February 2013, six months before Iran's presidential election, the ayatollahs' regime is toppled. There has been no need for military intervention because simultaneously, the freedom spirit of Cairo and Damascus arrive at Teheran, and sanctions have undermined Iran's economic stability. The import of refined petroleum shrinks and its price soars, unemployment reaches record levels, and inflation is rampant. Worst hit are the lower strata of society, from which the ayatollahs had drawn most of their political support. The opposition grows stronger. The middle class stages demonstrations to protest the rocketing prices and the long lines at gas stations, and the elites, urged by tail wind from successful revolts in neighboring countries, renew their fight for freedom.

Indeed, the outside pressure has fractured the regime's ostensible harmony. As Syria's civil war had drowned the country in blood, Tehran's defense pact, set up by the ayatollahs with Syria and Hezbollah, is completely dismantled. Assad has been toppled, Turkey's army invades Syria's northern region, and in Lebanon, a mini civil war erupts, as Hezbollah's paramilitary units battle Christians' militias.

The ayatollahs are divided. Some of the heads of the Council of Sages and the majority of the Majlis demand that the Supreme Leader, Ali Khamenei, depose Ahmadinejad. The president's associate, Revolutionary Guard commander Mohammad Ali Jafari, responds by threatening to disperse the parliament. The civil uprising gains momentum, with millions demonstrating in the streets and members of the Revolutionary Guard defecting from their units and joining the protests, until the regime finally collapses in a mirror image of the Khomeini revolution of 1979.

Relying on experience from other Arab Spring events, of these two scenarios, the latter seems to me the more realistic—in the case of Iran, an external intervention would not be necessary. The global coalition against Iran is powerful enough to bring its regime down. The key is not in China or Russia, but in the Middle East. If the united front of moderate Arab states headed by Saudi Arabia shows determination against a nuclear Iran, the international sanctions will be tightened until the ayatollahs' rule falls. Of course, that determination depends on Israel's withdrawal from the occupied territories as a step toward a solution of the conflict between Israel and the Palestinians. If a settlement is formulated on the basis of the Arab (formerly the Saudi) plan, the entire Middle East will undergo a momentous change.

The international stand against Iran's nuclear project and the negotiations between Israel and the Palestinians are therefore closely linked. The Bush administration did not emphasize this linkage, but the Obama administration, after closely studying the situation, has changed America's course, and rightly so. Regarding the negotiations for a Middle East settlement, Obama's salient advantage over his predecessor—perhaps over all his predecessors in the last two decades—is that he has undertaken to play the role of an unbiased mediator. Because of this, and also because he is the first American president with Muslim antecedents, moderate Arabs are less suspicious of him trying to force a deal favoring Israel on them than they were of his predecessors. Maureen Dowd, the acerbic *New York Times* columnist, aptly described Obama's attitude to Islam: "This is the man who staked his historical reputation on a new and friendlier engagement with the Muslim world."[3]

Since the early part of 2010, at meetings in Washington and Jerusalem, emissaries of the president, including then CIA director Leon Panetta, explained to Netanyahu that the Israeli-Palestinian conflict affected every one of the fronts on which the United States was active in the Muslim world, from Yemen through Iraq and Iran to Afghanistan and Pakistan. In order to weaken the extremists in Afghanistan and Pakistan and to form an effective coalition against Iran and its proxies—Syria and Hezbollah—America needed the support of moderate Muslims, the American envoys told Netanyahu. If there is not significant progress in the negotiations between Israel and the Palestinians, it is unlikely that we will get that support, and if the moderate Muslims are not on our side, it is unlikely that the international front against Iran's nuclear project will garner sufficient force to compel the ayatollahs to desist from pressing ahead.

Outwardly, Netanyahu never showed any sign that this message was persuading his government to stop dragging its feet in the negotiations with the Palestinians. It is possible that he was behaving like a bazaar peddler and holding out to see whether Washington was capable of delivering the goods on Iran, and only if it turned out that Tehran would give in to international pressure and drop its nuclear plans would

Israel oblige and advance the talks with the Palestinians. On the internal political front, this was a convenient solution, because any hint of any concession, even on a marginal matter, could have led to the breakup of Netanyahu's government. His coalition partners on the right kept a careful watch on the prime minister to make sure that he did not deviate from the hawkish line, and the leader of the Kadima party, Tzipi Livni, was waiting on his left flank for the opportunity to set up an alternative government.

Unable to drag Netanyahu's government to the negotiating table with the PA through conventional means, the Obama administration experimented with an unconventional tactic: taking advantage of Israel's unique sensitivity to any foreign involvement with its nuclear capabilities.

19

The Bomb Is Still in the Basement

IN ORDER TO force the Netanyahu government to adopt a policy of compromise with the Palestinians, the Obama administration carried out serious preparatory work and identified the two most sensitive points in the way Israel sees its security. One is its own nuclear option, and the other is that of the Iranians. The two are related, of course. Israel is prepared to pay a high price to ensure its nuclear monopoly in the region, and to this end it must block Iran from acquiring nuclear status. How can both goals be reached? By reaching a territorial compromise with the Palestinians in a give-and-take deal in which the United States undertakes to neutralize the Iranian nuclear project in exchange for Israel's withdrawal from most of the West Bank, enabling the establishment of a Palestinian state. This has been the formula through which the Obama administration has tried to set a number of measures in motion—a settlement between Israel and the Arabs on the basis of the Arab Peace Plan (based on the Saudi Arabian initiative of March 2002), stopping Iran from producing nuclear weapons, and blocking the Iran-Syria-Hezbollah Axis of Evil. The changes that these measures would bring about in the region would boost relations between the West and the Muslim world, weaken support for al Qaeda, and strengthen moderate Muslim elements.

Ever since Israel acquired nuclear capability, its strategy has been to prevent other states in the Middle East from drawing level with it. For decades, Israel's technological edge over its neighbors has steadily increased, particularly in the last fifteen years. The advantages of globalization have been more marked in Israel than in the other countries in the region because it is a democracy with open channels to the rest of the world and with a free economy. In the regional balance of power in which only conventional arms are taken into account, Israel may well be ahead, although this is not certain, but when Israel's nuclear option is included in the equation, its lead is absolutely ensured, and it is not interested in giving up its nuclear monopoly and entering a balance-of-terror situation.

In Israel's eyes—and this has been true for all of its governments since it reached nuclear capability in the late 1960s and up to this day—the possession of a nuclear bomb by the enemy is unacceptable, mainly because it would weaken Israel's deterrent stance. Imagine Hezbollah ambushing one of the sensitive points along the border with Israel, attacking an IDF patrol, capturing two soldiers, and taking them to Lebanon. Such an incident led Israel into the Second Lebanon War in the summer of 2006. Israel did not hesitate and responded at once in great force. It had to restore its deterrent capacity against Hezbollah, and it therefore immediately sent ground, air, and naval forces into action, bombing the headquarters of the organization in Beirut as well as its arms stockpiles all over Lebanon, inflicting a severe blow against it and its supporters. Since then Hezbollah has restrained itself, not daring to challenge Israel, and its leader, Hassan Nasrallah, is still holed up in the bunker in which he was compelled to take cover when Israel attacked. How would Israel respond to a similar incident if it were to occur at a time when Iran possesses a nuclear option? A balance of terror with Iran would obligate Israel to behave differently—and it is doubtful that Israel would be able to react in the preferred time and with the force that it deems necessary. In other words, losing its nuclear superiority means losing its capability of deterrence, and therefore there is no chance that Israel would ever come to terms with such a balance-of-terror situation with the ayatollahs' regime in Iran.

A glance at the more distant horizon, beyond Israel's desire to preserve its deterrent capability, reveals a similar picture. A bomb in Iran's hands would substantially reduce the ability of the United States to protect its interests in the Middle East. The change would be dramatic. On the one hand, the Gulf states would be threatened constantly, and protection of their oil wells would be complex and very expensive. On the other hand, elements fighting against American interests would be strengthened: the insurgents in Iraq, local militias like Hezbollah and

Hamas, and international terror groups like al Qaeda and other fundamentalist parties and organizations that have declared war on the Western way of life. At the same time, the bases of support for American interests will be weakened: the Saudi royal family, fragile Iraqi democracy, the Hashemite dynasty in Jordan, and the emirates in the Gulf. And of course, the nuclear option would empower the regime of the ayatollahs inside Iran and diminish the prospects of the opposition ever ousting them. Furthermore, at least three Muslim countries in the region—Turkey, Saudi Arabia, and Egypt—would feel compelled to join in the nuclear arms race in order to remain in the power game, and this could bring disaster in its wake to the Middle East.

And if we look east, to Pakistan, India, and Afghanistan, and to the eastern republics of the former Soviet Union, similar developments could be expected. Protected by a nuclear umbrella, extremist Shi'ite Iran will be able to disseminate its ideology among vast populations. Because of this, America's interest in Iran is identical to Israel's: stop Iran from acquiring nuclear capability.

And against this background, how can a right-wing Israeli government negotiate with the Palestinian government over the core issues? By threatening to expose Israel's secret weapon to the world. That's what the U.S. government has actually done. They subtly threatened to deprive Israel of the special status it enjoys, with its nuclear capability immune from international inspection. Statements by senior members of the Obama administration (including the president himself), some of which were vague and others more explicit, created the impression in Israel that if the Netanyahu government refused to go along with the peace initiative that the president was conducting in the Middle East, the United States would cease giving unbridled support to Israel's nuclear policy, as it had done so far.

On May 6, 2009, in a United Nations debate on the Nuclear Non-Proliferation Treaty (NPT), Assistant Secretary of State Rose Gottemoeller declared surprisingly that the United States believed that Israel should join the treaty. "Universal adherence to the NPT itself, including by India, Israel, Pakistan and North Korea," said Gottemoeller, "remains a fundamental objective of the United States."

The government of Israel was taken by surprise. For forty years, America had stubbornly defended Israel's policy of "nuclear ambiguity,"[1] and now, before President Obama had even warmed his seat in the White House, Washington's attitude to Israel's most touchy issue had changed fundamentally. Washington had trodden on a sore point, and the Jerusalem government panicked. From Israel's point of view, the American demand that Israel join the NPT was a recipe for calamity because it meant one thing: the exposure of its nuclear installations to international inspection.

A few days after that, Netanyahu met Obama in the White House and made an effort to get Israel's nuclear program back into the locked drawer where it had been kept for so many years, but he failed. The president demanded an unequivocal Israeli undertaking to strive for a two-state solution, the freezing of construction in the settlements, and direct talks with the Palestinians on the core issues, but the prime minister refused to commit himself.

The Obama administration took its next step in September 2009, at the annual conference of the IAEA in Vienna. For the first time in its history, the agency's general assembly passed an Arab resolution calling on Israel to join the NPT and demanding that all its nuclear activities be subject to international inspection, including the nuclear reactor in Dimona. This was a telling blow, because in the past, the Arab states had frequently demanded a vote on a similarly worded resolution, and each time the United States had persuaded its friends to oppose it or to abstain, thereby blocking the move. But in 2009, the American delegation made no effort to neutralize the Arab demand, and the resolution passed. From Israel's point of view, therefore, a dangerous precedent had been set. If the international demand for barring its nuclear project grew stronger, and if the United States refrained from acting to block that demand, Israel probably would not be able to preserve its unique nuclear status, with the Iranians and their supporters ceaselessly asking the world why what was permitted for Israel was forbidden for Iran.

Netanyahu, however, had not yet worked out what made Obama tick and how determined the president was to carry his plans through. In late March 2010, the prime minister came to the White House again, and the ritual was repeated: the president demanded that Netanyahu begin negotiating directly with the Palestinians on the core issues and reach an agreement within a year, and Netanyahu dodged the issue. Obama responded in an unanticipated manner, leaving the room and going about his business, telling Netanyahu, "Let me know if there's anything new." This was a humiliating experience for the Israeli, and he found himself in a bind. The president was treating him like the leader of some obscure nation, and not one of America's prime allies. No photographs of the two men were permitted. Netanyahu decided to leave immediately with his aides to discuss the crisis in the Israeli Embassy, not within reach of the White House microphones.

Despite everything, the prime minister refused to budge, and in mid-April there was further erosion in the American attitude to Israel's nuclear position. At a press conference, as host of a conference on nuclear non-proliferation, the president himself urged Israel to sign the NPT. Replying to a reporter's question in an ostensibly off-hand manner, he mentioned Israel: "Whether we're talking about Israel or any other country, we think that becoming part of the NPT is important, and that, by the way, is not a new position. That's been a consistent position of the United States government, even prior to my administration."

The president knew that his last sentence was misleading. The demand that Israel sign the NPT and unveil its nuclear installations to the world had not been heard in Washington since the 1960s, under Presidents Kennedy and Johnson, and even then not in public but in secret contacts between the two governments. Since the early 1970s, in accordance with the decision of President Nixon and National Security Adviser Kissinger, the United States had adopted the opposite policy. The Nixon administration created a new world order: On the one hand, American disengagement from Vietnam, détente with the Soviet Union, and a thaw in relations with China. On the other hand, for the sake of balance, a strengthening of the components of the Western alliance. In America's stance with regard to the proliferation of strategic weaponry, there was a 180 degree turnaround. Kissinger believed that instead of waging a rearguard action against friendly countries that develop nuclear weapons, including India and Israel, it was better to help them, or at least not hinder them, in order to bolster the Western camp. He explicitly stated that friendly states must not be pressed to sign the NPT. Of course, Israel was on his side in this matter. In September 1969, then prime minister Golda Meir came to Washington intending to hold a serious and sincere discussion on the nuclear option that Israel now possessed and, for the first time, to tell the Americans the truth.

If Israel's nuclear capability is a fait accompli and if there's no possibility of doing away with it, Kissinger believed after Meir's visit, it would be best for Israel to keep it under terms that would further American interests. This pragmatic reasoning led the Nixon administration to the conclusion that Israel should not be coerced into signing the NPT or pressured into revealing its plans or the inventory of its strategic arsenal. From Israel's point of view, a new era had opened up. Yitzhak Rabin, who was serving as the Israeli ambassador in Washington, described the situation in his memoirs: "The various arms of the Nixon administration left Israel alone on the subject of signing the NPT, and the matter dropped off the agenda."

The precise understandings that were reached by Meir and Nixon and Kissinger are still classified, but statements by politicians and officials on both sides in the past forty years make it possible to draw the outlines of a picture that is probably close to the reality. The United States accepted the fact that Israel had nuclear capability, stopped insisting that Israel sign the NPT, and waived the demand that American experts be permitted to examine what was going on at Dimona. Israel agreed to three limitations: no publication, no testing, and no use of its nuclear capability as a provocation against the Arabs. According to foreign publications, Nixon was told that Israel would not take the bomb out of the basement and would use it only in extremely dire circumstances. In exchange for this commitment, Nixon promised Meir that as long as he was president, Israel would never reach a situation in which it was weak in conventional military terms, and that was enough for her.

Since then, a silent agreement has prevailed between the two countries. Israel behaves as if it does not have a nuclear weapon, and the United States does not insist that it unveil what it denies that it has. All the presidents since Nixon accepted this arrangement, and none of them demanded publicly that Israel sign the NPT and open its installations to international inspection until the Obama administration threatened to cancel the understandings if the Israeli government refused to enter serious discussions with Palestinians on a compromise. What the president was saying in effect was that the United States would help Israeli interests if Israel helped American interests. You want a nuclear monopoly in your region, and we want to restrain the Muslim extremists by means of a peace agreement between you and the Palestinians.

In May 2010, the Obama administration made another threatening move. At the Review Conference of the Parties to the Treaty on the NPT in New York, the United States supported a final document that, if put into practice, was liable to oblige Israel to open its nuclear facilities to scrutiny. In the declarative section of the document, there was nothing new: Israel, India, and Pakistan were called upon to join the NPT immediately and unconditionally to allow IAEA inspectors into their nuclear installations. But the document also instructed the UN secretary general to convene an international conference in 2012 to discuss the declaration of a nuclear-weapons-free Middle East.[2] As Israel is the only country in the region that allegedly possesses nuclear weapons, the United Nations intends to institute a debate on disarming it of those weapons. Iran was not mentioned in the resolution. Although the United States supported the final document, it announced that it deeply regretted that it focused on Israel.

In Israel, the nuclear issue is still taboo, and the local media and think tanks have therefore refrained from seriously examining the measures that the Obama administration has taken. But behind the scenes, the defense establishment felt betrayed and was seething with anger.

Now the Arab states sensed that the Obama administration was executing a change in America's traditional policy toward Israel's nuclear option, and in August 2010, about a month before the annual conference of the general assembly of the IAEA, the Arab league urged the United States and other countries that had supported Israel's nuclear policy to vote for a resolution phrased similarly to that adopted by the agency in 2009, calling on Israel to join the NPT and demanding that its entire nuclear program come under international inspection.[3] But this time the Arab request was turned down, because by now Israel had given in on the Palestinian issue. In order to enable resumption of negotiations with the Palestinians, the Netanyahu government had accepted the principle of two states for two peoples, frozen construction in the settlements for ten months, and agreed to discuss the core issues with the Palestinians in direct talks: borders, Jerusalem, and refugees. In July 2010, after a meeting at the White House, Obama and Netanyahu agreed that at the IAEA conference, both of them would "work together to oppose efforts to single out Israel." In other words, unlike 2009, the United States would act to ensure that the vote at the IAEA conference in September would be in Israel's favor. And that is what happened. The Arab resolution was rejected by a majority of fifty-one opposed, forty-six for, and twenty-three abstentions. The United States, all the member states of the European Union, Canada, Japan, Australia, and New Zealand voted against it, and several states of the "unaligned bloc" abstained. China and Russia voted with the Arabs.

The United States had seen to it that the bomb that Israel keeps in its basement—according to foreign sources, of course, because although Israel admits that it has nuclear capability, it does not admit that it has already done so—would not be exposed to outsiders' eyes. The nuclear option remained as opaque as it had been since its inception in the late 1960s. IAEA inspectors would not be allowed to examine what Israel was hiding in Dimona and at other sites where its nuclear option was located.

The Obama administration probably did not plan to depart from the policy that America had held since Nixon and force Israel to open these sites up for inspection, but the veiled threats were enough to force it to toe the line. Defense Minister Ehud Barak traveled the Tel Aviv–Washington route several times and spent many hours in the White House and the Pentagon, and Netanyahu met Obama alone twice before the threat was removed. In July 2010, at a White House summit, Netanyahu for the first time handed the president a detailed plan for a settlement with the Palestinians, and Obama believed that Israel was ready to carry out a far-reaching compromise.

So in the end, was this strategy successful? It certainly could have been, if the Democrats had kept their absolute majority in Congress. But in the midterm election on November 2, 2010, Democrats were defeated. Republicans won control of the House of Representatives; Democrats retained control of the Senate, although their majority margin decreased. For the Israelis and the Palestinians, this change was crucial. While Netanyahu's relationship with the Obama administration was built on mistrust and suspicion, his relationship with the Republican Party had blossomed. Under Republican pressure and as the campaign for the 2012's elections intensified, the Obama administration was compelled to delay its peace initiatives for a later time. Consequently, the Palestinians lost their trust in Obama being an impartial broker and Abbas was forced to shift his efforts from Washington to the UN. On the other side, supported massively by the Republican-controlled House of Representatives, Netanyahu's rightist government was able to make a shift by pulling the Palestinian problem from the administration's foreign policy agenda and replacing it with Iran's nuclear threat. The two-state solution was out and Iran's bomb came in, and until the November 2012 elections, any attempt to compel Israel to seriously negotiate the core issues with the Palestinians was over and done with.

How could the Israeli government make such an exchange of issues and priorities within the United States' foreign policy agenda? The GOP pursuit of the Jewish financial and political support for the 2012 elections made it possible. So willingly had Republican presidential candidates sought to please the Jewish vote that former speaker of the house Newt Gingrich, a historian, proclaimed that the Palestinians are "invented people." Speaking to the national Republican Jewish Coalition, Gingrich made another proclamation: "In a Gingrich administration, the opening day, there will be an executive order about two hours after the inaugural address; we will send the [U.S.] embassy from Tel Aviv to Jerusalem as of that day." The status of Jerusalem is one of the most delicate issues in dispute between the two sides of the conflict, and any change in the present situation has an impact on the whole Islamic world.

A few months earlier, when Obama declared that the borders predating the Six-Day War of 1967, adjusted to some degree, should be the starting point for negotiations, former Massachusetts governor Mitt Romney accused the president of throwing Israel "under the bus," although the 1967 borders have been viewed by previous U.S. administrations as the foundation for the peace agreement.

Some Republican candidates expressed strident viewpoints on the question of the settlers' harsh treatment of the Palestinian population in the territories. One example was the staged uproar by right-wing Jewish groups over public comments expressed by Howard Gutman, the U.S. ambassador to Belgium. On December 2011, addressing a Brussels conference on antisemitism in Europe, the diplomat said that some antisemitism had stemmed from Israeli-Palestinian tensions, which is common knowledge for any reasonable person. Consequently, Romney and Gingrich urged Obama to dismiss the ambassador, a Jew and the son of a Holocaust survivor. Hoping to grab his piece of the Jewish vote, former ambassador to China (under Obama) Jon Huntsman Jr. was even more assertive. Huntsman said that Gutman's comments reflected "deeper anti-Israel attitudes" within the Obama administration. "These aren't speeches that are cooked up at the local level and at the embassy," Huntsman said. "They go high up within the State Department." This last remark comes close to accusing the Obama administration and the State Department's higher echelons of being antisemites. Nevertheless, the Obama administration said that it has full confidence in Gutman.

Another Republican presidential candidate, Michele Bachmann, added her share of hypocrisy. Speaking to NBC News, Bachmann portrayed Iran's malicious intents by overstating the level of perilousness, as if an atomic war is a fait accompli: "Iran will take a nuclear weapon, they will use it to wipe our ally Israel off the face of the map, and they've stated they will use it against the United States of America," Bachman said. Well, Iran has never threatened to use a nuclear bomb against the United States.

In fact, while debating Middle East topics over the course of the 2012 presidential campaign Republican leaders (and some Democrats as well) moved wildly to the right, taking unrestrained pleasure in being persuaded, almost hypnotized, by aggressive concepts and showing their seeming toughness. Far-right groups in Israel were pleased, and the Israel government could take advantage of that madness for its benefit.

In 2011 Israel's defense establishment was busy devising plots in order to persuade the Obama administration to impose significant sanctions against Tehran. Netanyahu's team launched a genius campaign against governments that had pledged to block Iran's nuclear project but not held up their end of the bargain. It was primarily aimed at the White House, although the effect had a wider range. Suddenly foreign observers noted an unprecedented phenomenon: the nuclear weapon issues, which for decades were held by Israel's official censors as top secret, had suddenly become public knowledge. A huge widening of the public discourse took place, including exceptional public declarations by ex-heads of Mossad, official announcements about Air Force training in distant regions, and the formation of a new military command for "depth" operations carried out far from Israel's borders. Retired generals debated in public, and cabinet ministers and Knesset members released statements. Day after day, the headlines were busy examining the capabilities and probabilities of a preventive Israeli strike on Iran. This kind of uproar was unusual for a country that strictly guarded any publicity of security topics. Israel's message to the free world: "Either you break Iran's resistance, or we might send F-16 fighters to bomb Natanz."

The timing was perfect because precisely as the Israeli campaign reached its peak in mid-November, the IAEA released a special report containing evidence that Iran had conducted work on a highly sophisticated nuclear triggering technology that could only be used for setting off a nuclear device. Furthermore, the report stated that the agency was "increasingly concerned about the possible existence in Iran of past or current undisclosed military nuclear activities including those related to the development of a nuclear payload for a missile."

The combination of the IAEA's revelations together with Israel's aggressive campaign confused many pundits. Columnists questioned how many aces were in Israel's poker hand. Would Netanyahu and Barak really order their air force to hit nuclear sites in Iran, in spite of the generally accepted prediction of formidable consequences? Because these questions remained open, Washington could not stay impassive, and in October 2011, the Pentagon estimated that an Israeli military option is available. Leon Panetta, now secretary of defense, was again sent to caution Israel about the dangers of attacking Iran. He delivered a forceful message. Because targets in Iran are dispersed and hard to destroy, an attack would probably delay Iran's nuclear weapon by only one to two years, the secretary said, and he specified some "unanticipated consequences," among them the likelihood that the United States would be blamed and might be included in retaliatory response, and the possibility of an escalation that could broaden into a larger war in the region. Several weeks later, on December 2 in a speech at the Saban Center, he stated that "at this point, we believe that the combination of economic and diplomatic sanctions that have been placed upon Iran have had a serious impact." Because of the Revolutionary Guard's attack on the British embassy on November 29, Panetta added, "Iran is isolating itself from the rest of the world" and has become "a pariah in that region." Teheran's government "is off balance in terms of really trying to establish any kind of stability within Iran." He later said, in response to a question from the audience, that military action could make "a backlash in the region that would serve to strengthen a regime that is now weak and isolated." Any military attack, Panetta concluded, should be a "last resort."

But Israel continued pushing. Ten days after Panetta's harsh warning, "top government officials" in Israel were quoted by the media, proclaiming that "the administration is still not acting in full force to impose significant sanctions against Tehran." One Israeli official praised French president Nicolas Sarkozy and British prime minister David Cameron "for having begun to act determinedly" and another official complained that "the Obama administration has yet to formulate a policy that is sufficiently severe."

Consequently, Republican candidates preparing themselves for the first race in the Republican presidential contest intensified their aggressive declarations. Except for libertarian Ron Paul, all the candidates came close to declaring war on Iran. Thus, the patriotic ball had been thrown from Netanyahu's government in Jerusalem to the GOP's candidates wrestling in Iowa and back to Jerusalem, and back again in an astonishing exchange of deceptive statements, which actually were motivated with the goal of embarrassing the Obama administration.

This anti-Obama campaign was wrong. His administration conducted the struggle with the ayatollahs skillfully. Certainly, Obama's opening position has been weak because of the war that his predecessor started against Iraq. In its first two years, the Obama administration had to dismantle the mines and obstacles that its predecessor had placed all across the region: in Iraq, shoring up self-government and getting American troops back home; in Afghanistan, reorganizing the fight against al Qaeda, eliminating bin Laden, and planning a pullback strategy; in the Israeli-Palestinian conflict, mediating between the sides in proximity talks in order to restart the negotiations on core issues; and in the Gulf, weakening the ayatollahs' regime by stepping up international sanctions, and bolstering the defensive capabilities of Saudi Arabia and the other oil-producing entities—Qatar, Bahrain, Kuwait, and the United Arab Emirates.

There was no disagreement between Washington and Jerusalem on the nature of the Iranian threat and its gravity. It is a conflict over hegemony on the most important world's assets, and the West should be seeking to defend at all costs its predominance. Both the American and Israeli intelligence services assumed that the Islamic Republic wanted to get nuclear capability, was accumulating low-grade enriched uranium, and was building nuclear warheads for ballistic missiles. Moreover, both the United States and Israel believed that if and when Iran gets a nuclear weapon, the power game in the Middle East will change fundamentally. Official personages in Israel and the United States have refrained from direct threats of waging war against Iran—many of them, including Bush, Obama, and Netanyahu, used the phrase "all options open"—but Tony Blair did not hesitate to describe the situation clearly. On September 1, 2010, in an interview with the BBC, the former prime minister, who was closely involved in the agreed strategy of the leadership of the United States and Europe, said, "It is wholly unacceptable for Iran to have a nuclear weapons capability, and I think we have got to be prepared to confront them, if necessary militarily. There is no alternative to that if they continue to develop nuclear weapons. They need to get that message loud and clear."

Obama's statements regarding Iran are carefully formulated and never reaching beyond the familiar expression "considering all options," but nevertheless some White House sources suggest that inside closed doors, Obama's views about the use of power against Iran are not different from Blair's. "The President didn't hesitate to use force when it is necessary," said his former advisor on Middle East affairs Dennis Ross, "and he would not hesitate to do so against Iran, but only as a last resort." On December 13, 2011, speaking at the Washington Institute for Near East Policy, Ross said that in order to avoid a sharp increase in the price of oil, the United States prefers to operate in a "gradual manner."

One week later, Chairman of the Joint Chiefs of Staff Gen. Martin Dempsey went a big step further and said in an interview with CNN that the United States is preparing for a possible strike in Iran. It was the first time that a member of the highest U.S. defense echelons literally warned the Tehran regime with a military assault. "My biggest worry is they will miscalculate our resolve," he said. "Any miscalculation could mean that we are drawn into conflict, and that would be a tragedy for the region and the world."

Iran is a country with a considerable technological capability and a weak military. Its air force and air-defense systems are obsolete. Its offensive power lies in its Shahab and Sejil medium- and long-range solid-fuel, surface-to-surface missiles with ranges that cover the whole Middle East.[4] Iran's ally Syria possesses Scud missiles that cover most of Israel, although the acute and chronic conflict inside Syria drastically limits its capabilities to attack Israel. Hezbollah has thousands of short-range missiles that can reach targets in a large part of Israel. If it is attacked by Israel, in the worst case-scenario, Iran will presumably respond with prolonged bombardment of Israeli targets with Shahab missiles with conventional warheads. It has several hundred missiles capable of reaching Israel, but conventional missiles do not decide wars, and therefore as long as Iran does not possess nuclear weapons, they almost certainly cannot threaten the existence of Israel.

This method of operation has obliged Israel to devise a solution, and with generous American assistance, the country's ability to defend itself against missile attacks has greatly improved in recent years. With mainly American funding, Israel is developing three defensive systems: Iron Cap, to intercept medium- and short-range missiles; Magic Wand (also known as David's Sling), to knock out medium- and long-range missiles; and Arrow-3 to hit long-range ballistic missiles.[5]

In addition, the U.S. Department of Defense has deployed in Israel radar stations (operated by American soldiers), which are capable of differentiating between missiles that will hit populated areas and those that will fall in empty spaces so that only the former will be intercepted.

For the fiscal year 2012, the House Appropriations Defense Subcommittee approved $235.7 million for U.S.-Israeli missile defense programs, a record budget. This aid package will fund the jointly developed missile defense programs Arrow-2, Arrow-3, and Magic Wand.[6] It will come on top of the $205 million special grant for the procurement of more Iron Dome antimissile batteries announced by Obama and in addition to the $3 billion in annual U.S. military aid. (For the fiscal year 2011, U.S. aid for joint missile defense programs with Israel totaled $217.7 million.)

For its part, Israel could hit targets in Iran with its F-15 and F-16 warplanes, as well as its advanced ballistic missiles. According to foreign sources, Israel possesses the robust medium-range missile program Jericho,[7] whose missiles are launched from the surface or the air, and a space launch vehicle that essentially gives Israel intercontinental ballistic missile capability. According to foreign sources, three Israeli Dolphin-class submarines, built in Germany, have been fitted with American Harpoon cruise missiles with nuclear warheads. At least one of these submarines is permanently patrolling near the Persian Gulf.

When it comes to its existential interests, Israel has a fast trigger finger, and nuclear capability in the hands of Iran's ayatollahs was defined by the Jewish state as an obvious existential threat. Israel is unlikely to ask the United States to approve any attack on Iran. This insight was verified on November 30, 2011, when General Dempsey told Reuters that he didn't know whether Israel would alert the United States ahead of time if it decided to attack Iran. A few weeks later, U.S. ambassador to Israel Dan Shapiro countered Dempsey's claim. Briefing reporters in Tel Aviv, the ambassador said, "There is no issue that we coordinate more closely than on Iran."

Indeed, there is a large amount of intelligence sharing between the two countries, but an operational coordination does not exist. An agreement in principle regulates the way in which Israel may rightfully respond to the threat of weapons of mass destruction. This agreement was framed in a document drawn up in 1998 and signed by Clinton and Netanyahu (in his first term). It states that the United States is "very concerned" by the nonconventional threats in the Middle East (without mentioning Iraq or Iran, although it was clear at the time that Saddam Hussein's Iraq and Iran were the subject of the statement) and that it understands that Israel needs defensive capabilities in the face of the threats. This is apparently the first written agreement between the two countries that refers to nonconventional threats against Israel and the manner in which it may respond to them. The agreement provides for a permanent apparatus for joint discussion on nonconventional threats in the Middle East. This machinery is separate from the working groups that have been meeting twice a year since the 1980s in the framework of the "strategic dialogue" between the two countries. On April 14, 2004, at the end of a series of discussions by the nonconventional threats panel, Bush and Sharon exchanged letters. Sharon released a section of one of these letters for publication, including the following American statement: "Israel has the right to defend itself with its own forces." This statement was a direct message to Tehran that the United States recognized Israel's right to use its defensive capacity in the event that Iran develops nuclear weaponry.

The first time that Israel had implemented its "No WMD in the Hands of My Enemy" doctrine was the destruction of Iraq's nuclear reactor in the summer of 1981. It was a historical precedent: for the first time ever, a regional power with nuclear capability had gone on the offensive to prevent a neighbor with considerable military power from developing nuclear weaponry. For the seven years prior to the attack, Israel had tried in various ways to stop Iraq from acquiring the installations and materials that would enable it to build a bomb. Straight after the attack, Prime Minister Menachem Begin made the following declaration: "Israel will not tolerate any nuclear weapons in the region"—a principle that is still in force today. Israel conducted this air force operation near Baghdad without giving Washington advance notice.

The second situation in which the "No WMD in the Region" doctrine was put into effect happened in 2006. Syria secretly erected a nuclear installation, apparently a reactor capable of producing plutonium. The facility had been built with North Korean aid at a remote site in northern Syria called Al Kibar (aka Dair Alzour). Early in 2007, a short while after the Pyongyang regime had seemingly given in to an international demand and halted uranium enrichment and making a nuclear bomb, North Korea transferred radioactive materials to the Al Kibar site.

Reports in the media outside Israel have said that in the spring of 2006, an Israeli spy satellite relayed photographs of the suspicious site. Intelligence surveillance identified a North Korean presence in the area. About a year later, members of an Israeli commando unit called Shaldag ("Kingfisher" in English) landed nearby and collected soil samples that were found to contain radioactive materials. Israeli intelligence feared that the Syrians intended to use the radioactive material it had obtained from North Korea to arm its Scuds with nuclear warheads. American intelligence feared that the facility had been built at Iran's initiative and with its assistance with the intention of stockpiling its nuclear materials outside the country and far from the eyes of international inspectors, and perhaps even to enrich uranium there.

Just as it had done in Iraq in the summer of 1981, Israel dispatched warplanes to destroy the suspicious installation in Syria. In September 2007, with the agreement of the United States, Israeli Air Force F-15s bombed the Al Kibar site and demolished it. Syria's air-defense systems were out of action during the attack. Israel never admitted that its planes carried out the operation, and Syria denied that the bombed building housed nuclear materials or installations. An official Syrian declaration condemned what it called "fabrication and forging of facts." Nevertheless, on April 24, 2008, the Bush administration announced that it was "convinced" that Syria had been building a "covert nuclear reactor" that was "not intended for peaceful purposes." Two months later the IAEA dispatched a team of inspectors who identified traces of radioactive material near the ruins of the building. The IAEA report stated that "a significant number of natural uranium particles," produced as a result of chemical processing, were found at the site. Consequently, in June 2011 the IAEA's board of governors reported Syria to the UN Security Council and General Assembly over noncompliance with its nuclear safeguards obligations by failing to declare the construction of a nuclear reactor.

John Bolton, a former undersecretary for arms control at the State Department who constantly warned of the dangers of Iran's nuclear dream and demanded that it be eliminated, said at the time that Iran and North Korea had "outsourced" some of their nuclear activities to Syria.

The feasible removal of Assad would almost certainly cause the Tehran-Damascus partnership to collapse. If the post-Assad transitional period for democracy will bring about a stable regime, the chances for restarting peace negotiations between Israel and Syria are good.

20

Post-Assad

SYRIA IS INTERESTED in regaining the Golan Heights, and in recent years, in speeches and media interviews, Assad has frequently called upon the United States and Israel to resume negotiations with his government. He has stated explicitly that in exchange for the return of the Golan Heights, he would be ready to sign a peace treaty with Israel and indeed, during 2010 and 2011, both administrations, Obama's and Netanyahu's, in a coordinated course secretly examined in Damascus if Assad's positions were negotiable. The outcome seemed to be positive, except for the internal conflict's deterioration in Syria, which hindered the setting up of indirect orderly negotiations.

Netanyahu's predecessor as prime minister, Ehud Olmert, also tried to get the talks with Syria going using Turkey as a mediator but failed. It is doubtful that Turkey, with Recep Tayyip Erdogan as prime minister, would be capable of mediating, and apparently it would be impossible to come to an agreement without active American involvement.

Of course, as long as Syria's civil war continues, any peace initiative is not an option, yet from Israel's point of view, resumption of negotiations with Syria would embody the best possible cost-effectiveness ratio: low cost and tremendous benefit. The process and its outcome, including a withdrawal from the Golan Heights, would be much easier to achieve than the processes that led to the signing of a peace agreement with Egypt; it would be less complex than the path to achieving a settlement with the Palestinians, and even easier than the unilateral disengagement from the Gaza Strip carried out during Ariel Sharon's term as prime minister. Once the post-Assad era begins, common sense should lead Israel to make a supreme effort to get talks going again and reach a settlement with any Syrian government. After all, the Golan Heights is not part of "the Whole Land of Israel," and most of the settlers there are not messianics. All signs indicate that most of them belong to the center of the political spectrum.

In fact, most of the path leading to an agreement between Israel and Syria has already been paved. Most of the details have been discussed at several rounds of direct and indirect negotiations, and many disputed points have been settled. At least two prime ministers, Rabin and Barak, and apparently Olmert and Netanyahu as well, agreed to the basic principle of Israel withdrawing from the Golan Heights and returning it to Syria.

The first meaningful attempt to reach peace between Israel and Syria was registered by Yitzhak Rabin during his second term as prime minister (1992–1995), when the term "Rabin's deposit" was coined to describe a letter of intention that Rabin gave Clinton stating that in exchange for a peace agreement, and if its requirements on security, normalization of relations, agreed borders, and water sharing were met, Israel would be prepared to withdraw to the pre–Six-Day War borders, in effect returning the entire Golan Heights to Syria. From then on, at a number of negotiations carried out by third-party emissaries as well as at face-to-face meetings between high-ranking officials of both countries, agreement has been reached on most of the issues raised, apparently with two exceptions: the precise location of the border at the north eastern side of the Sea of Galilee, and the formula for the allocation of water that flows from Syrian territory into Israel. The latter issue was not a substantial obstacle, but demarcating the border along the lake shore aroused sharp disputes. The Israeli prime ministers conducting the negotiations with the Syrians could not bring the process to a culmination.

Of the four prime ministers who negotiated with Syria (Rabin, Netanyahu, Barak, and Olmert) the two belonging to the Labor Party, Rabin and Barak, went the furthest and were on the verge of creating an agreement. Barak's failed effort was the most conspicuous because at the most dramatic point in the talks, which took place in early 2000 in Shepherdstown, West Virginia, he was sitting face to face with Syria's foreign minister, Farouk al-Sharaa, the envoy of the late Syrian president Hafez al-Assad, and everyone there saw that the Syrian was ready to take out his pen and sign, but Barak hesitated and missed his opportunity.[1]

Before that meeting, Barak's representative, reserves general Uri Saguy, a former head of military intelligence, had conducted highly detailed negotiations with the Syrians. According to statements by Saguy in a book he had published in Hebrew (*The Hand that Froze*) and in several media appearances, borne out by one of those involved in the talks in a conversation with me, both sides drew their proposed borders on maps. Clauses were formulated pertaining to security arrangements, open trade, and normalization of relations, including the exchange of ambassadors. The Syrians agreed to the positioning of an early warning station on their territory, atop Mount Hermon. U.S. intelligence would keep an eye on Syrian military movements. Simultaneously, in Israel detailed plans were drawn up for the resettlement of the evacuees from the Golan Heights, mainly in the Galilee. Barak took part in meetings where plans for the payment of compensation to these displaced settlers were discussed.

The two countries exchanged draft treaties drawn up by the State Department's deputy legal adviser, Jonathan B. Schwartz. All parties agreed on most matters. The few clauses that remained unapproved were to be discussed at the Shepherdstown summit. Before Barak set out for the meeting, Israeli military intelligence reported that the Syrian president had given his foreign minister a mandate to sign.

In effect, what was on the table was an almost complete treaty, and even the gap on the issue of border demarcation on the north eastern shore of the Sea of Galilee was not too wide for Barak and al-Sharaa to bridge. Israel had, after all, informed the Syrians that it was prepared to go back to the pre–Six-Day War line, and Syria had declared that in exchange, it would agree to security arrangements and the establishment of full peace. Even if Israel had been compelled to give up the short stretch of lakefront that the Syrians were demanding, it was clear that its citizens and tourists would still have been able to enjoy most of the shores and the lake itself, because almost the entire circumference of the lake and its waters are inside the Green Line and belong to Israel.

In the end, at what was to have been the decisive meeting, Barak refused to discuss the two pending issues. Al-Sharaa was surprised and interpreted the refusal as an act of deception. Saguy quoted al-Sharaa as telling Barak, "You said we would discuss borders and water here. That is what I relayed to my president, and it hasn't happened. What shall I tell him now, that you deceived me?"

Barak explained that he had political constraints, and he had to examine the issues further. Al-Sharaa asked, "Who is left for you to consult? You have your best experts here.[2] You are a military man. Shahak [Amnon Lipkin-Shahak, a member of the Israeli team] was chief of staff. Saguy was head of military intelligence. Who else do you need?"

Not only al-Sharaa was disappointed. So was the host, Clinton. Saguy was highly critical of Barak: "We were very close to reaching a peace settlement with Syria, closer than ever, it would have happened if we kept our promises to ourselves, the Americans and the Syrians." Saguy thought that Barak "caught cold feet," and he called Barak's refusal to carry the negotiations through "a missed opportunity of profound historical significance." In his opinion, for some of the Israelis, "seeing the Syrians dipping their feet in the Kinneret (Sea of Galilee)" would have been like "a harsh blow to the national honor. . . . What we had there was a matter of ethos, of wounded pride."

Is Israel forgoing a strategic agreement of untold importance for the sake of a few hectares of land? Clinton probably would not have invited the sides to meet at Shepherdstown if he had not been convinced that the common denominator achieved at earlier meetings ensured a positive outcome to the talks. And if Barak had misgivings, why did he agree to go to the summit? He has never given a satisfactory answer to Israelis.

As mentioned, I have spoken to a member of the Israeli team who accompanied Barak at the talks, and whose identity I am not free to reveal. He told me, "True, al-Sharaa refused to shake Barak's hand when they met, but the talks were good, and the Syrian came with a mandate to reach an agreement. President Assad wanted an agreement." He added that some of the Israeli team felt that they were witnessing a historic act and were partners to a strategic change of direction. Barak did not share his misgivings with them. Most of the time they rested, took walks, and exercised. Barak never explained to my source why he refused to sign.

And so, it is strange that ten years later, in February 2010, Ehud Barak, now defense minister in the Netanyahu government, in a speech to the Israel Defense Forces senior officers corps, made the following declaration: "In the absence of a settlement with Syria, we are liable to get into a violent confrontation with that country that could turn into an all-out war." Furthermore, he observed, "As is known to happen in the reality of the Middle East, straight after such a war we will sit down to negotiate and we will discuss precisely the same things that we have already been discussing with the Syrians for fifteen years."

Indeed, the blunder of not resuming negotiations with Syria could cost Israel dearly. If Syria attacks Israel at some future date with the goal of retaking the Golan Heights, this would be a war that Israel could have averted, just as in the early 1970s, if Golda Meir's government had accepted the Egyptian president's invitation to begin negotiations, the lives of the thousands of the dead who fell on both sides in the Yom Kippur War would have been spared.

In the course of the last decade, Israel's defense establishments, including the army intelligence corps' chiefs, consistently advised the governing politicians to exchange the entire Golan Heights for a peace treaty with Syria. The Council for Peace and Security—a voluntary Israeli association of about one thousand retired high-ranking army officers, ex-Mossad senior agents, and retired top-level diplomats has provided the same professional advice to the government. "Peace with Syria is a strategic necessity," this group of defense experts keeps stating.

Moreover, the military intelligence annual appraisal for 2012 (which was presented to Netanyahu's cabinet on November 2011) includes a prognostication that Assad's fall might increase the prospect for Israel to negotiate a political agreement with his successor.

21

The Next Cycle

SYRIA IS UNDER siege from within, Iran is under heavy economic pressure from the outside, and Hezbollah is rapidly losing ground not only with the Shi'ites in Lebanon but across the entire Middle East. Once, Hassan Nasrallah was worshiped by the masses. Today, from Morocco to Yemen, millions of Muslims swear at him. One day Nasrallah denies rumors that his militia's fighters help Assad's army suppress Syrian demonstrators, and the next day he declares his support for Assad's regime and ignores the very existence of a revolt in Syria.

Most of the experts and analysts refuse to accept that Hezbollah's tumble is not a consequence of the uprising in Syria, but it actually began six years ago, in the summer of 2006, when the Second Lebanon War ended. Furthermore, the conventional assumption that Israel's security interest was harmed by that war is not correct, but the opposite is true: the results of the war bolstered Israel's deterrent power, and it was Hezbollah and Iran that were substantially harmed. That second war that Israel had waged in Lebanon foreshadowed the current events.

True, on the Israeli side there were a considerable number of snags, both in the conduct of the war by the cabinet, the preparations for war, and the military actions themselves, but nevertheless, from the strategic point of view, the final outcome was favorable to Israel.

The war broke out after two Israeli soldiers were abducted by a Hezbollah squad that crossed the border with Lebanon and ambushed a routine IDF patrol. It happened soon after daybreak on July 12, 2006. The ambush took the patrol by surprise, and after a brief exchange of fire, the militiamen killed three soldiers, injured two, and captured two and took them into Lebanese territory. Five more Israeli soldiers were killed the same morning in a failed rescue attempt.

Israel saw the abduction as a casus belli and immediately attacked targets in Lebanon with great force, using both artillery and airplanes. Hezbollah responded by bombarding northern Israel with Katyusha rockets and missiles. The Israeli government ordered the mobilization of several tens of thousands of reserve troops and set the aims of the war for the IDF: the release of the abducted soldiers, destruction of Hezbollah's military infrastructure and missile stockpiles, and the removal of its militiamen from the border area. The political aim was defined as getting the Lebanese army and a UN force to deploy in South Lebanon to keep Hezbollah out.

I am convinced that when the news of the successful ambush reached the Iranian leaders, they roundly cursed Nasrallah. The charismatic and arrogant Hezbollah leader had ordered the operation out of a desire to exchange the abducted soldiers for Lebanese citizens who had been sentenced to long jail terms in Israel for carrying out acts of terrorism,[1] and the mullahs in Tehran were certainly happy about that. But from the standpoint of Iranian strategic interests, the outcome of this provocation of Hezbollah was calamitous because it prematurely exposed to the eyes of the world the eastern flank of the front that Iran had built up in advance of the decisive battle over the nuclear option that it was developing. This was not the way that Tehran had planned its campaign. The thousands of missiles that Hezbollah had deployed with funding and training from Iran, in stockpiles in Shi'ite villages, and in underground bunkers and dugouts in open areas, were meant to be fired as part of a response to a scenario in which the United States or Israel, or both together, would attack its nuclear installations. In anticipation of such an attack, Iran had prepared a massive assault on American interests across a broad front in the Middle East, including Israel, and had invested hundreds of millions of dollars in it. This Iranian deployment in South Lebanon was meant to be hidden until the order was given, but from the time that Nasrallah gave in to the temptation and provoked Israel, the sophisticated network was exposed and severely damaged.

Of course, the Iranian involvement in Lebanon and the assistance Tehran gave Hezbollah were known to the intelligence agencies of the countries involved in the struggles of the Middle East, but their knowledge was general, and most of the details remained secret. Israeli intelligence lacked specific information on the location of most of the short-range rockets and the methods of firing them.

Aside from Israel, under whose very nose this military buildup had taken place, those most taken aback by its existence were the moderate Arab countries. The intelligence agencies of Saudi Arabia and Egypt were alarmed when it became clear to them how far westward and to what extent the Iranian Revolutionary Guard had penetrated. Iran had identified in Lebanon's Shi'ite population the weakest link in the Arab world and had exploited the lack of alertness among the Sunni communities in order to place a center of power at the heart of the Arabs' sphere of influence, right on the shores of the Mediterranean Sea.

The war that Nasrallah forced on Israel had therefore speeded up the formation of a moderate Arab front in the Middle East. It turned out that the interest of Saudi Arabia, Egypt, the Gulf emirates, and the Kingdom of Jordan was identical to the Israeli interest: the negation of Iran's nuclear capability, in order to stop it from achieving hegemony over the region. This was the most striking feature of the diplomatic sphere in the course of the fighting: the public reservations expressed by the moderate Arab states about Hezbollah's warlike initiative against Israel. Arab states had never denounced a military action against Israel by a Muslim entity since the Jewish state was established, and their actions attested to the extent to which the Arab states felt threatened by Iran's growing power and the spread of its influence.

This reality was projected by the Saudi king Abdullah urging the United States to demolish Iran's nuclear program. According to a U.S. State Department cable released by WikiLeaks, during a conversation with an American diplomat in Riyadh, on April 2008, Saudi ambassador to Washington Adel Al-Jubeir "recalled the King's frequent exhortations to the U.S. to attack Iran and so put an end to its nuclear weapons program." The Saudi ambassador added: "He [the King] told you to cut off the head of the snake."

The war in Lebanon lasted 34 days, and most experts (along with most Israelis) agreed it ended indecisively. Lebanon suffered 1,191 fatal casualties compared to Israel's 163 and also sustained enormous destruction. The damage in north Israel was considerable, but not as severe. Yet when the ceasefire was reached, Nasrallah declared a "divine victory," and many experts and columnists around the world seemed to accept it. Many high-ranking Israeli politicians and many of the regular and reserve officers and soldiers who were involved in the war were also confused by the outcome of the war.

But looking at the outcome with six years of hindsight shows that a degree of perspective is necessary. In actuality, Hezbollah declared a victory that had not happened, and the Israelis bemoaned a defeat that had not happened.

For one thing, Israel has deterred Hezbollah for six years. The border has been quiet, and Nasrallah's militia has not dared to act provocatively. Nasrallah himself is still holed up in his bunker, afraid of moving around freely even in areas exclusively controlled by his organization in the Shi'ite neighborhoods of Beirut. At Hezbollah rallies, he appears only on large screens, making speeches relayed from his hiding place. In October 2010, when Ahmadinejad visited Lebanon, Nasrallah did not dare to appear in public at his side.

Second, at Israel's insistence, the Lebanese Army and units of the United Nations Interim Force in Lebanon (UNIFIL) were deployed in Southern Lebanon and to a certain degree have managed to keep the Shi'ite militia away from the border with Israel.

Third, and most importantly, Israel learned the lessons of the war and drew the proper conclusions. The minister of defense and the chief of staff were ousted; senior officers of the Northern Command were replaced and the logistical problems solved; and military intelligence has improved its pinpoint knowledge of the targets in Lebanon.

True, with the generous assistance of Iran and Syria, Hezbollah has continued to arm itself. According to Israeli military intelligence estimates, in late 2011 the organization had more missiles at its disposal than it did before the 2006 war, but this is something that Israel cannot prevent. The main point is that in the wake of the Second Lebanon War, Iran has lost the element of surprise. Israel knows exactly what it can expect and what it should prepare for.

Iran's massive military involvement in Lebanon reflects the aspiration to spread the Shi'ite Islamic revolution, but it is not enough to constitute a threat to Israel's existence. The fate of the Iranian nuclear project and the fate of the revolution will not be decided in Lebanon or in a confrontation between Israel and Hezbollah, but rather on the international game board, and here, too, the dice are weighed in Israel's favor. The chain of linked internal events accumulating during the last two years—the enfeeblement of the alliance with Syria and the Hezbollah as a consequence of Syria's prolonged internal conflict, the effects of the economic sanctions imposed by the West on Iran, the brutal political struggles in the regime's highest echelons, the revelations of huge corruption affairs, and the undermining of the legitimacy of the regime by the Green opposition—are constantly undermining Iran's political stability.

The broad front that the free world has formed against the ayatollahs' regime strengthens my opinion that Iran is on the verge of a new historical cycle. The failure of the Iranian Islamic revolution is likely to occur in parallel with the culmination of negotiations between Israel and the Arabs. When the Shi'ite eruption that Iran has led dies down, so will the need of the Sunnis, and chiefly the Saudi Wahhabis, to struggle for the primacy of their legacy. Then, each one of the Arab countries would be able to manage its own crisis. The current reactionary cycle, which began in 1979 with the return of Ayatollah Khomeini to Iran from Paris and reached its peak with the terrorist attacks that the Saudi Osama bin Laden launched on September 11, 2001, is about to end. The Arab Spring that began in December 2010 in Tunisia symbolizes a new dawn for the Muslim world. We have seen the start of an internal rectification process, tikkun ("repair" in Hebrew). Kabbalah teaches us that tikkun requires a toll. It could be high, sometimes bloody and agonizing. It could last for as long as a decade or two. In the case of South Africa, the exchange of apartheid for a nonracial democracy was done smoothly, thanks in part to Nelson Mandela's amazing character. Muslims need their Nelson Mandela. I truly believe that when the savior appears, there is a good chance that from the absolute evil of indiscriminate suicide terrorism and the current revolutionary chaos, the buds of salvation may yet spring.

22

Critical Mass

WHEN DOES A mass become critical? In physics, the answer is clear: When the necessary amount of fissile material (about 3.6 kilograms of uranium 235) accumulates and an atom is split, a chain reaction sets in, and when it is over, there is an explosion.[1] In the social sphere too, when a mass of frustration and anger builds up because of oppression or enslavement, or alternatively a mass of love and fraternity is formed because of feelings of satisfaction and contentment, or even a mass of disappointment, of mental anguish, or of sadness—when any such mass crosses the critical border, no opposing force is capable of withstanding its expansion, and it creates a consensus on the formation of a new reality that changes the way the world is ordered.

How do we know when the mass is critical? It is hardly possible to calculate at any given moment how much of a general consensus has accumulated in society and whether it is sufficient to produce a social or political upheaval. To do this, public opinion surveys are not adequate, and what is needed is an examination of complex processes, measurement of inclinations and emotions, and understanding of the way in which power is divided among the groups that are active in the community and the communications between them. Sometimes, a dramatic action by individuals could cause the rapid accumulation of a critical mass—like the Tunisian revolution had sparked the Arab Spring when twenty-six-year-old fruit seller Mohamed Bouazizi set himself on fire in protest against harassment by local authorities—but their potential for influencing general consensuses also cannot be measured, and this is why political and social upheavals usually come as a surprise; they are noticed only after society has already absorbed them and the new reality has become a fact.

With the benefit of hindsight, the experts will usually say that the writing was on the wall. But in real time, the directors of the huge Western intelligence apparatus, with their mega computers and tens of thousands of sophisticated analysts, time and again are amazed and confused as masses become critical, bursting the most influential (and most expected, post factum of course) events into existence: Egypt's and Syria's armies storming Israel on October 6, 1973; the Soviet Empire's collapse; Berlin Wall's knocking down; the three hijacked passenger planes, flown into the most emblematic American institutions on September 11; and many other powerful upheavals.

I have been fortunate enough to be able to closely observe several political and social upheavals that took place in the last quarter of the twentieth century. I was a student in California in the late 1960s, and I mentioned previously my participation in some of the largest demonstrations against the war in Vietnam. I served as a foreign correspondent based in West Germany in the second half of the 1970s, when urban terror was buffeting a tense and anxious society that was constantly reminded of how the Nazis had seized control of the country. I was stationed in Moscow when the Soviet Union began its collapse, starting on the night of August 21 and the morning of August 22, 1991, at the climax of the attempted rebellion that some of the leaders of the state launched against their president, Mikhail Gorbachev. It was an astounding spectacle. Tens of thousands of Muscovites barricaded themselves around the parliament building and courageously faced up to the Tamanskaya armored brigade that surrounded the area. Hearts were pounding with emotion that night because no one knew whether the plotters would order the tanks to open fire on the civilians or whether the tank crew would obey such an order. But when the sun came up, it became clear that the tyrants had lost the power that their positions had given them and the ability to impose their will, and at the same time the Soviet citizens had lost their fear of their rulers. The plotters had to surrender and were arrested. One may say that those were the hours when the Soviet Union crumbled, but it is clear that it actually collapsed long before. However, only when that night's confrontation in Moscow was over did it emerge that the mass of popular opposition had accumulated to the critical point. In reality, the communist dictatorship had been dying for a long time before that. When did the oligarchy begin losing its ability to maintain control over the empire? As long as it controlled the communications media, putting its own spin on everything, describing capitalist society as decadent and flawed, the common citizens were not able to make comparisons. The communist lie started being exposed when communications satellites began relaying images from the West. In the early 1960s, Nikita Khrushchev was compelled to admit to Stalin's crimes. In the 1970s, Leonid Brezhnev held on to power until his last days. In the mid-1980s, Gorbachev was forced to give in. The Old Guard made a pathetic attempt to turn the wheel of history backward—the putsch attempt that I witnessed in August 1991—but the mass of opposition was already critical by then.

I am prepared to take the risk of stating that a critical mass of sane citizens has already formed among Israelis and Palestinians and has determined that there must be a compromise solution to the conflict. This is the good news. The fanatics have lost, although they are not yet aware of it, and those holding the reins of government in Jerusalem are also still living in a bygone period.

23

Apology and Compensation

ONE CANNOT SAY that the Jewish public in Israel is prepared to acknowledge its responsibility for the enormous price that the Palestinians have had to pay for the consummation of the Zionist goal of establishing a Jewish state in the Middle East. Assimilating and internalizing the heavy onus is no mere technical process. Not only individuals but communities and states have to undergo a complex process of soul searching and self-repair in order to reach a stage where they will be ready to admit that they are responsible for unjust acts. But when the political power of messianic circles and the settlers in Israeli society weakens, willingness to conduct a moral stock-taking will grow, and the ethical significance of what occurred in the occupied territories after 1967 will be internalized, errors will be admitted, and sins and evil acts atoned for.

Reducing the harm sustained by the Palestinians must be implemented in four areas:

First, Israel has to admit that Zionism is responsible for a considerable part of the injustice suffered by the Palestinians during the twentieth century and to issue an official apology.

Second, the territory controlled by the Jews since the end of the 1948–1949 war must be completely separated from the West Bank that was conquered in 1967.

Before 1949, the Jewish takeover of the western part of Palestine was achieved with the backing of most of the world's states (in particular on the strength of the UN partition resolution of November 29, 1947) and in the wake of the war that the Arabs forced on the Jews. From the ethical point of view, and on the basis of the population exchanges that occurred during the 1948–1949 war and in its immediate aftermath, as previously described, there is a great deal of logic in establishing the Green Line for the State of Israel in the 1949 Armistice Agreements. This situation would not be an extreme departure from similar arrangements for self-determination and population exchanges that have occurred many times in world history.

In contrast, the West Bank, which was conquered in a war between two neighboring states, and consequently the world does not recognize Israel's right to settle Jews there, will be returned to its indigenous inhabitants and declared an independent Palestinian state. The Arabs will waive the right of return of the refugees, and the Jews will surrender the land they conquered in 1967. This would be a compromise that truly reflects the aspirations of the founding fathers of the Israeli nation. On May 14, 1948, if they had been told that this would be the settlement with the Arab world, they would have jumped for joy and danced in the streets.

Third, the 1948 refugees must be given compensation for the property they were forced to leave behind in Israeli territory when they were driven out or fled to neighboring lands. An international commission will set the compensation arrangements.

Fourth, in the light of the continual and severe damage that Zionism has caused the Palestinians, it is clear that Israel has to manifestly help the Palestinian state consolidate itself. Beyond the essential individual compensations for the refugees' property, Israel should make up for the suffering of West Bank and Gaza Strip Palestinians during the long period of the occupation. One reasonable possibility is for Israel to pay the new Palestinian State a fair compensatory amount for a prolonged period, say 2 percent of Israel's gross national product (GNP) each year for fifty years.

In the past generation, Israel has developed and accumulated wealth to the extent that today it is one of the top thirty countries in terms of per capita GNP. In 2011, Israel's GNP totaled some $240 billion, so the compensation would amount to $4.8 billion a year. Analysts have evaluated the annual GNP of the PA in 2011 at approximately $14 billion, so we are speaking of an annual supplement of around one-third of the present value of the Palestinian GNP. According to this calculation, the total compensation to the Palestinians based on Israel's 2011 GNP would come to around $240 billion. This amount is approximately equal to the output that all the Israelis alive today produce in one year of work, and it is therefore possible to say that each Israeli would be called upon to give one year of work to make up for the suffering caused to the Palestinians.

These four compromise measures on Israel's part—sincere confession, apology, personal compensation, and national compensation—will make it possible to exorcise some of the evil spirits and demons that have seized control of the conflict over the years and deflected it from a pragmatic course. It will be a time for chastening, a time to discard the messianic mindset that created this inherently flawed arrangement.

In this way, the physical damage to the Palestinians will be diminished, and the Jews will have to bear the responsibility not only for the injustices caused to a large population of innocent people, but also for the fact that after 1967 they have been overbearingly arrogant and devoid of compassion and their behavior as occupiers has been shameful. Israel owes itself such reparation.

NOTES

PREFACE

1. According to the plan put forward by King Abdullah of Saudi Arabia, in exchange for an Israeli withdrawal from the territories it occupied in June 1967 in the Golan Heights, the West Bank, and East Jerusalem; the establishment of a Palestinian state; and a "just solution" to the Arab refugee problem, the Arab states would make peace with Israel. In March 2007, the plan was endorsed by a conference of the Arab League. Israel never expressed a readiness to discuss the plan, but in November 2008, in a speech in the UN General Assembly in Abdullah's presence, Israeli president Shimon Peres praised the initiative, saying:

> We cannot change the past. However, we can shape our future. This seems more feasible today in light of the Saudi proposal which evolved into an Arab peace initiative. The initiative's portrayal of our region's future provides hope to the people and inspires confidence in the nations. Yes—in order to change the world we have to change ourselves. The Arab peace initiative states that "a military solution to the conflict will not achieve peace or provide security for the parties." Israel agrees with that assumption. Further on, the initiative states that "a just and comprehensive peace in the Middle East is the strategic option of the Arab countries." This is Israel's strategy as well. It continues that its goals are to "consider the Arab-Israeli conflict ended, and enter into a peace agreement with Israel, and provide security for all the states in the region. Establish normal relations with Israel in the context of comprehensive peace. Stop the further shedding of blood, enabling the Arab countries and Israel to live in peace and good neighborliness, and provide future generations with security, stability and prosperity." These expressions in the Arab peace initiative are inspirational and promising—a serious opening for real progress.

2. The other major parties in the current Knesset are Yisrael Beytenu ("Israel our Homeland") a far-right party with fifteen seats, which is part of the government coalition; Shas, ultra-Orthodox, eleven seats, part of the coalition; Kadima, center, twenty-eight seats, leading the opposition to the government; and Labor, left, eight seats, part of the opposition. Eight other smaller parties are also represented in the legislature, among them three parties representing the Israeli Arabs minority with eleven seats together. The largest party, Kadima ("forward" in Hebrew), was formed in 2005 by then prime minister Ariel Sharon, who quit the Likud party with a group of parliament members and created a new centrist party with a mission of disengaging from the Gaza Strip as part of a wider plan for compromising with the Palestinians on West Bank territories. Kadima seized Labor's seniority position at the center-left political arena.
3. During the twenties, Israel's creator, David Ben-Gurion, urged his comrades to display solidarity with the Arab peasant: "We have not come here to steal a country," Ben-Gurion said, "but to build it and revive it"—for the Arabs as well as the Jews. This was Zionism's moral justification. The Arabs "should understand this," primarily because "they are incapable of building the country themselves," and secondly because "they aren't strong enough to eject us." In a 1920 article titled "On the Arab Peasant and in His Land," Ben-Gurion wrote, "The encounter between the Hebrew elite and the Arab laborer should be an encounter of working comrades," in phraseology reminiscent of a Russian revolutionary. He wrote: "Only between two free national groups of workers, each of which can stand on its own, will it be possible to establish the harmonious and comradely life which we must place at the foundation of our settlement enterprise in the Land." According to this concept, Ben-Gurion expected two societies to develop in parallel in Palestine, each helping the other. Characteristically, he prepared detailed plans for achieving economic and agricultural cooperation, and he expounded on them to both Jews and Arabs. "The Land of Israel will be for both the Hebrew nation and the Arabs who live in it," he wrote in another article, "The Hebrew Worker and the Arab," in 1926. Three years later, following the August 1929 Palestinian riots, the first significant anti-Jewish outbreak initiated by the national Palestinian movement in which hundreds of Jews and Arabs were killed and wounded, Ben-Gurion discarded his romantic view of the Arabs and adopted a pragmatic realism: two national liberation movements were fighting for the same country.
4. In the middle of the twenties, a small and elitist association, Brit Shalom (the Peace League), was established by the philosopher Martin Buber;

Hadassah founder Henrietta Szold; the kabbalah researcher Gershom Scholem; the first president of the Hebrew University of Jerusalem, Yehuda Leib Magnes; and Joshua Radler Feldman (whose pen name was Rabi Benjamin and who was my father's uncle). It advocated the establishment of a joint Jewish-Arab government in a binational state in Palestine. But Ben-Gurion mocked the naïveté of the Brit Shalom circle and called its members "rootless," meaning they had lost their fundamental national consciousness.

1. HISTORICAL CORRECTION

1. According to the UN, the number of registered Palestine refugees grew from about 750,000 in 1949 to 5 million today. They live in 58 recognized refugee camps in Jordan, Lebanon, Syria, the Gaza Strip, and the West Bank, including East Jerusalem.
2. The following are the first six sentences of the Declaration of the Establishment of the State of Israel of May 14, 1948: "The Land of Israel was the birthplace of the Jewish people. Here their spiritual, religious and political identity was shaped. Here they first attained to statehood, created cultural values of national and universal significance and gave to the world the eternal Book of Books. After being forcibly exiled from their land, the people kept faith with it throughout their Dispersion and never ceased to pray and hope for their return to it and for the restoration in it of their political freedom. Impelled by this historic and traditional attachment, Jews strove in every successive generation to re-establish themselves in their ancient homeland. In recent decades they returned in their masses."
3. Until World War I, Palestine was part of the Ottoman Empire. In 1917 the British-led Egyptian Expeditionary Force occupied Palestine, and between 1920 and 1948 Great Britain administered it with a mandate from first the League of Nations and then the United Nations. In early 1947, Britain announced its desire to terminate the mandate, and on November 29th of that year, the UN General Assembly confirmed a plan to partition the territory into separate Jewish and Arab states. The Jewish state was to receive 56 percent of Mandatory Palestine and the Arab state 43 percent. (Jerusalem, the other 1 percent of the territory, was declared international and placed under a special international regime, administered by the UN.) On May 14, 1948, the same day that the State of Israel was declared, the Arab League launched an attack on the new Israeli state. At the end of the war, the territorial division was different from the UN Partition Plan. In addition to the partitioned area, Israel captured and incorporated a further

22 percent of the Mandate territory; the Kingdom of Jordan annexed the West Bank, incorporating 21 percent of the Mandate territory; and Egypt controlled the Gaza Strip, which holds 1.4 percent of the Mandate territory.

4. Efraim Karsh, a professor of Middle East and Mediterranean studies at King's College and the author of *Palestine Betrayed*, wrote that between 1948 and 1967, "when Egypt and Jordan ruled the Palestinians of the Gaza Strip and the West Bank, the Arab states failed to put these populations on the road to statehood." See Karsh, "The Palestinians Alone," *New York Times,* August 1, 2010.
5. The following is Article 3 of Khartoum Resolutions: "The Arab Heads of State have agreed to unite their political efforts at the international and diplomatic level to eliminate the effects of the aggression and to ensure the withdrawal of the aggressive Israeli forces from the Arab lands which have been occupied since the aggression of June 5. This will be done within the framework of the main principles by which the Arab States abide, namely, no peace with Israel, no recognition of Israel, no negotiations with it, and insistence on the rights of the Palestinian people in their own country."
6. In 1964, when it was established, the PLO proclaimed its wish to establish an independent Palestine state in the whole territory that was governed till 1948 by the British Mandate, meaning the territory of the State of Israel, the West Bank, and Gaza Strip.
7. A small Jewish population inhabited the Holy Land all along history. Permanent Jewish communities existed in Jerusalem, Tiberias, Safed, and Hebron. According to Ottoman records, around 1880, in the area that comprises today's Israel, the West Bank, and the Gaza Strip, there was a population of about half a million Arabs alongside approximately 20,000 Jews. The first wave of Zionist immigration began in 1882 as Jews fled pogroms in Eastern Europe. Around the outbreak of World War I, the population of Jews in Palestine had risen to about 60,000, and the Arab population was around 700,000. The British Mandate's Palestine census of 1931 listed 760,000 Muslims, 89,000 Christians (most of them Arabs), and 175,000 Jews.
8. Although this sentence may remind the reader of New York University professor Norman Finkelstein's observations in his 2003 book *The Holocaust Industry: Reflections on the Exploitation of Jewish Suffering,* I want to make clear my disapproval of Finkelstein's allegation that the Holocaust has become the Israelis' chief ideological justification for the oppression of the Palestinian people.
9. To understand the reality that prevailed in Europe at the end of World War II, I recommend reading the description of population transfers and ethnic

cleansings that occurred then in the first chapter of Tony Judt's book *Postwar: A History of Europe since 1945.*

10. In 1951 the UN Conciliation Commission for Palestine estimated that the number of Palestinian refugees was 711,000. Four hundred Arab villages were left empty, and after the war ended, most were demolished by Israel. Only about 170,000 Arabs stayed in Israel and became citizens.
11. A few examples: In the 1830s, the United States relocated many Indian tribes and groups living east of the Mississippi River in so-called Indian Territory in the west. Stalin deported more than 1.5 million people to Siberia and the Central Asian republics from the European parts of the Soviet Union. Following World War II, 88,000 Romanians were moved from Bulgaria to Romania, and 65,000 Bulgarians were moved to Romania. Also following the World War II, 2.1 million Poles who were living east of the newly established Poland-Soviet border were deported to Poland, and 450,000 Soviet Ukrainians were moved to the opposite side.
12. Following World War II, the United States consolidated the hold of American companies on Saudi Arabia's oil industry, and the Saudis granted the Americans the right to build an airbase in Dhahran, the oil area. Oil started flowing from Saudi Arabia immediately after the war, as the U.S. role in the region grew.
13. Over one million Greeks and half a million Turks were moved from one side of the international border to the other.
14. More than 6 million Muslims moved from present-day India to present-day Pakistan, and more than 5 million Hindus moved from Pakistan to India.

2. WITHOUT COMPASSION

1. One of the positive results of the Jewish return to the Holy Land was the Faisal-Weizmann Agreement signed on January 3, 1919, by Emir Faisal, the future king of Iraq, and Chaim Weizmann, the head of the Zionist Movement. This short-lived agreement was part of the post–World War I Paris Peace Conference. Both parties committed themselves for Arab and Jewish in developing a Jewish homeland in Palestine and an Arab nation in a large part of the Middle East; carrying out the Balfour Declaration of 1917; and encouraging immigration of Jews into Palestine on a large scale while protecting the rights of the Arab peasants and tenant farmers. The Muslim Holy Places were to be under Muslim control. The Zionist movement undertook to help the Arab residents of Palestine and the future Arab state "develop their natural resources and establish a developing economy."

2. Breaking the Silence is a nonprofit organization established in 2004 by ex-soldiers with the aim of disseminating information about the activities of the army and the settlers in the occupied territories. They collect statements made by soldiers and distribute them to the media for publication.
3. Arab permanent residents are entitled to receive Israeli citizenship if they swear allegiance to the state, give up foreign citizenships, and demonstrate a minimal knowledge of Hebrew. The vast majority of the East Jerusalemites have refrained from applying for citizenship. Those who have obtain "blue" ID cards that enable them to move freely anywhere in Israel, a right that some have used to carry out terror attacks inside Israel. Noncitizens need special permits to travel out.
4. Since the Arabs constitute about a third of the population of Jerusalem, if they organized for massive participation in the elections, they could take over key positions in the city government and perhaps even get an Arab mayor elected.
5. The major East Jerusalem settlement organizations, including Elad and Ateret Cohanim, have American auxiliaries that accept tax-deductible donations. In January 2010, a few weeks after President Obama issued a statement condemning new Israeli construction in East Jerusalem, Israeli authorities approved a new Jewish settlement on the campus of an American-funded yeshiva in East Jerusalem called Beit Orot. The group constructing the new settlement is a subsidiary of the previously mentioned Elad, a settlement organization that received $2.7 million in 2007 from its tax-exempt American affiliate. In 2010, a *New York Times* investigation revealed that since 2000, at least forty American organizations have donated more than $200 million for Jewish settlement in the West Bank and East Jerusalem.

3. THE MESSIAH IS BACK

1. Prominent among the settlers movement's opponents was the late Israeli philosopher Yeshayahu Leibowitz, who forewarned that the occupation will be "as harmful for the nation as a malignant growth."

4. THE ORIGINAL SIN

1. With one significant difference: the American Revolution's cornerstone was the principle of a free market, while the Zionist revolution's basic doctrine was socialistic. It began slowly changing into a free market structure only during the last quarter of the last century.

2. The Central Bureau of Statistics examined the segmentation of the Jewish population according to attitude toward religious practice: 44 percent are secular, 27 percent are traditional but not religious, 12 percent are traditional-religious, 9 percent are definitely religious, and 8 percent are ultra-Orthodox (Haredim). The survey was done in 2004, and because the procreation rate of the ultra-Orthodox and religious groups has been higher than in the nonreligious, it is reasonable to believe that the current percentage of the religious and ultra-Orthodox in the population is higher by 1 to 2 percent at the expense of nonreligious groups. My assumption is that today the Jewish population is segmented roughly as follows: 40 percent secular; 30 percent traditional but not religious, 20 percent traditional-religious and definitely religious, and 10 percent ultra-Orthodox. The more religious one is, the less he or she will agree to exchange territories for peace. Among secular and traditional, 70 percent are pro-peace. Among religious and ultra–Orthodox, 70 percent are pro-territories. Adding these suppositions provides a rough conclusion that currently around 70 percent are pro-peace and approximately 30 percent are pro-territories.
3. In the United States, the ultra-Orthodox account for about 9 percent of the Jewish community. Unlike the Israeli Haredim, the American ultra-Orthodox work for their living, as there is no external factor that would provide a livelihood for them, and they are committed by oath to be loyal to the U.S. Constitution.
4. The Haredim are obligated by God's instruction to Adam and Eve, "Be fruitful and multiply and fill the earth" (Genesis 1:28), and according to their interpretation of it, women have to conceive as often as they can. Married couples are barred from using contraceptives, and the average number of children in a Haredi family is very high. Families with at least ten children are common.

5. "JEWISH AND DEMOCRATIC" OR "STATE OF ALL ITS CITIZENS"

1. As of August 2012, Israel has a population of approximately 7.94 million inhabitants, and about 1.64 million of them are Arabs.
2. Currently, out of 120 members of the Knesset, 11 are Arabs, who represent 4 Arab parties.
3. A slight change in this matter is noticeable. Prominent companies have displayed readiness to change their employment policies and to adopt a more multicultural position. Leading this trend are multinational corporations active in Israel, including Indigo, HP, Matrix, IBM, Intel, and SAP.

4. Christian Arabs—a small minority of around 130,000 people comprising 9 percent of Israel's Arab community—enjoy as high per capita GDP standards as the Jewish population.
5. Nevertheless, the Arab birthrate is in steady decline. In 1965 Arab women had an average of 8.5 births, as compared to 3.6 in 2008.
6. A demographic forecast released by the government's Central Bureau of Statistics in February 2010 predicted that by 2030, the number of Arabs is expected to reach 2.4 million, or 24 percent of the total population.
7. The term "sane secular" refers to those Israelis who are against the establishment of a theocracy and who do not believe that the borders of the state must match with biblical precedents but should be determined according to today's demographic reality. There is a minority of religious people (Modern Orthodox) and even some ultra-Orthodox Israelis whose conduct and attitudes conform with modern, western, democratic patterns and who fall into this "sane secular" category, just as there are many right-wing non-religious Israelis who believe in the "Whole Land of Israel" concept.

6. WAR AND PEACE

1. Henry Kissinger, *Crisis: The Anatomy of Two Foreign Policy Crises* (New York: Simon & Schuster, 2003). Kissinger relates that within a day after the war broke out, Sadat's security adviser, Muhammad Hafez Ismail, sent Kissinger a secret message through the Cairo CIA station outlining his strategic plans for the war and for the negotiations that would come in its wake. Sadat wrote to Kissinger that he did not seek to "widen the confrontation" and outlined his territories-for-peace plan, which was implemented afterward almost exactly as he planned it. Sadat's letter remains classified by the U.S. government, but Kissinger in his book outlined its main points. Unclassified State Department documents and interviews with retired Egyptian military commanders verify Kissinger's depiction.

7. "THEY HAD LEARNED NOTHING FROM HISTORY"

1. The Separation of Forces Agreement between Israel and Syria was signed on May 31, 1974. It provided for a buffer zone termed the "separation line" that was under UN control. The town of Kuneitra was given back to Syria, and its inhabitants were allowed to return. UN forces were also stationed in a number of positions that Israel had conquered on Mt. Hermon.
2. He was responding to a question asked by Hanna Zemer, the editor of *Davar*, the Labor Party's daily newspaper.

3. Among them: the poets Nathan Alterman, Haim Guri, Zrubavel Gilad, and Jacob Orland; authors Haim Hazaz, Moshe Shamir, and Yehuda Burla; the physicist Yuval Ne'eman; Labor Movement ideologists Yitzhak Tabenkin, Rachel Yanait Ben-Zvi (wife of the second Israeli president, Yitzhak Ben-Zvi), Zvi Shiloach, and Eliezer Livne; and Zivia Lubetkin and Yitzhak "Antek" Zuckerman from kibbutz Lohamei Haghetaot. (Both took part in the Warsaw Ghetto's uprising and were regarded as heroes by the Labor Movement.) Nobel laureate Shai Agnon also joined the Great Israel Movement, although he was not part of the Labor Movement, and therefore it is impossible to say that he crossed the lines to the right. In contrast, some of the Labor Movement founding fathers like David Ben-Gurion, Yitzhak Ben-Aharon, Pinhas Lavon, Yaakov Hazan, and Arie "Lova" Eliav had recommended an Israeli unilateral retreat from the West Bank to what they called a "security border."
4. Regarding the "triple cord," see my analysis of the secular messianic perception of right wing leaders like Netanyahu in chapter 13.
5. The Israeli daily *Maariv*, June 16, 1967.
6. The nationalist Revisionist faction was founded by Ze'ev Jabotinsky in 1925 and defined its territorial aspirations in the slogan coined in the lyrics of a poem written by Jabotinsky himself: "Two Banks has the Jordan (river)—this is ours and, that is as well." It implies the goal of achieving control over not only western Palestine but also over Transjordan, granted by Great Britain to the Hashemite dynasty, which established there today's Kingdom of Jordan. The revisionists advocated "Zionist activism" and were the chief ideological competitors to the dominant socialists, led by Ben-Gurion. In 1931, when the socialist majority in the Zionist Congress refused to debate Jabotinsky's demand to declare that the aim of Zionism was the "establishment of an independent Jewish state in the Land of Israel," the Revisionist faction left the Zionist Movement and set up its own parallel body, which was considered by the majority in the *yishuv* (the body of Jewish residents in Palestine) outside the mainstream. During the 1930s and 1940s, their underground paramilitary group, the Irgun, conducted an armed struggle against the British Mandate authorities and Arab paramilitary groups. The Revisionist faction opposed the partition plan, and their leaders refrained from signing Israel's Declaration of Independence (although three moderate Revisionists did sign it).
7. Tuchman offers three tests for historical folly: first, when the outcome of the folly is evident at the time it is committed and not afterward; second, when it's clear there was an alternative that was not tried; and third, when the mistake is not committed by a lone ruler, but collectively, and it remains in effect for an extended period, at least one generation. All these

conditions exist in Israel's policy toward the occupied territories. Among the variety of acts of folly that Tuchman enumerates and analyzes, there are at least two with elements similar to Israel's errors in the territories: the Trojan Horse and the American policy in Vietnam.

8. IMPOTENT LEADERSHIP

1. Netanyahu was prime minister between 1996 and 1999; Barak, 1999–2001; Sharon, 2001–2005; Olmert, 2005–2009. Netanyahu's second term started in 2009 and will end in the beginning of 2013, following the scheduled January 22 elections.

9. SECULAR MESSIANISM

1. The occupation price has been estimated because Israel's state budget is not specifying money allocations, which are explicitly financing the settlement enterprise and the West Bank's occupation. Most of the budget invested in the settlements and occupation is hidden in other budget articles.
2. In Paris, in 1960, French president Charles de Gaulle asked his guest, Ben-Gurion, "Tell me, what are your inner most wishes, what are the borders you would like to reach for the State of Israel?" Ben-Gurion replied, "I want more Jews and no more territory." De Gaulle: "And if more Jews come to you, where will you settle them?" Ben-Gurion: "We have enough land for another five million Jews, or even more." In 1960 the number of inhabitants was 2.2 million.
3. The result of the Knesset vote on February 16, 2005, was fifty-nine for, forty against, with five abstentions.
4. More than half of the Knesset members from Netanyahu's party, Likud, would support a compromise, together with all the MKs from the Labor Party (including Barak's "Independence" group, which had broken apart from the Labor, as it would from the opposition), almost all the MKs from Kadima, all the Arab MKs, and the Meretz Party. This combination creates a majority of 65 to 70 out of 120. It is possible that they would also be joined by some moderate members of the ultra-Orthodox parties.
5. My book *Murder in the Name of God* (New York: Henry Holt, 1998, co-author Ina Freidman) describes in detail the incitement campaign that was carried out by the Right in Israel and the United States against Rabin and the Oslo Accords.
6. Their spiritual mentor, Rabbi Mordechai Eliyahu, an extremist and racist who served as a chief rabbi of Israel from 1983–1993, swore that Sharon's

"evil decree" would not be carried out and the settlements would not be evacuated. "It will surely not be," he declared, and explained, "This is both the prayer and, with God's help, a factual statement." His disciples in the settlements in Gaza believed in his power to remove the threat and they therefore refrained from getting ready to relocate. But his connection to the Holy Spirit did not prove itself, and they were all compelled to leave. The late Rabbi Eliyahu was the most influential spiritual leader of the Israeli national-religious movement.

7. Sixteen settlements in the Yamit region with a total population of twelve thousand were evacuated in April 1982.

10. THE DEMOGRAPHIC THREAT

1. Al Hourani's article was also published in *Encounter* 29, no. 5 (November 1967).
2. Ahmad Khalidi, "Thanks, But No Thanks," *The Guardian*, December 12, 2007.

11. A BULLDOZER THAT BUILT AND DESTROYED

1. Speeches and declarations by Arafat have been quoted in Israel's media, and it can be understood that the PA's chairman issued orders to prepare the uprising. Israeli officials connected the outbreak of the second intifada to the final withdrawal of Israeli forces from Lebanon in May 2000. They claimed that the leadership of the PA interpreted the withdrawal as a victory for Hezbollah and proof of Israel's vulnerability.
2. The idea of building the barrier was actually approved by the cabinet in April 2002, but its path was not set, and only four kilometers were initially built, as a trial. Sharon, right-wing politicians, and the settlers held up the planning and construction until the bloodshed caused by Palestinian suicide terrorists became so severe that there was no choice but to plan and go ahead with construction.
3. As of December 2011, about 65 percent of the barrier is complete; a further 5 percent is under construction, and 30 percent is planned but not yet constructed.
4. In an agreement on the final status, the depth of the withdrawal in the West Bank is what will determine which settlements will be evacuated. In negotiations conducted with the PA, both Barak and Olmert expressed readiness to give up 96 settlements, while the Palestinians insisted on 107. In terms of area, the difference between the two sides is not large. According to leaked reports from the negotiations, Israel apparently wants to annex 115,000

dunams, almost 29,000 acres, or some 2 percent of the area of the West Bank. The Palestinians are ready to give up 85,000 *dunams,* or 1.5 percent. Israel is ready to evacuate 70,000 settlers, and the Palestinians demand that 110,000 be evacuated, about one third of the 330,000 settlers living in the West Bank, excluding the Jewish neighborhoods in East Jerusalem.

5. The Geneva Initiative was a public initiative taken in 2003 by left-wing Israeli personages and leading Palestinians from the Fatah movement. Following serious negotiations, the initiators produced a draft of a peace agreement that recommended an end to the conflict: Palestinian recognition of the Jewish people's right to a state of its own; establishment of a demilitarized Palestinian state; an international inspection apparatus for checking compliance by both sides with their undertakings; demarcation of a final border between Palestine and Israel; division of Jerusalem with Jewish neighborhoods going to Israel and Arab ones to Palestine and Temple Mount and the Old City—except the Jewish Quarter—belonging to Palestine; and right of return of Palestinian refugees to Israeli territory only with Israel's agreement.
6. On May 16, 2008, in a speech in South Dakota, then presidential candidate Barack Obama attacked the Bush administration's Middle East moves and blamed it for Hamas's seizure of Gaza because it supported the holding of elections in the PA. Obama was responding to a speech made by Bush the previous day in the Knesset in Jerusalem in which he suggested that Obama wanted the United States to negotiate with terrorists. In fact, it was the Bush administration that complicated matters in the PA by insisting that Hamas should be allowed to participate in the elections.

12. TWO PALESTINES

1. An IMF investigation revealed that in the years 1995–2000, Arafat had transferred some $900 million in donations to the PA to his personal accounts. It is possible that some or all of the money was used to fund PA operations, bypassing the inspection procedures of the donor countries.

13. SOFTENING THE HARDEST

1. According to the Torah, Esau is the son of Rebecca and Yitzhak, twin brother to Jacob. Jewish tradition has it that each twin represents different nationalities, cultures, and faiths. Jews are descendants of Jacob, and Edomites are descendants of Esau, and from the Edomites all other nations grew. When Rebecca was pregnant with the twins, she could feel them kicking and fighting, and God told her, "The two children inside

you will become the fathers of two nations. Just like the two are fighting with each other now, the two nations will struggle with each other. One will be stronger than the other and the older, Esau, will serve the younger, Jacob." That was the beginning of Esau's (Edom's) perpetual hatred toward Jacob (Israel). Rashi, the most renowned commentator of the Old Testament and the Talmud, wrote: "It is a known fact that Esau hates Jacob" (Rashi, Genesis 33:4).

15. THE RIGHT OF RETURN

1. This ruling cannot be challenged. Decisions issued by the ECHR are binding and final.
2. In 2004, the Turkish community accepted the UN peace plan for Cyprus, which included a right of return for some Greeks to places that were taken by the Turks and compensation for the others, but the Greek community rejected it.

16. DELAYED IGNITION

1. Avigdor Evet Lieberman is the head of the ultranationalist party Yisrael Beytenu. Eli Yishai is the leader of the ultra-Orthodox Shas party. Both are Netanyahu's government coalition cornerstones.
2. Obama received 78 percent of the Jewish vote, 25 points higher than the electorate as a whole (53 percent), 53 percent higher than the white vote (43 percent), and 11 points higher than the Hispanic vote (67 percent). Only the black community vote for Obama was higher at 95 percent.
3. For details, see chapter 5 in *Murder in the Name of God.*
4. See a study by sociologists Steven Cohen and Ari Kelman from 2007. They found that American Jews' linkage to Israel drops off with each subsequent generation. Nearly 40 percent of Jews over 65 were found to be highly attached to Israel, compared with just over 20 percent of Jews under 35.
5. On this subject, read Peter Beinart, "The Failure of the American Jewish Establishment," *New York Review of Books*, May 12, 2010, http://www.nybooks.com/articles/archives/2010/jun/10/failure-american-jewish-establishment/?pagination=false.

17. A STATE OF ISOLATION

1. See Judith Butler, "No, it's not anti-semitic," *London Review of Books* 25, no. 16 (August 21, 2003), 19–21.

18. IRAN—TWO SCENARIOS, ONE REALISTIC

1. During that time, in 2008, Suleimani, using a phone text, approached the then commander of the U.S. forces in Iraq, Gen. David Petraeus, telling the general that if he wanted to discuss Iranian foreign policy he should speak with Suleimani. "General Petraeus, you should know that I, Qassem Suleimani, control the policy for Iran with respect to Iraq, Lebanon, Gaza, and Afghanistan," the text said.
2. A forty megawatt research reactor that planned to become operational in 2014.
3. "Our Mosque Madness," *New York Times*, August 18, 2010.

19. THE BOMB IS STILL IN THE BASEMENT

1. For a detailed description of how different U.S. administrations have dealt with Israel's nuclear status, see my book *The Bomb in the Basement—How Israel Went Nuclear and What That Means for the World* (New York: Simon & Schuster, 2006).
2. Paragraph VII, 7, of the final document says: "The Secretary-General of the United Nations . . . in consultation with the States of the region, will convene a conference in 2012, to be attended by all States of the Middle East, on the establishment of a Middle East zone free of nuclear weapons and all other weapons of mass destruction, on the basis of arrangements freely arrived at by the states of the region, and with the full support and engagement of the nuclear-weapon states."
3. In a letter sent on August 8, 2010, to U.S. secretary of state Hillary Rodham Clinton, the secretary general of the Arab League, Amr Moussa, asked the United States to vote at the IAEA's general assembly for the Arab motion. The same letter was sent to Belgium's foreign minister, the EU's relieving president at that time, and the foreign ministers of the permanent UN Security Council members, Russia, China, Britain, and France.
4. The Shahab class of missiles is derived from the North Korean No-dong missile. The advanced Shahab-3 is the first intermediate-range ballistic missile that Iran developed. It has a range of 2,000 kilometers and carries a heavy warhead. Its control system is able to change its trajectory several times during re-entry, although its accuracy is largely speculative. The most advanced type of Sejil is believed to be a two-stage missile carrying two engines with combined solid fuel.
5. The Arrow-3 is designed to destroy salvos of Iranian Shahab and Sejil missiles.

6. David's Sling, which is sometimes called Magic Wand, was jointly developed by Rafael Advanced Defense Systems, an Israeli armament development corporation, and the American company Raytheon, designed to intercept medium- to long-range rockets.
7. Jericho III is a three-stage solid propellant missile equipped with a single 750 kilogram nuclear warhead, or two or three lower-yield MIRV warheads. Its estimated range is 2,982 to 7,180 miles (4,800 to 11,500 kilometers).

20. POST-ASSAD

1. A short time later, in Geneva in March 2000, on behalf of Barak, Clinton tried to persuade Hafez al-Assad to surrender land on the shore of Lake Galilee, but the Syrian president refused. A few weeks later Assad died.
2. Barak was accompanied in Shepherdstown by then foreign minister David Levy; then attorney general and later Supreme Court justice Elyakim Rubinstein; and retired Chief of Staff Amnon Lipkin-Shahak and Uri Saguy.

21. THE NEXT CYCLE

1. In mid-July 2008, following German mediation, Israel and Hezbollah exchanged prisoners. Israel freed three Lebanese prisoners and received the bodies of the soldiers who had been fatally wounded in the ambush.

22. CRITICAL MASS

1. Here is a simplistic description of the way it works: the nucleus of the fissile material emits two or more neutrons, and at least one of them hits another nucleus and splits it, and again two neutrons are emitted, and at least one hits another nucleus, and so on. If the mass of the fissile material is big enough—that is, if it is a critical mass—then within a fraction of a second, a huge amount of energy will be released. If the mass is too small—that is, sub-critical—the chain reaction will die out on its own.

BIBLIOGRAPHY

BOOKS

Benvenisti, Meron. *Intimate Enemies: Jews and Arabs in a Shared Land.* Berkeley: University of California Press, 1995.

Chomsky, Noam. *Gaza in Crisis: Reflections on Israel's War against the Palestinians.* London: Hamish Hamilton, 2010.

Cordesman, Anthony H. *Lessons of the 2006 Israeli-Hezbollah War.* Washington, DC: Center for Strategic & International Studies, 2007.

Crist, David. *The Twilight War: The Secret History of America's Thirty-Year Conflict with Iran.* New York: Penguin Press, 2012.

Dershowitz, Alan. *The Case for Israel: Exposing Jimmy Carter and Others Who Stand in the Way of Peace.* Hoboken, NJ: John Wiley & Sons, 2003.

Finkelstein, Norman. *The Holocaust Industry: Reflections on the Exploitation of Jewish Suffering.* New York: Verso, 2001.

———. *Image and Reality of the Israel-Palestine Conflict.* 2nd ed. New York: Verso, 1995.

Indyk, Martin. *Innocent Abroad: An Intimate Account of American Peace Diplomacy in the Middle East.* New York: Simon & Schuster, 2009.

Judt, Tony. *Postwar: A History of Europe Since 1945.* New York: Penguin Press, 2005.

Karsh, Efraim. *Palestine Betrayed.* New Haven, CT: Yale University Press, 2010.

Kissinger, Henry. *Crisis: The Anatomy of Two Major Foreign Policy Crises.* New York: Simon & Schuster, 2003.

Kurtzer, Daniel C., and Scott B. Lasensky. *Negotiating Arab-Israeli Peace: American Leadership in the Middle East.* With William B. Quandt, Steven L. Spiegel, and Shibley I. Telhami. Washington, DC: United States Institute of Peace Press, 2008.

Lewis, Bernard. *The End of Modern History in the Middle East.* Stanford, CA: Hoover Institution Press, 2011.

———. *What Went Wrong? Western Impact and Middle Eastern Response.* New York: Oxford University Press, 2001.

Lynch, Marc. *The Arab Uprising: The Unfinished Revolutions of the New Middle East.* New York: PublicAffairs, 2012.

Mackay, Charles. *Extraordinary Popular Delusions and the Madness of Crowds.* CreateSpace, 2012.

Miller, Aaron David. *The Much Too Promised Land: America's Elusive Search for Arab-Israeli Peace.* New York: Bantam, 2008.

Morris, Benny. *One State, Two States: Resolving the Israel/Palestine Conflict.* New Haven, CT: Yale University Press, 2010.

Quandt, William B. *Peace Process: American Diplomacy and the Arab-Israeli Conflict since 1967.* Berkeley: University of California Press, 2005.

Rabinovich, Itamar. *Waging Peace: Israel and the Arabs, 1948–2003.* Princeton, NJ: Princeton University Press, 2004.

Robinson, Glenn E. *Building a Palestinian State: The Incomplete Revolution.* Bloomington: Indiana University Press, 1997.

Ross, Dennis. *The Missing Peace: The Inside Story of the Fight for Middle East Peace.* New York: Farrar, Straus & Giroux, 2005.

Said, Edward W. *The Question of Palestine.* New York: Vintage, 1992.

Sayigh, Yezid. *Armed Struggle and the Search for State: The Palestinian National Movement, 1949–1993.* New York: Oxford University Press, 1997.

Shadid, Antony. *House of Stone: A Memoir of Home, Family, and a Lost Middle East.* Boston: Houghton Mifflin Harcourt, 2012.

Sharon, Gilad. *Sharon: The Life of a Leader.* New York: Harper, 2011.

Tuchman, Barbara. *The March of Folly: From Troy to Vietnam.* New York: Knopf, 1984.

Wright, Robin B. *Dreams and Shadows: The Future of the Middle East.* New York: Penguin Press, 2008.

ARTICLES & ESSAYS

Beinart, Peter. "The Failure of the American Jewish Establishment." *The New York Review of Books,* May 12, 2010. http://www.nybooks.com/articles/archives/2010/jun/10/failure-american-jewish-establishment/?pagination=false.

De Zayas, A. "International Law and Mass Population Transfers," *Harvard International Law Journal* 16, no. 2 (Spring 1975): 207–258.

Dowd, Maureen. "Our Mosque Madness." *New York Times,* August 18, 2010.

Hamzawy, Amr. "The Key to Arab Reform: Moderate Islamists." Carnegie Endowment for International Peace Policy Brief 40 (August 2005). http://www.carnegieendowment.org/files/pb40.hamzawy.FINAL.pdf.

OFFICIAL REPORTS

European Court of Human Rights. "*Demopoulos v. Turkey and 7 other cases.*" March 1, 2010. http://hudoc.echr.coe.int/sites/eng/pages/search.aspx?i=001-97649#{"itemid":["001-97649"]}.

United Nations Commission on Human Rights. "The Realization of Economic, Social and Cultural Rights: The Human Rights Dimensions of Population Transfer, Including the Implantation of Settlers." July 6, 1993. http://www.unhchr.ch/huridocda/huridoca.nsf/0/683f547c28ac785880256766004ecdef?OpenDocument.

United Nations Human Rights Council. "Human Rights in Palestine and Other Occupied Arab Territories: Report of the United Nations Fact Finding Mission on the Gaza Conflict—Conclusions and Recommendations." September 24, 2009. http://www2.ohchr.org/english/bodies/hrcouncil/docs/12session/A-HRC-12-48_ADVANCE2.pdf.

INDEX

ABOUT THE AUTHOR

Michael Karpin is an Israeli broadcast journalist and the author of *The Bomb in the Basement: How Israel Went Nuclear and What That Means for the World* (2006) and *Murder in the Name of God: The Plot to Kill Yitzhak Rabin* (coauthored with Ina Friedman, 1998), among other books. For most of his television career, Karpin was engaged with Israel's public TV and radio, serving as news reporter, anchor, and foreign bureau chief in Bonn and Moscow. He lives in Tel Aviv.